THE PRISON SCHOOL

THE PRISON SCHOOL

EDUCATIONAL INEQUALITY AND
SCHOOL DISCIPLINE IN THE AGE OF
MASS INCARCERATION

Lizbet Simmons

 UNIVERSITY OF CALIFORNIA PRESS

University of California Press, one of the most distinguished university presses in the United States, enriches lives around the world by advancing scholarship in the humanities, social sciences, and natural sciences. Its activities are supported by the UC Press Foundation and by philanthropic contributions from individuals and institutions. For more information, visit www.ucpress.edu.

University of California Press
Oakland, California

Library of Congress Cataloging-in-Publication Data

Names: Simmons, Lizbet, 1971– author.
Title: The prison school : educational inequality and school discipline in the age of mass incarceration / Lizbet Simmons.
Description: Oakland, California : University of California Press, [2017] | Includes bibliographical references and index.
Identifiers: LCCN 2016026093 (print) | LCCN 2016027482 (ebook) | ISBN 9780520281455 (cloth : alk. paper) | ISBN 9780520281462 (pbk. : alk. paper) | ISBN 9780520293144 (ebook)
Subjects: LCSH: Juvenile corrections—Louisiana—New Orleans. | African American young men—Education—Louisiana—New Orleans. | African American young men—Louisiana—New Orleans—Discipline. | School discipline—Louisiana—New Orleans.
Classification: LCC HV9106.N4 S56 2017 (print) | LCC HV9106.N4 (ebook) | DDC 365/.66608350976335—dc23
LC record available at https://lccn.loc.gov/2016026093

Manufactured in the United States of America

25 24 23 22 21 20 19 18 17 16
10 9 8 7 6 5 4 3 2 1

CONTENTS

ACKNOWLEDGMENTS

In writing this book, I aimed to keep a promise I made to Albert "Chui" Clark, who put his trust in me, that I would tell the story of the Prison School. I am indebted to him and to Jamal and Spider and their families, who invited me into their lives and made it possible. I also want to thank Orissa Arendt, the late Llewelyn Soniat, and the staff of Juvenile Justice Project of Louisiana, who helped me along the way.

Two outstanding mentors, Pedro Noguera and Angela Y. Davis, supported this project from its infancy. They each influenced my thinking about what equality means in theory and practice, and I am deeply humbled by the opportunity I have had to work with them. Didi Heller, my undergraduate advisor, inspired me to find beauty in reading and writing; Anne Haas Dyson taught me the art of ethnography; and the late John Hurst remembered to take me out on a boat when I needed a new perspective. I wish to thank Mona Lynch, Jonathan Simon, Carol Stack, Dick Walker, Michael Omi, Torin Monahan, Aaron Kupchik, Michael Musheno, and Jessica Fields, who helped me situate the work in a larger community of scholarship.

I was exceptionally fortunate to have been given support for my research from San Francisco State University through the Affirmation Award and the President's Award. I completed the manuscript with funding from the Office of Diversity and Faculty Development at the University of California, Los Angeles, and with support from the Civil Rights Project. At UCLA, Christine Littleton, Ali Behdad, Gary Orfield, and Patricia Gandara provided assistance in critical stages of the writing.

Several anonymous reviewers provided astute comments on the manuscript and shaped the project in significant ways. Please accept my sincere thanks for engaging in the work and contributing to it so productively. I am particularly appreciative of Dylan Rodriguez and Peter Scharf, whose openness and keen intellect represent the very best of the scholarly community. Maura Roessner, my editor at the University of California Press, ushered this project into print. I cannot imagine a more thoughtful or caring editor. Her support and advocacy were unyielding, and, just as importantly, she offered constructive criticism when it was necessary. I wish to thank Jack Young at UC Press for writing an impassioned call to arms when the manuscript was due. Thanks as well to all the support staff at the University of California Press, and especially Richard Earles, who worked behind the scenes to bring this book into the world. It was my honor to collaborate on the graphics with Rigo 23, who drew all the original charts in the book by hand, and with Ingo Giezendanner, AKA GRRRR, who drew the cover image of the Orleans Parish Prison.

I began this book while I was a graduate student at the University of California, Berkeley, where I was surrounded by some of the most thoughtful, diligent, and hilariously clever people I have ever known. Thank you to Sarah Hamill, Mike Kunichika, Sylvan Brackett, Jenny Wapner, Ariel Evnine, Barrie Brouse, Diana Anders, Andrew Weiner, Freya Read, Heather Nicholls, Elizabeth Meyer, Bernie Jungle, Rachel Stevenson, Jessica Green, Steve Green, Catherine Geanuracos, Kristin Hull, and Myriam Casimir. Lucia Neare, you get five stars and a cake for being so good. Likewise, Nancy Prior. Helen Mirra, Natascha Unkart, Mike Milley, Lucy Jordan, Lisa Tarlow, Alexa Green, Miranda July, and Mike Mills, you are truly excellent friends to have. I found my way in New Orleans with the help of Annie and Nick Pieper, Betty DeCell, and the inimitable Jann Darsie and Señor George Gattoni. John Allen was always ready with a plan B.

I am deeply grateful to my family, especially my parents, the late Elizabeth McCrary Simmons, and my father, Charles Harriss Simmons. My mother modeled kindness in all things and gave me the freedom to shape my future in ways that made sense, at times, only to me. My father stood behind me at every moment and pushed me forward with his endless curiosity and his belief that no one in this world is a stranger. Special thanks go to my sister Ann, a giant in my life for her ethics, care, and compassion. This book is indelibly marked by my enduring love and respect for the late Ida Mae Williams.

I dedicate this book to Louise Hornby. That is ultimately much easier than describing her role in this. So that it is written down somewhere for my children, Philo and Queenie, I'll write it here: Find something, or many things, that you care about; it will work out somehow.

Finally, thanks to Otto and Ladle. They spent almost as much time on this book as I did.

Introduction

In 2002, the criminal sheriff in New Orleans, Louisiana, opened a new public school at the Orleans Parish Prison. The school enrolled a group of African American boys who had previously been removed from regular public schools, most for nonviolent disciplinary offenses such as tardiness. Five days a week, these students were escorted to the school for nearly twelve-hour days on the prison grounds, despite the fact that they had not been charged with, tried for, or convicted of anything other than *status offenses*—actions designated as law-breaking only when committed by certain groups of people. The building that contained their school was a low-slung space in the shadows of the larger prison complex.[1] Small barred windows, a tall fence, and surveillance cameras surrounded the property, clearly marking it as a correctional site. The young boys, ranging in age from twelve to seventeen, were supervised by the warden, who was the criminal sheriff of Orleans Parish, and a school principal who served under him half time.[2] The students were taught by inexperienced and uncredentialed teachers relying on a remedial curriculum and were surveilled and disciplined by the sheriff's deputies, who monitored the students' movements and responded to all disruptions, large and small. Locals called it "the Prison School."

All too frequently, when I have told the story of the Prison School, it has been dismissed as an anomaly, symptomatic of New Orleans's own peculiarity, marginality, and precariousness. The city's unique cartography, demanding climate, and relative geographic isolation seem enough to set it apart from other American cities, and the spectacle of Mardi Gras and the jubilant local bar and music scene only elaborate on this notion.

New Orleans was once an unusually wealthy city. With a plantation economy, enslaved labor, and a location at the mouth of the Mississippi River, the city became a leader in trade and served as the financial capital of the United States in the first half of the nineteenth century (Germany, 2007). More recently, though, New Orleans has been distinguished by intense poverty. In 2005, the number of families living in destitution in New Orleans was the second highest in all of urban America (Berube & Katz, 2005; Berube & Holmes, 2015). The gap between rich and poor in New Orleans is also the second largest in the country, which puts New Orleans on par with Zambia in southern Africa in terms of income inequality (Germany, 2007; Bloomberg, 2014).

High concentrations of poverty radically shape opportunities in neighborhood public schools, and New Orleans provides a quintessential example of this (Berube & Katz, 2005). The grim profile of public schooling in the city is drawn by a long combined history of economic hardship and academic inadequacy in segregated and low-income black communities (Bankston & Caldas, 2002; Germany, 2007). A study of social welfare levels in New Orleans in 1964 reveals that almost three-quarters of the black male population ages twenty-five to forty-four had an elementary level of education or lower (Kerns as cited in Germany, 2007). In the post–civil rights era, this legacy of educational failure has largely endured. Until Hurricane Katrina virtually leveled the public educational infrastructure, the school system made up a sprawling configuration of decrepit and outmoded neighborhood schools. The classrooms themselves were grossly overcrowded and under-resourced, and the students ranked at the bottom of the nation on all levels of standardized academic measurement (Louisiana Department of Education, 2001–2002, 2002; Morgan Quinto Press, 2003). Many of the New Orleans public schools remain de facto segregated, and children continue to go to schools named after a once prominent slave-owner, John McDonogh (Louisiana Department of Education, 2002–2003, 2013; Sims & Vaughn, 2014).

Given this dramatic rendering of New Orleans, it would be hard to deny altogether the ways in which the city is a study of extremes with variations on the themes of failure and disenfranchisement. As Americans learned in the aftermath of Hurricane Katrina, however, the city of New Orleans lays bare extant socioeconomic inequalities that low-income communities of color contend with in every urban locale (Berube & Katz, 2005). New Orleans reflects the structures of racialized oppression that sponsored the nation's growth and prosperity up to the Civil War and now serves as a warning for the ways in which racialized inequality produces the kind of vulnerability that is life-threatening and ultimately unsustainable on both the local and the national scale.

In the tough-on-crime era, marginal investments in the academic curriculum combined with aggressive crime control measures meant that it was even more difficult to get an education in schools that were inadequate to begin with. Public school campuses in New Orleans were routinely guarded by armed police officers; thousands of students in New Orleans Public Schools were suspended each year; and, in an arrangement that signaled an unprecedented coordination of local school and prison leadership, the criminal sheriff opened his own public school within the Orleans Parish Prison (Louisiana Department of Education, 2004; Tuzzolo, 2007; Tuzzolo & Hewitt, 2006).[3]

Positioning the Prison School as a case study, this book examines the link between school failure and mass imprisonment in the era of the "War on Crime." It is a study of how and why public schools take a punitive approach to education and an investigation of how this criminalizing mode influences a student's approach toward correctional custody. How did schools and prisons, two very different kinds of public institutions, become so intertwined in the War on Crime era, and what does this combination mean for students, communities, and, ultimately, a democratic society? How do we begin to unravel the many ties that bind the racialized realities of school failure and mass incarceration? Throughout the book, I am concerned with the ramifications of such ties, which have meant that large segments of the population—in particular, African American males—have been systematically removed from schools and from society. As I will argue, the carceral conditions experienced by young black men have facilitated their disappearance into and dispersal through a black prison diaspora.

The construct of the black prison diaspora explains how African American youths have been simultaneously pushed out of school and pulled toward the criminal justice system by punitive ideologies and policies. It describes an internal human migration—from one part of the country to another—and reflects the understanding of that movement as catalyzed by both push and pull factors (Lee, 1966; Gregory, 2012). I consider the forces that push disenfranchised youths away from school and pull them toward correctional control and show how these practices of undereducation and overcriminalization, which have allowed for continued, systemic failure of urban schools, have shaped a migration of diasporic proportions leading black American males to prison. This integrated analysis of the public education and criminal justice systems helps to explain the mutual implications and connections between two major racialized social problems: school failure and mass incarceration.

The term *mass incarceration* has been used by scholars to refer to the vast and unprecedented expansion of the American prison system, which began in the mid-1980s and led to acute rates of African American male imprisonment (Garland, 2001a, 2001b; Pettit & Western, 2004; Clear, 2007; Alexander, 2010; Tonry, 2013; Wildeman, 2014). According to an oft-cited statistic, the lifetime likelihood of imprisonment for black males was approximately one in three in 2001 (Bonczar, 2003). This rate is two times greater than the lifetime probability of imprisonment for Latino males and almost six times greater than the rate for white males (Bonczar, 2003; Sentencing Project, 2016). Given these racial disparities, the term *mass incarceration* is actually quite misleading. *Mass* as an adjective is defined as a general and standard condition, and while the prison boom in America has affected a large population, there is nothing wholesale or universal about it. I use the term *mass incarceration* throughout this book (and in its title) with this problem in mind. The language that is meant to represent racialized oppression in the context of the American criminal justice system diffuses and obscures the dynamic through generalization. Used as a noun, the term *mass* is more accurate; indeed, the correctional system in America holds a large mass of black males behind bars.

In advancing the notion of a black prison diaspora and articulating the complex dynamics of school failure and mass incarceration in historical contexts, I am working against the construct of the "school-to-prison pipeline." This analytical framework is used to describe how groups of disenfranchised youths tend to move rather fluidly from schools to prisons under tough-on-crime school disciplinary policies (Wald & Losen, 2003a, 2003b; Kim et al., 2010; Bahena et al., 2012). In the sociology of education, the school-to-prison pipeline model was the first rubric to explicitly link harsh school disciplinary policies and correctional risk. It has galvanized educators and other youth advocates around the need to address disproportionate minority confinement with both improved educational opportunities and more thoughtful and less adversarial school disciplinary practices. As the ideologies and practices of the criminal justice system have become further embedded in public schooling, however, the disciplinary dynamic in schools is neither so linear nor so unidirectional as the pipeline analogy would suggest. Schools and prisons do not sit on opposite sides of a metaphorical path, and the criminal justice system is not merely at the end of the pipeline—it is implicated all along the way.

To understand the relationship between racialized school failure and racialized incarceration, it is necessary to look beyond the surface of school disciplinary policy and examine the historical context of racial oppression. The logic of the school-to-prison pipeline might present an overly simplistic solution to the kinds of educational inequality that render black youths more vulnerable to the correctional system. As Damien Sojoyner suggested in his similar critique of the pipeline analogy, we would be remiss to assume that by changing student behavior and rewriting school disciplinary policy, we will ensure that black males will no longer be pushed out of school, arrested, or incarcerated (Sojoyner, 2013, 2014). This is because the social, political, economic, racial, and gendered dynamics at the root of these phenomena remain intact, in spite of efforts to dismantle the pipeline. If we don't pay attention to the underlying conditions in the campaign for educational equality, we run the risk of concealing the struggle for black liberation (Sojoyner, 2013, 2014).

It is difficult to imagine how a concerted effort to dismantle the mechanism of the school-to-prison pipeline could disrupt the larger racial power structure in a meaningful way. Michelle Alexander argues in her book *The New Jim Crow* that one mechanism for racial control, such as Jim Crow, can simply be exchanged for another, like mass incarceration (Alexander, 2010). Racially disproportionate school punishment, Jim Crow laws, mass incarceration, and even the urban ghetto itself are expressions of disciplinary power that allow for the cordoning off of black bodies (Wacquant, 2001; Simmons, 2009a).

We can think about the exclusionary tactics of disciplinary power in light of Michel Foucault's *Discipline and Punish*, in which he yokes exclusion to practices of enclosure, finding the roots of educational exclusion in traditions of monastic isolation (Foucault, 1979/1995). Early penitentiaries were designed with this model in mind, removing transgressive individuals from society and encouraging penitence (Peters, 1995). In our late modern society, so many individuals—though from relatively few communities and disproportionately black and male—have been taken out of schools and into correctional custody that isolation has become a normal part of black life (Kurgan, 2013). This social disenfranchisement builds within schools, in the context of an educational system that has increasingly turned to the criminal justice system as a model for discipline, adopting the very same strategies that were designed to fight drugs and crime on the national stage. When public schools began to systematically adopt versions of the correctional system's isolation practices, with aggressive suspension and expulsion policies that excluded children from school, they sponsored a secular condemnation of students that has had parallel effects. Suspension and expulsion exclude and isolate students, and as youths lose positive, or even remotely positive, academic affiliations (as might be true for any student attending a failing urban public school), they lose relevance as potentially productive members of society. These youths can be characterized in many of the terms used to describe inmates in the era of mass incarceration: they are disposable, banished, and invisible (Advancement Project, 2010; Beckett & Herbert, 2010; Giroux, 2011; Pettit, 2012).

The condition of racialized invisibility, which was famously explored by Ralph Ellison in his 1952 novel *Invisible Man*, has been a significant part of contemporary critiques around the recent deaths of Michael Brown, Eric Garner, Freddie Gray, Tamir Rice, and other black males at the hands of police. Critics of these brutalities have raised a banner stating that "Black Lives Matter," a declaration of the obvious and the necessary that is relevant only in a radically unbalanced society in which the humanity of black lives might, in fact, not matter much at all. As Judith Butler has noted, black lives have historically been disposed of readily and easily in the interest of protecting white privilege, and until they are disposed of, they are targeted and hunted by law enforcement (Yancey & Butler, 2015). In each of these recent cases of police brutality, black males were perceived as a threat even when they held no deadly weapon. The threat was embodied instead by blackness and by masculinity. The invisibility of black bodies—their very expulsion from community norms and institutions—is arranged paradoxically, then, by a certain kind of brutal visibility that Ta-Nehisi Coates describes in his epistolary memoir as "being naked before the elements of the world" (Coates, 2015). Invisible unless criminalized, the black masculine body is a subject for discrimination, capture, containment, neutralization, and/or disposal. This book is driven by a methodological imperative to make the experience of youth criminalization visible for critique, insisting that these youths and their communities be accounted for as a way of intervening in the institutional arrangements that would have them disappear.

PUSHED AND PULLED IN NEW ORLEANS, LOUISIANA

I learned about the school at the Orleans Parish Prison quite by accident. In April 2002, I was attending a large education conference in downtown New

Orleans. Late in the morning, as I left one hotel to attend a panel in another location across Canal Street, I was drawn to a loud protest on the sidewalk. A tall, broad-shouldered, older African American man in a white baseball cap was at the center of a small group comprising two men, several women, and one young girl, and he was leading them in protest chants. He was wearing a white t-shirt, faded denim shorts that covered his knees, black sneakers, and white ribbed socks pulled up tight around his calves as if a single wrinkle would have undone him. The man held a large poster in his hands showing an image of a fortified structure with the caption "Schools not Incarceration."

As I stood alone in front of the group, the rush of the conference carried on, its attendees seemingly indifferent to the local protestors chanting "Close Foti's Dungeon."[4] I approached the tall man in the white cap, and as he stepped forward to talk to me, other members of the group took the lead and the chanting continued. It was so noisy that he had to lean in close to me and cup his hands around his mouth to shout in my ear. In time, I grasped that he was protesting the recent establishment of a public school at the Orleans Parish Prison, which was opened by Sheriff Charles Foti with the consent of the Orleans Parish School Board.

The protestor's name was Albert "Chui" Clark, and I told him that I wanted to see the school. Chui Clark turned and spoke to the sole white woman in the group, who was in her late fifties, with a willowy build and long, straight gray hair. One of her eyes was fully covered by a black patch that was strapped around the back of her head. "She'll drive you," Clark said. The woman introduced herself as Orissa Arendt, and we walked to her car. On the drive, we talked about her work as a local freelance reporter for the *Louisiana Weekly* and the *New Orleans Tribune*, periodicals serving the African American community. She told me about her kids and about the "haves" and the "have-nots" in New Orleans Public Schools. Her kids "are haves," she said, but "most local kids are have-nots." Halfway across town, we passed the Orleans Parish Prison and turned down a small road just beyond it. We stopped in front of a tall red fence and she said, "Well, this is it." We got out of the car together. Looking up, I saw one chain-link fence after another, each topped with dark coils of barbed wire. Orissa pointed to the low-slung building in the foreground—the public school on the Orleans Parish Prison grounds.

The school building had bars on the windows, and the surveillance cameras surrounding it suggested an institution of high security. Coming from behind the tall wooden privacy fence that tightly surrounded the property, I heard male voices—one older and several younger—but I could not make out their words. Occasionally, over the fence top, we could see a basketball being lobbed toward a makeshift goal. It was late afternoon, a time when most public school students would have left school and gone home. Within minutes of our standing there, a gold sedan pulled in behind us and parked. The driver, a well-heeled white woman in her fifties with hair cut in a precise bob, got out of the car and introduced herself as the sheriff's assistant. She must have been alerted to our arrival by someone on staff or by the exterior surveillance camera capturing our images. I introduced myself as well and began asking questions to which she offered measured answers.

The school had opened in January 2002 and served African American boys between the ages of twelve and seventeen. The goal of the program was to redirect youths who seemed to be on a destructive path. "Once they get into the [criminal justice] system," she said, "they can't get out." That spurred the sheriff's efforts to reach the youths before their problems became real. According to the assistant, the sheriff was an experienced educator, having started a successful GED program for inmates in the prison in the 1990s. This time, he wanted to reach children prior to incarceration, so he opened his own school. I turned from her to look again at the sheriff's school and the backdrop of the Orleans Parish Prison.

> L: What did these kids do to get here?
> Assistant: They were disciplinary problems.
> L: Were any of them violent?
> A: Only one. He hit another kid in the nose, but the rest, no.
> L: What did the other kids do?
> A: They were hard to manage.
> L: What do you mean?
> A: They were disrespectful, talked back to their teachers.
> L: I heard people talking about this school downtown. I was told that when it opened, it served only students who were black and male.
> A: When it opened. We have since added a white student.
> L: I study schools. Could you let me inside to see it?
> A: For your safety and the safety of the children, we can't allow that.

I left the school with Orissa, but in the days that followed I stepped up my efforts to gain access to the children inside the Prison School through formal channels. I made nearly seventy more contacts—in person or by phone or mail—with the sheriff's office, the school's principal, the school board, and school district administrators, all of whom reinforced the total inaccessibility of this particular site. After months of these efforts to gain access, I was finally given permission to do research in any school in the district—*except* the Prison School. It struck me that I had an easier time gaining entry to San Quentin Prison in Marin County, California, where for two years I taught weekly classes in English literature and composition.

I later learned that I wasn't the only person who had pressed for entry to the Prison School and been denied. A month after my efforts, C. C. Campbell-Rock, a local reporter and youth advocate, attempted to storm through the Prison School gate. She was threatened with arrest. Eventually Rock returned to the school with Ellenese Brooks-Simms, the president of the Orleans Parish School Board, and they were met with strong resistance too. At the perimeter of the school, Brooks-Simms was told that she should talk to the president of the school board, to which she replied, "I am the president of the school board!" Brooks-Simms and her companion Campbell-Rock finally gained entry to the school by pulling rank, and Campbell-Rock published a small piece in a local newspaper about what she saw inside: "I toured the . . . program . . . and was alarmed at what I saw. Four armed sheriff's deputies sat around watching four television monitors; the bathroom had no stalls, but a row of stainless steel toilets and a camera were mounted on the wall . . . there was no principal on the premises" (Campbell-Rock, 2002). My efforts to tour the school never did pan out, and within a few months the school closed. In making their decision to shut the school, the school board, with Brooks-Simms at the helm, vowed to take a new direction in serving public school students, saying that "the law enforcement environment of the school was not the direction the board [wanted] to take" (Thevenot, 2002).

The school's closure, however, does not address the question of how it was that a public school could have opened in a correctional institution in the first place. What does this instantiation of punitive school relations signify in terms of trends in school discipline more broadly? How does the school fit into the local experience of the public education and criminal justice systems and the historical conditions of racial inequality in the city? The stakes of these questions push beyond the intellectual or historical and toward the ethical, cutting to the heart of the critical import of ethnographic and qualitative research. At every turn, I was refused access to the school, whose inaccessibility was fiercely protected. But what would it mean for a researcher to choose *not* to study a site because she cannot gain admittance? Were I to acquiesce to the demands of the sheriff's assistant and the administration at the Orleans Parish Schools that I not study the school, it would be as though I were tacitly acknowledging that (A) a correctional facility might be an acceptable place to educate black children in America or that (B) the story of racial discrimination in New Orleans Public Schools discipline had ended with the closure of the school. Put slightly differently, I would either be complicit in the project or naive about the enormous depth of its significance. Later in the year, I moved to New Orleans to study the emergence of the Prison School and its place in the complex set of historical relations shaping the move toward harsh school punishment locally and nationally. I set out to build local relationships that would yield insights into how intergenerational inequality structures urban educational opportunity and correctional vulnerability.

Evidence mounted that the Prison School was, as locals like Chui Clark had suspected, not an isolated example of harsh youth criminalization in New Orleans Public Schools. Furthermore, the school board had not, in fact, taken an entirely new direction in serving the local students subsequent to the school's closure. The board had set aside $51 million of the local school budget to secure a private contract with Community Education Partners, Inc., to open a school emphasizing discipline for one thousand children in a low-income African American neighborhood. Community Education Partners held strong ties with the correctional industry and had a reputation for running "soft jails" for kids (Lewis, 2002; Fuentes, 2005). Chui Clark called the Prison School "a pilot project" for this larger initiative that would reconstitute public education for all local African Americans in a correctional vein. The Prison School proved to be neither the beginning of the story nor the end of it. It is a piece in a much larger puzzle depicting the perpetual undereducation and overcriminalization of blacks in American cities, and in New Orleans in particular.

ETHNOGRAPHY OF THE PAST AND PRESENT

The Prison School is a historical ethnography and uses a macro lens to remain attentive to the experiences of participants in both the past and the present. I examine the educational and correctional experiences of Chui Clark in the second half of the twentieth century as well as the experiences of two Prison School students, Jamal and Spider, in the early part of the twenty-first century.[5] Historical ethnography offers a way of "working up the past," as it is called in a German tradition of cultural anthropology, and it responds to the idea that "ethnographic research should open itself, draw more on historical dimensions, and more fully investigate the many relationships and connections between past and present" (Fenske, 2007). As the scholar Michaela Fenske has put it, this methodology "quits the present as the key (or sole) point of departure and point of reference" in order to develop a "deeper understanding of what makes culture, or the human experience, possible" (Fenske, 2007).

Historical ethnography is conceived in the midst of the "historical turn" in social and cultural anthropology, in which scholars have attempted to provide "ethnographic studies of how the past is known, represented and understood in the world" (Palmie & Stewart, 2013). This epistemology underwrites inquiries in various sites of "past-making," including archives, popular memory, oral history, and contested minority accounts of the past (Palmie & Stewart, 2013). I position these sources of knowledge alongside ethnographic data collected as they unfold in the present, to allow for an understanding of the historical conditions and present coordinates that led to the formation of the Prison School. This open approach imagines the methodological capacities of ethnography as ever more expansive and ever more necessary for uncovering sociocultural meaning in and around sites, such as criminal justice institutions, where access is limited. Rather than heed the sheriff's assistant's advice that I take my research elsewhere, I sought access to the Prison School by way of the past as well as the present and was guided by the historical and contemporary narratives of the local participants.

At the core of this book is an overarching concern about the ways in which urban youths are burdened by the long arm of the criminal justice system. Recent microethnographies of juvenile offenders, such as Victor Rios's *Punished* and Alice Goffman's *On the Run*, have clearly elucidated youth criminalization with regard to street-based law enforcement (Rios, 2011; Goffman, 2014). As the title of Goffman's book makes clear, these practices render youths as fugitives in their own country. *The Prison School* contributes to this scholarship by examining the particular role urban schools have played in shaping youth vulnerability to the criminal justice system through the practices of undereducation and school-based criminalization. The students featured in this book, fourteen-year-olds Jamal and Spider, are markedly different from the characters in both Rios's and Goffman's accounts, a distinction that is critical for understanding the precise argument that I am making about the racialized collaboration of schooling and punishment. When Goffman meets her youngest subject, Chuck, for the first time, he is just out of county jail on charges of a school fight, assault, and running from the police (Goffman, 2014). Likewise, most of Rios's teens and young adults had "gang involvement" and were "going in and out of jail" (Rios, 2011). The students at the Prison School, such as Jamal and Spider, were not involved in gangs, had not spent time in juvenile detention, and were not on the run. In other words, they had neither committed nor been charged with any crime beyond what might be considered status offenses.

Jamal had skipped classes, which he said was a "knucklehead idea," and the behavior meant that he was charged with the status offense of absenteeism, an action designated as lawbreaking only when committed by a school-aged child. Spider was also a status offender by virtue of tardiness. Though he had never been late to his first-period class at 9:00 A.M. when academic instruction began, he had been consistently late to his 8:30 A.M. homeroom class. This was the check-in time at the beginning of the day, during which "they'd just be in the cafeteria, and wait until the teacher comes to get [them]." When Jamal and Spider were pushed out of school for these infractions, they didn't run further away—they essentially banged on the door to get back in. "I attempt to go to school every day," said Spider, "and you sending me home! . . . I want to go to college." Jamal's positive view of school was similarly reflected in his aspirations: "I wanted to be a math teacher," he said, though by the time he shared this ambition with me, he was fourteen years old and already using the past tense to reflect on his former ambitions as a way of explaining what it meant to him to have his education derailed.

FINDING THE INVISIBLE

The broad scope of *The Prison School* builds on a body of qualitative research on school discipline, work that is scaled to the public school classroom or the school campus. *Punishing Schools* by William Lyons and Julie Drew, *Homeroom Security* by Aaron Kupchik, and *Police in the Hallways* by Kathleen Nolan are three notable ethnographic accounts of punitive relations at traditional schools (Lyons & Drew, 2006; Kupchik, 2010; Nolan, 2011). Nolan's recent examination of school disciplinary practices at an urban public high school in the Bronx has a particular resonance for the stakes of my argument. She finds that "institutional discourses [at the school] . . . were explicitly influenced by the logic of the criminal-justice practices" and that a "criminal-justice framework had become normative at the school" (Nolan, 2011). She writes that as a school-based ethnographer, she was used to seeing "teens in handcuffs"; "kids with a pocketful of summonses"; and accustomed to "tidal waves of blue in the hallways, security agents corralling students during sweeps, and the image of youngsters with their arms stretched out in front of them as agents moved scanners over the contours of their bodies" (Nolan, 2011). Though Nolan sees students being tracked toward the criminal justice system by way of school arrest and court summonses, she maintains the institutional parameters of her school-sited study.

I build on this work in *The Prison School* by following students on their way out of the system and toward correctional control. Educational research sited on school campuses cannot adequately account for the growing number of students who—suspended, expelled, or truant—are not on school grounds. These youths, especially African American males, exist in a liminal state in between institutions—no longer formally in school and not yet formally in the criminal justice system. For a large percentage of these disconnected students, prison is on the horizon. Of African American male dropouts who were born between 1975 and 1979, 68 percent spent at least a year in prison by 2009 (Pettit, 2012). The question is how to find these students, if they cannot be found in school.

The Prison School was a citywide program, which meant that the fourteen students who attended the now closed school did not necessarily live near the prison. In fact, they could have been anywhere in New Orleans. My instincts and the national and local data on educational disenfranchisement, school discipline, and youth criminalization led me to look for the boys in the most marginal spaces of the city (Louisiana Department of Education, 2002–2003; Moore, 2010; Rios, 2011; Terriquez et al., 2013; Berube & Holmes, 2015). I began by mapping the ghettos of New Orleans, and I walked through them, starting with the Ninth Ward. This ward, made famous in subsequent years by Hurricane Katrina, was segregated and impoverished, and the schools serving the neighborhood were very poor (Moore, 2010). Students in the Ninth Ward schools dropped out or were pushed out in high numbers every year (Louisiana Department of Education, 2002–2003).

Walking the streets as a means of study has a long sociological history, allowing direct observation to guide the research process. W.E.B. Du Bois conducted his social history of Philadelphia's Seventh Ward, titled *The*

Philadelphia Negro (1899/1996), by walking through the streets "with a house-to-house canvass" (Bulmer, 1984). Robert Park, the famed Chicago School sociologist, walked street by street to delineate the lines of racial segregation and made "tour[s] of exploration," a habit of walking the city to gain impressions of the field and acquaint himself with its denizens (Hayner as cited in Bulmer, 1984, p. 97). Central to this research orientation of the Chicago School, as Bogdan and Biklen have argued, was a consciousness about "the importance of seeing the world from the perspective of those who were seldom listened to—the criminal, the vagrant, [and] the immigrant—and a belief in the ability for urban research to make visible those people who are most marginalized in society" (Bogdan & Biklen, 1998).[6] Recalling the effort by Burgess to interview old residents in local communities and rely on their "exact and complete knowledge," I walked to the edge of each mapped neighborhood and worked my way in, street by street, door by door (Burgess as cited in Bulmer, 1984).

By most accounts, New Orleans was a dangerous city at the time of my research. There were high incidents of violent crime, and the city had the nation's highest per capita rate of homicide, which was about six times the national average (DeSilver, 2014). At several points of my research I was one degree of separation from local murder victims. A boy named Harman, one of the students at the Prison School, and one of his friends were murdered before I could interview them, and my university colleague's girlfriend was shot and killed in New Orleans, apparently for her purse, one night when she rode her bike home alone from a concert. There was a quintuple murder in the Central City neighborhood in 2006, at an intersection where I spent time a week afterward (McCulley, 2006). In the later phases of my research, my wife was coincidentally hired to join the faculty at Tulane University in New Orleans. At the new-faculty orientation, her dean advised her and her new colleagues to avoid walking on the city streets at night. I found this advice striking, especially given the city's vibrant nightlife and the music that spills out into the streets. Despite what I was told, I did not approach the city as a dangerous place, nor did I understand the people I spent time with as dangerous. I hung out with Chui Clark, a formerly incarcerated man, who led the protests of the Prison School, and with kids who had been kicked out of school. I understood them as everyday people who were struggling to make their lives work in the context of rampant socioeconomic inequality (Rios, 2011).

Sitting in his car, Chui told me, "You can't just come into the black community." He said this in the context of a discussion about another white woman who had gotten involved in a race-reconciliation campaign, and I was similarly implicated for my research. I was a white outsider looking into his world and, as Chui suggested in this comment to me, there is something presumptuous about embedding yourself in a community that is not your own and having expectations of acceptance. I heeded Chui's warning and developed a stance, similar to the one advocated by the sociologist Michael Burawoy, in which I was neither distanced nor totally immersed (Burawoy et al., 1991). I took Chui's lead and listened as he put the Prison School into context, and I participated in those conversations with ease. Over time, Chui and I developed a relationship based on trust, of which he said, "You know, I am trusting you with all this, because you hear me, and you know what I am saying."

Chui and I spent a lot of our time together talking in his white sedan. He picked me up at my apartment and took me across the city, showing me everything he thought I needed to know about how the public school at the Orleans Parish Prison came to be. Over time, he charted the history of race relations in New Orleans and explained that the Prison School emerged from the kinds of racial discrimination that undergirded plantation ideologies, slavery, Jim Crow laws, school segregation, racialized policing and disciplinary practices, prison expansion, and mass incarceration. He drove me down Jefferson Davis Parkway, so named to honor a champion of slavery who served the cause of white supremacy as president of the Confederacy. We drove around and around Lee Circle, as if tethered to the statue of Jefferson Davis's successor, Robert E. Lee, at its center. The bronze statue of Lee stands atop a towering Doric column like a sentry guarding the city's Central Business District, so that all commerce in the city takes place under the scrutiny of Lee's racist logic.[7] We went to John McDonogh High School, named—along with nineteen other schools, many of which are still operating—after a prominent slave owner. We stood below Confederate flags on billboards and buildings, and watched white men walking down the street wearing the flag on their belts, suspenders, and hats. Cars and trucks passed us with Confederate-flag license-plate frames. "What does all this tell you?" Chui would ask in an exasperated drawl. Sometimes Chui pulled over to the side of the road and stopped the car to frame the phenomena he was pointing to in the city's history of racialized politics. When the car engine was quiet, I could audio record our conversation. On occasion, we sat parked on the side of the road talking for hours.

Every now and then, Chui found ways to make me useful. He asked me to make inquiries about the sheriff at sites like the roadside fish market, where he, a formerly incarcerated black man and potentially recognizable local agitator, was kept at arm's length. He said:

> They won't talk to me, but maybe they'll talk to you. You tell them you want to know where that fish come from. I know it come from Foti. He has that fish-farm up in his prison. I showed you all those boats parked. What does a criminal city sheriff need with all those boats? He is farming fish with inmate labor, and he is trying to sell those fish to you. He has a real prison industry.

I found out from the fishmonger that the fish had indeed come from Foti's "little fishing program," which was supported by a prison-run hydroponics laboratory and a tilapia fish farm. "They sure did talk to me," I told Chui. "We should do this more often." We also stopped a few times to eat at his favorite po-boy shop, and over lunch he suggested other people for me to interview and people to "study up on." When I followed these leads, I usually did so independently.

In the course of my research, which ultimately spanned a period of three and a half years, I logged over a thousand hours in the field. I did not ultimately find all fourteen boys who were matriculated at the Prison School, as I had once imagined. Instead, I found two students, Jamal and Spider, whose experiences are knitted into a broad cultural and historical fabric that spans the local and the national, past and present. I learned from them by spending time with them at their homes, talking with their family members, and visiting them at work and at a series of schools. I sat down with Jamal's mother and grandmother and interviewed them as well as two of his teachers. I interviewed both of Spider's parents and two of the teachers from the traditional public school he had attended before being pushed out. I spent several days shadowing Spider at a school-to-work program that he attended for youths who hadn't finished high school. There I interviewed his jobs program director and two more teachers. None of the educators I talked to about Jamal or Spider seemed to know either of them very well. The director of his jobs training program knew what Spider presented on paper and said things like "Just looking at his administrative record, I think he is improving. . . . [He has] two weeks attendance, of being physically here." As such, those particular interviews were revealing in their lack of in-depth knowledge and pointed to Jamal and Spider's disconnectedness. After the Prison School closed, Spider ended up in a group home in New Orleans, for reasons that he remained very vague about, and I hung out with him there on two occasions. After Katrina, I lost track of

Spider, and his old neighbors said he had moved to Texas. I spent time with Jamal in the aftermath of the storm at his family's FEMA trailer, and I visited him at his place of employment, which was a nearby McDonald's. Jamal and Spider had been so alienated by their experience at the Prison School that they could not recall ever knowing the names of the other students, with the one exception of Harman, who had, by then, been murdered.

Grounded theory—the idea that theory emerges from data and from whatever shape the data take to reveal what is actually going on in the research field—allowed me to see what was happening in the community from the perspective of many people and not just students (Glaser and Strauss, 1967; Glaser, 2001, 2002). The fact that the students were so hard to find—that records were lost and kids were unaccounted for—speaks broadly to the larger point that I make in this book about the extreme vulnerability and liminality of certain populations, and the ways in which this vulnerability is enforced. My aim was to understand the local and national conditions underlying the emergence of the Prison School as a case study of the punitive trend in public schooling in the War on Crime era. In searching for and finding two students from the Prison School through a chain of connections, I had collected data from across the local community that penetrated the subject of intergenerational school failure and racialized youth criminalization. While Chui, Jamal, and Spider remained my primary informants, I also learned about the punitive dynamics in New Orleans from other protestors and locals, including but not limited to Orissa Arendt, who first took me to the Prison School; Chui's colleague Llewelyn Soniat, a retired postal worker; C. C. Campbell-Rock, introduced above; and Robert Hillary King, a former Black Panther Party member and member of the Angola 3. I interviewed the criminal sheriff who opened the Prison School, his assistant, sheriff's deputies, and the professors who served as consultants to the program. On the whole, the data I collected from individuals in law enforcement were the most limited, which ultimately suggested an intentionality to their obfuscation, but I was also given the runaround by the school board, school administrators, teachers, and record keepers, which made it seem like they, too, willingly lost sight of these students.

THEORIZING DIFFICULTY

My practice of historical ethnography responded to the intricacies and difficulties of access presented by the site, which required me to approach historical archives as themselves ethnographic field sites (Fenske, 2007). Subscribing as well to Glaser's notion of grounded theory that "all is data," I documented, analyzed, and theorized my difficulty in these archives, and especially in local and state institutions, to reveal sociological meaning (Glaser, 2001). As Glaser explains, "all is data" means that "exactly what is going on in the research scene is the data, whatever the source, whether interviews, observations, documents in whatever combination. It is not only what is being told, how it is being told, and the conditions of its being told but also the data surrounding what is being told" (Glaser, 2001, 2002). My quest for Spider's school records offers one example of what difficulty looked like in the archival sites of New Orleans. When I went to Spider's former neighborhood middle school to collect his school file, with Spider's and his mother's permission, the school secretary told me that they had absolutely no record of him. I responded to this claim with some degree of incredulity, and she pointed me to the cabinets containing all recent student files and suggested that I look for myself. After I made a dedicated but unsuccessful search, the secretary then proposed that I look for the files in the basement of a local church on the other side of the Mississippi River. A church seemed an unlikely place for students' public school files and possibly problematic with regard to the Establishment Clause of the First Amendment of the U.S. Constitution, if the arrangement suggested that the public schools of New Orleans, as institutions of the state, were excessively entangled with religion (Scruggs, 2015). Pushing the student files out of the system was also rather like pushing out the students themselves. There seemed to be a total lack of accountability.

Despite my skepticism, I went to the church in search of the lost student files. When I arrived, I found that the basement had flooded—not because of Hurricane Katrina, which was yet to come, but because the space was well below sea level. Basement flooding was to be expected in much of New Orleans, which made the site a poor one for storing anything intended to be preserved. When I arrived, an African American male janitor was standing in the muck of the church basement, stooped over a mop. He told me that there *had* been public-school file boxes there, but mold grew after the water rose, and everything had been thrown out.

"Everything?" I said.

"Yes, everything!"

"Why would they put school files in a church basement that is under sea level?"

"More of the same, ma'am . . . *more . . . of . . . the . . . same.*"

I grew to interpret these disappearances and the difficulty of gaining access—to the files, to the students, to the school—as evidence of systemic concealment strategies, veiling long-standing traditions of racialized disregard and neglect. Relegating student files to a flood-prone church basement was a way of discarding them, leaving little evidence that these youths had ever existed in New Orleans Public Schools. If they could be said to have never existed in the system, there was also no record of their having been pushed out. While examining data archives on district school performance, I found evidence that twelve of seventy schools in the Recovery School District had been omitted from the performance reports by way of a data-formatting scheme, thus skewing the performance data upward. Dr. Barbara Ferguson, writing for the Research on Reforms organization, calls this strategy a "creative data manipulation" that allowed "low-performing schools to evade" inclusion and allowed the state to "hide its failures" (Ferguson, 2013). As the data mounted, I began to understand young African American boys in New Orleans as "invisible men" in the making, whose invisibility is constructed by these interlocking strategies of concealment, along social, economic, political, and educational axes. This notion of invisibility comports with Becky Pettit's claim, in her recent book *Invisible Men*, that mass incarceration conceals racial inequality (Pettit, 2012). Punitive school discipline works similarly to conceal extreme educational disparity along the lines of race, class, and gender.

AN EDUCATION WORTH FIGHTING FOR

In the summer of 2005, I had returned to California to teach for the fall semester at UC Berkeley and had begun writing up my findings based on eighteen months of data collection. Thus, I was in the Bay Area and not in New Orleans when Hurricane Katrina flooded the city on August 29, 2005. From afar, with all lines of communication severed, I studied news images, looked for faces I recognized, and worried over who had survived. I looked back at the data I had collected, which was evidence of their lives, and I thought about how, yet again, the plight of African Americans in New Orleans was patterned by the themes of racial exclusion, abandonment, isolation, disposal, invisibility, and disappearance. In other words, Katrina echoed the janitor's refrain, revealing "more of the same."

It was five months or so after Katrina before New Orleans had begun functioning at a very basic level. When I returned in early 2006, I found myself walking the streets again, mourning the loss of so many lives and thinking of all the stories gone untold. In the Ninth Ward and the areas surrounding it, where I had walked before in my search for the students of the Prison School, I encountered miles of storm wreckage. Travel was difficult. The buses and streetcars were off line, making it hard for locals who relied on public transportation to get to work. After a couple of weeks of long walks across the city, my father drove his old Buick down to me from North Carolina. I punctured the tires on that car so many times on hurricane debris that I finally bought a bicycle to get around town. In traveling across New Orleans, I saw many homes torn open to the street, each with a story to piece together from water lines, overturned sofas, and family portraits still clinging to flood-stained walls. I toured one empty shell of a school after another, stepping over huddled desks and kicking aside mildewed textbooks and fallen bulletin-board fliers. The absence of human life was haunting. Most days, I could go for many blocks without seeing another soul. These excursions brought me into spaces where all humanity appeared lost, but as I exited the residences and institutions that lay in ruin, I sought a life again in the city streets, the public spaces of accountability, democracy, and hope. The absence I felt everywhere inspired my need to find presence and promise somewhere in what remained. Along the way, I started writing this book.

I established a permanent home in New Orleans and continued data collection from the summer of 2007 to the spring of 2010. In the years after Katrina, the city felt abandoned. New Orleans lost over half of its residents in the aftermath of the storm, to become a small metropolis of a little more than two hundred thousand residents (Fussell, 2007; U.S. Census Bureau, 2005; Louisiana Public Health Institute, 2007). The crisis forced a large exodus to neighboring states and to locations nationwide, based on family ties and work prospects. Many residents were slow to return to the city after the storm, precisely because there was no public school system for their children to return to. This fact offered a reminder that public schools are central to our communities and, as such, remain institutions worth fighting for. In New Orleans, a highly dysfunctional public school system had shaped the severe socioeconomic marginalization of the local population, which had implications for the kinds of resources that people had at their disposal to protect themselves from the rising water. After the storm, the community was more marginalized educationally, socially, and economically than it had been before. Were local youths to find new channels of opportunity, they would need the local public school system to open the doors and let them in.

I begin this book by charting the complex dynamics that have pushed students from school and pulled them toward the criminal justice system, setting up the terms of a black prison diaspora that are maintained throughout the book. Chapter 1 argues that harsh school disciplinary policies, emerging from the punishing culture of the War on Crime era, curtail youth academic achievement and accelerate incarceration risk in the African American community. The chapter describes how the concentrated effect of punishment has a destabilizing effect on the African American community and the American democratic project as a whole, while benefiting larger social, political, and economic strategies in a neoliberal and postindustrial context.

Chapter 2 explains how and why public schools and prisons have collaborated in the War on Crime era. It shows that the punitive shift in education catalyzes youth correctional vulnerability while serving larger social and political needs. Specifically, the chapter documents the powerful influences of market forces in shaping school security expansion and what has been called the "at-risk youth industry." As public schools have employed a correctional approach to education, they have established students' initial approach to correctional custody. In demonstrating how youths experience punitive schooling within the correctional spectrum of the at-risk youth industry, nationally and in New Orleans, the chapter revisits and revises current theories of the school-to-prison pipeline.

Chapter 3 looks closely at New Orleans to show how punitive school disciplinary measures endorse the War on Crime, compounding the academic problems of African American students within the city's historically dysfunctional school system, in a state that has the highest incarceration rate in the world (ACLU, 2008). I draw a picture of the dismal educational and disciplinary conditions in the public schools of New Orleans across two generations of African American men and show their role in extending correctional vulnerability.

Chapter 4 offers an investigation of the New Orleans Prison School—a public school in a prison—where African American male students, like Jamal and Spider, were sent as punishment for nonviolent status offenses. Through the voices of local residents, including students and their families, teachers, local activists, and law enforcement officials, this chapter explains what the push-pull factors of punitive schooling mean for their lives and their community. I situate this examination in the historical context of urban school failure, youth criminalization, and mass correctionalization from the post–civil rights era of New Orleans forward. The work is theoretically framed by scholarship in the sociology of punishment, which articulates mass incarceration as a disappearing act playing out on the stage of the postindustrial and neoliberal state (Wacquant, 2009; Schept, 2015). The chapter ends by returning to New Orleans in the aftermath of Hurricane Katrina. While the city's schools were physically demolished by the tremendous floodwaters, the punitive ideologies of the city's criminal justice system, which were undergirded by larger sociostructural forces, remained intact. These ideologies resurged and were made manifest as the school system was rebuilt. Activists who took to the streets in post-Katrina New Orleans included students, and they protested criminalization policies and technologies that continued to compromise their efforts to achieve academically. The protest is ongoing, as individuals and communities continue to struggle against racialized school failure and the push-pull factors of a black prison diaspora.

In the Conclusion, I revisit the push-pull factors of punitive schools and review their role in expanding dependency and correctional vulnerability. In a brief discussion of what it would mean to divest from punitive policies—to cease practices of suspension and expulsion—I argue, quite simply, that we have no other promising choice.

CHAPTER I

Public Schools in a Punitive Era

Unless you have been inside a sanitarium you do not know that madmen are *made* there, just as criminals are made in our reformatories.

—André Breton, *Nadja*, 1928

The road to prison is long. Rarely are individuals catapulted into the criminal justice system. A vulnerability to incarceration accrues over time, through relations and power structures that play out in personal and institutional spaces (Nolan, 2011). By the time individuals actually find themselves at the mercy of the criminal justice system, most have already experienced a profound degree of alienation stemming from social, economic, political, geographic, and educational disenfranchisement (Pettit, 2012; Clear, 2007). People marginalized on many or all of these structural fronts prior to being criminally charged are overrepresented in America's prison population: inmates tend to be urban, low-income, undereducated, and African American (Bonczar, 2003; Pettit, 2012; Clear, 2007; Kurgan, 2009). That men, and African American men in particular, are disproportionately represented among prison inmates points to how gender constitutes a primary axis of disenfranchisement for men in the sphere of the criminal justice system, especially when conflated with minority racial status (Bonczar, 2003; Pettit, 2012; Clear, 2007). One in every six African American men has been incarcerated at some point (National Association for the Advancement of Colored People, 2009–2016; Bonzcar, 2003). At the current rate, prisons will house one in three African American males and nearly three-quarters of African American high school dropouts (Simon, 2007; Bonczar, 2003; Pettit, 2012).

This book charts the long road to prison and shows how the punitive dynamics that influence the early educational experiences of African American youths

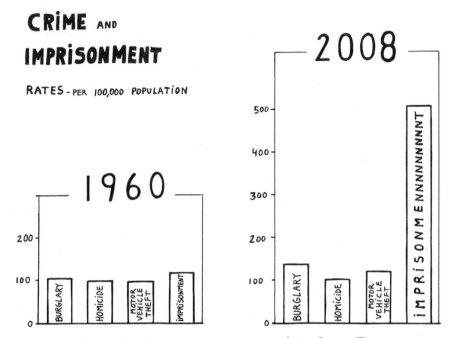

FIGURE I. Crime and imprisonment rates per 100,000 population. Sources: Tonry, 2013; National Research Council, 2014. Graphics courtesy of Rigo 23.

lead to youth exclusion, alienation, and invisibility and help generate correctional trajectories. *The Prison School* is an excursion into the push-pull dynamics that have shaped the migration of African American males from school to prison in the War on Crime era. Accordingly, the book inaugurates a new understanding of how prisons grew in the War on Crime era as public schools failed. That the criminal justice system expanded in this period, despite significant and simultaneous declines in crime, challenges a popular etiological argument that crime causes punishment (Zimring, 2007; Davis, 2005, p. 40).

Figure I compares crime and imprisonment rates between 1960 and 2008. While crime rates fluctuated during this period (rising and falling over the course of time in approximate synchronicity), the rates for homicide and common crimes like burglary and car theft in 1960 look very much like the rates in 2008 (Rand, 2009; Cooper & Smith, 2011; Tonry, 2013). Imprisonment rates, however, look radically different. They reflect the punitive ideologies and severe sentencing practices in the criminal justice system from the mid-1980s onward, such as harsh mandatory minimum sentences and "three strikes" laws (Tonry, 2013).

Rather than the result of crime, the growth of the prison—indeed, the rise of the prison industrial complex—is the result of a complex set of coordinated policies and engagements that answer to much larger structural conditions. For example, as the criminologist Michael Tonry explains, the tough-on-crime agenda was inspired by a set of goals that were significantly political in nature (Tonry, 2013). While policymakers were seeking to prevent crime, they were campaigning for political support and attempting to bolster public confidence by espousing values that were in political favor (Tonry, 2013). Tonry names the values of the tough-on-crime era in terms like *expulsion, denunciation, ostracism,* and *severity,* thus illuminating the cultural context for both mass incarceration and school-based youth criminalization (Tonry, 2013).

My examination of such forces as they operate in New Orleans shows how the disciplinary collaboration between public schools and the criminal justice system generates the racialized push-pull factors of the black prison diaspora. Nationally, too, black male students, more than any other demographic across the nation, have disappeared from schools under the punitive mechanisms of the War on Crime and disappeared once more into the prison system during the era of mass incarceration. This phenomenon poses a central sociopolitical problem, since the black prison diaspora is enabled by racialized criminalization processes within public schools, the very institutions charged with providing for achievement and advancement in a democracy (Dewey, 1944/1916).

THE BLACK PRISON DIASPORA

The correctional trajectory of African Americans is so clearly mapped in our landscape today that it recalls the patterns of the Great Migrations, which drastically changed the regional demographics of America between 1910 and 1970. In those years, millions of African Americans moved from the rural South to the North and the Northwest and into the ghettos of cities like Baltimore, Boston, New York, and Chicago; later, a second wave moved westward toward California (Sugrue, 1996; Massey & Denton, 1993). This southern diaspora was shaped by push-pull factors: Jim Crow racism and difficult farming conditions in the South drove the migration toward the northern promise of personal freedom, job opportunity, and property ownership (Sugrue, 1996). In 1980, only ten years after the Great Migrations officially ended, African American males, most undereducated, began leaving American cities in large numbers en route to prison, altering the terrain of urban America again in a third wave of migration conditioned by the War on Crime (Clear, 2007). This migration to prison has remade the American landscape as much as the previous dramatic shifts in population. By 2012, there were approximately ten million African Americans living in the United States who had experienced correctional supervision (Schmitt and Warner, 2010; Holzer et al., 2003; Hirsch et al., 2002; Travis et al., 2001; Freeman, 1992). Data from 2008 on the total ex-offender population of twenty-one million show that half were functionally illiterate and 70 percent were high school dropouts (Schmitt & Warner, 2010; Holzer et al., 2003; Hirsch et al., 2002; Travis et al., 2001; Freeman, 1992).

As millions of African American men have been captured by prisons in a third wave of migration, they have been rendered largely invisible (Pettit, 2012). Beckett and Herbert refer to these men in the custody of local law enforcement as having been "banished" (Beckett & Herbert, 2010). Once individuals are behind the carceral wall, they are removed from their social, economic, and political existence, with serious consequences for their own lives as well as the lives of everyone around them (Bernstein, 2005; Clear, 2007; Mauer & Chesney-Lind, 2002). Becky Pettit suggests that the disappearing act of mass incarceration has compromised the pledge of the civil rights movement by reobscuring a population that was made invisible by discrimination, segregation, and Jim Crow laws (Pettit, 2012). Michelle Alexander has called the phenomenon of mass incarceration a new form of "second-class citizenship" that uses well-disguised processes of racialized control to function "in a manner strikingly similar to Jim Crow" (Alexander, 2010).

In his book on mass incarceration and its community impact, Todd Clear describes the experience of going to prison as "a hole in the life span" (Clear, 2007). Inmates are hidden from the view of their family, their immediate community, and the public (Clear, 2007; Mauer & Chesney-Lind, 2002). Inmates have low rates of marriage and are absent as parents (Western, 2006). Approximately 25 percent of African American children have a parent who lives under correctional custody (Wakefield & Wildeman, 2014). Prison populations are also erased from our primary economic indices (Western et al., 2002). They are, for example, excluded from the data on employment rates, which means that the nation is always doing less well economically than the official employment figures suggest, and this is a particular concern when published employment rates are low (Western, 2006).

As political beings, inmates experience a civil death and are denied the right to participate in the electorate (Manza & Uggen, 2008). For many of those with a felony conviction, this denial extends in perpetuity. In some states, one in four African American men are denied the right to vote and are, thus, erased from the democratic sphere (Manza & Uggen, 2008). The U.S. Census Bureau does count inmates, but they are considered residents of the municipalities where they are incarcerated, and nearly a quarter of all inmates are incarcerated outside their own counties (Hunter & Wagner, 2007). Since voting districts are redrawn around total population counts that include nonvoting inmates, communities with large inmate populations gain voting power over the counties of inmate origin (Heyer & Wagner, 2004; Hunter & Wagner, 2007). This gerrymandering encourages prison growth and has the collateral effect of diminishing political capital in the urban, low-income African American neighborhoods that many inmates come from, thereby obscuring large-scale African American community interests (Heyer & Wagner, 2004; Hunter & Wagner, 2007).

It was not until the American prison population exploded in the War on Crime era that a misdirected education meant a likely future in prison, as became the case for most African American males in the 1990s (Mauer, 1999, p. 1; Arum & Beattie, 1999). One look at the present U.S. incarceration rates shows that prison is primarily a place for undereducated men of color. Over 90 percent of prison inmates are male; nearly 60 percent are racial minorities; and 75 percent of state inmates lack a high school diploma (Harlow, 2003; U.S. Census Bureau, 2000a; Glaze & Parks, 2012). There is a long-standing inverse relationship between correctional risk and educational attainment: correctional risk diminishes as education level rises. With the War on Crime, however, there was a further development in this risk formula. In the latter part of the twentieth century, the significance of education for correctional risk was magnified. Academic achievement began to matter more than at any point in the past in terms of lifetime risk of incarceration (Arum & Beattie, 1999).

Education matters, in fact, nearly three times more for white male high school dropouts in the War on Crime generation than for previous generations, and four times more for black male high school dropouts (Pettit & Western, 2004). The gravity of this rate hike for African Americans is revealed in the factoring; their incarceration rates were much higher to begin with, such that a fourfold increase in incarceration meant that 60 percent of African American males who came of age in the War on Crime era had served prison time by 1999 (Pettit & Western, 2004). After a 300 percent increase, the incarceration rate for white male high school dropouts was still just over

10 percent. These figures are high in actual terms but relatively low in comparison to undereducated blacks and also low in comparison to the incarceration risk in the total black male population (Pettit & Western, 2004).

As incarceration became a normal event in the lives of African American males and a probable one for African American male dropouts, a black prison diaspora took shape, whose complex push-pull factors are produced by schools and prisons. A map of this diasporic migration shows the primary penal catchment zones in the major metropolitan areas of the United States, and more detailed spatial analysis pinpoints the origin of migration to low-income and minority neighborhoods that typically have the lowest-performing schools (Anyon, 1997; Kurgan, 2009; Kozol, 1991/2012; Southern Education Foundation, 2015). While not all individuals respond to push-pull forces in the same way, migration theory holds that certain classes of people tend to respond similarly to the conditions they face at the point of migration origin and the point of destination (Lee, 1966).

THE CORRECTIONAL SPECTRUM

My engagement with a diasporic construct and with salient push-pull factors is a theoretical departure from the school-to-prison pipeline rubric that has characterized most recent analyses of school failure and correctional vulnerability. The school-to-prison pipeline, or the STPP as it is sometimes called, names the seemingly fated path of young minorities from school to prison. It draws the association between prisons and schools as an axial one, positioning schools at the beginning of a linear progression and prisons at the end. While this is a well-trod path, there is a broader context that the pipeline analogy fails to capture. It obscures the fact that large numbers of black and Latino students experience the presence of the criminal justice system by way of their public schools. These youths are criminalized by school security, by disciplinary policies, and by everyday school interactions in which adults cast them in a negative light or, worse, fashion them as public enemies to protect against (Meiners, 2007).

In the ethnography *Ghetto Schooling*, based on work in the early 1990s in a school serving primarily low-income and African American students in Newark, New Jersey, the sociologist Jean Anyon records the violence of a white fifth-grade teacher saying to her students, "If I had a gun, I'd kill you. You're all hoodlums," and the abusive language of a black first-grade teacher saying,

"You're disgusting. You remind me of children I would see in jail" (Anyon, 1997). Pedro Noguera, a sociologist of urban education, encountered similar conditions of youth criminalization while touring public schools in Northern California a few years later. During one elementary school tour, an assistant principal pointed Noguera's attention to a boy in the hallway who was young enough to be in third grade, saying, "Do you see that boy? There is a prison cell in San Quentin waiting for him" (Noguera, 2003b). In these accounts, teachers and administrators in public schools invoke the criminal justice system in their daily interactions with children. Racialized assumptions of native criminality and impending incarceration, even when expressed less explicitly than in these examples, are indicative of how low the expectations often are for black students (Ross & Jackson, 1991).

As schools became more punitive in the era of the War on Crime, teachers and administrators were provided with new opportunities to engage criminalizing ideologies. Public schools, especially urban public schools, formed tighter relationships with law enforcement. In the widening penal net, many school-aged youths made contact with the criminal justice system at an earlier age (Wilf, 2012). In 2009–10, nearly a quarter of a million students were referred to law enforcement by school administrators, and ninety-six thousand youths were arrested at school (Wilf, 2012). Seventy percent of those students were black or Latino (Wilf, 2012).

The current punitive dynamic in public schooling problematizes the linear rubric of a school-to-prison pipeline, since schools and prisons have in many ways merged, making the pipeline itself collapse in a state of punitive rupture. We can no longer limit our conceptual understanding of schools and prisons to a pipeline analogy, because it blurs the more complicated push-pull factors at play. Damien Sojoyner argues that the school-to-prison pipeline metaphor is, in fact, damaging in its simplicity (Sojoyner, 2013). If school disciplinary practices are reformed such that black youths continue to be harshly treated and even harshly disciplined—but no longer punished with the threat or deployment of suspension, expulsion, and arrest—the problem (as framed by the school-to-prison pipeline) is resolved, and yet racialized educational inequality remains and is sponsored by reformed disciplinary practices (Sojoyner, 2013). Though punitive tactics in education were newly expressed in the era of the War on Crime, long-held racist ideologies were always at their root. As Sojoyner writes, "the STPP framework may challenge the basic tenet that the meting out of discipline is disproportional, [but] . . . it fails to challenge the ethos of anti-Blackness as foundational to the formation and enactment of school discipline" (Sojoyner, 2013). By attending to the foreground of disciplinary policy, the school-to-prison pipeline rubric conceals foundational power dynamics and allows them to go unchallenged.

I offer a corrective to the metaphor of the school-to-prison pipeline by arguing that schools and prisons are coordinated institutions operating in a correctional spectrum. By evacuating educational opportunity across generations of African Americans and engaging harsh school disciplinary policies that have disproportionately affected this population, public schools participate in structuring a black prison diaspora. These conditions have forced an involuntary migration of youths away from formal schooling.

Suspended, expelled, and displaced by public schools, the children of the black prison diaspora bear a striking similarity to internally displaced persons. They share diasporic characteristics and conditions identified by the United Nations, the Red Cross, and other humanitarian agencies: their movement or expulsion may be coerced; they live in relative deprivation; they are in need of assistance, protection, education, and durable social and economic solutions; they are vulnerable and threatened on the grounds of race; they are at risk of physical attack and live in fear (International Committee of the Red Cross, 2000; European Commission, 2016; United Nations Human Rights, 2016). Globally, there is an extremely high death toll for persons who face these kinds of conditions due to violent conflict, human rights abuses, or natural or man-made disasters (United Nations Human Rights, 2016). The life-and-death stakes play out differently in the black prison diaspora, but the comparison to internally displaced persons remains significant.

Consider, for instance, the public health crisis and the exclusion from services that is uniquely part of African American life. Claiming that African Americans experience health care very differently from other racial and ethnic populations in the nation, Byrd and Clayton cite as evidence the "corrosive sociocultural, health and biomedical system legacies of 2000 years of being portrayed as being biologically and intellectually inferior; 246 years of chattel slavery, including a slave health deficit and a slave health subsystem; 100 years of legal segregation and discrimination and a 'Negro medical ghetto'; and contemporary social, political, and economic isolation, oppression, exploitation, and a 'dual' and unequal health system" (Byrd & Clayton 2002, 2003). Their description of racially disproportionate health care and the legacy of state-sanctioned neglect and dispossession does indeed make it sound like they are speaking of a migrant population, severed from the fabric of civic life.

GETTING TOUGH

The black prison diaspora—the migration of black men toward prison—began with the end of slavery but experienced a surge of epic proportions in the early 1970s, when the very character of crime control in America changed. In the midst of an unpopular war in Vietnam, President Nixon convinced Americans of a secondary engagement at home, which became known as the War on Drugs. He reasoned that domestic drug activity caused violent crime, which stoked fears among Americans that every doorstep was under attack (Simon, 2007). This could not have been further from the truth, but the bellicose spirit was infectious. In the vein of a counterinsurgency, even Americans who themselves had witnessed scant evidence of drug-related crime got behind Nixon's War on Drugs and its escalating instantiation—so much so that tough crime control and excessive punishment became characterizations of late-modern American society (Simon, 2007; Garland, 2001a, 2001b).

The War on Drugs, broadened and rebranded as a War on Crime, harnessed an American obsession with crime and crime control that was out of sync with the realities on the ground, making the perception of criminality larger than life. Unlike the War on Drugs, which had at least a referent in rising crime rates from 1960 to 1980, the War on Crime escalated outside of criminological contexts (Garland, 2001a, 2001b; Western, 2006). Zero-tolerance policies, three-strikes laws, and mandatory sentencing policies were instituted with a vigilance honed by the fight against drugs as primary mechanisms for getting tough on crime even as crime rates were diminishing (Zimring, 2007). Consequently, the criminal justice system tacked in the direction of punitive excess. In a case made famous for delivering punishment in extreme disproportion to the offense, a California man with prior strikes against him was sentenced to twenty-five years to life for stealing a piece of pizza (Leonard, 2010). That case represents the criminal justice system's range of motion under tough-on-crime laws, but a better measure of the institution's strength takes account of how the national correctional system amassed its sheer bulk and maintained it. Between 1973 and 1997, the inmate population in the United States rose by more than 500 percent (Loury, 2008). By 2008, there were 2.3 million people behind bars and another 5 million in jail, on probation, or parole, giving the United States the highest incarceration rate in the world (Loury, 2008; Pew Center on the States, 2008). The way this translates is that one out of every hundred adults in America was incarcerated, and one in every three adults was under some form of correctional control by 2008 (Pew Center on the States, 2008).

Major policy shifts at the base of the punitive phenomenon mechanized the stringent ideologies of crime control. Tougher prosecution meant that the link between arrest and incarceration grew tighter (Western, 2006). The risk of incarceration for nonviolent crime was multiplied by a factor of eleven (Loury, 2008). Incarceration for drug crimes was significant in this trend, increasing more than tenfold between 1980 and 2001 (Western, 2006). Drugs that plagued the black community, like crack cocaine, were uniquely targeted in this scheme (Provine, 2011). Prison terms grew longer as a result of harsh sentencing, and truth-in-sentencing measures eliminated parole in many states (Pew Charitable Trusts, 2015). Together, these policies meant that jails and prisons functioned a little less like a revolving door and a little more like a trap. More individuals went to prison and stayed longer (Mallik-Kane et al., 2012; Pew Center on the States, 2008a; Pew Charitable Trusts, 2015).

In this period of gross prison expansion, minority commitments outpaced those of other racial groups and were highly disproportionate to their percentages in the national population as a whole (Pettit, 2012). African Americans represent approximately 12 percent of the national population but nearly 40 percent of the U.S. prison population. For whites, the disproportion is reversed; in 2000, they made up three-quarters of the national population but only 35 percent of prison inmates (U.S. Census Bureau, 2000a; Glaze & Parks, 2012). It is precisely because young black men are incarcerated so disproportionately and in such large numbers that the criminologist David Garland has characterized the trend as one of mass imprisonment (Garland, 2001a, 2001b). The prison is the prime site for amassing black males and disconnecting them from their communities and their futures.

POLICING DISRUPTION

In the late twentieth century, public schools across the nation turned to the criminal justice system as a model for discipline, adopting the very same strategies that were designed to fight drugs and crime on the national stage. Public schools partnered with criminal justice agencies, tapped into homeland security monies, instituted zero-tolerance policies, invested in surveillance and metal detection, expanded security staff, and infused school campuses with a toughness that was endemic to the War on Crime itself (U.S. Department of Homeland Security, 2015; Nolan, 2011; Kupchik, 2010; Monahan & Torres, 2010).

In this period, national school suspension rates rose dramatically. In 1974, 1.7 million students were suspended from school, or 3.7 percent of the total student population (Schiraldi & Ziedenberg, 2001; Losen & Edley, 2001). In the 2011–12 school year, according to a study by the Civil Rights Project, almost 3.5 million public school students (7 percent of the total) were suspended— enough to fill forty-five years' worth of Super Bowl stadium seats (Losen et al., 2015). Almost half of those students, 1.55 million, were suspended more than once, and given that an average suspension is 3.5 days long, an estimated 18 million days of classroom instruction were lost that year as a result of forced exclusion (NCES, 2014; Losen et al., 2015). In most states, there are 180 instructional days in a school year, making 18 million days of lost instruction equivalent to 100,000 academic school years (Bush et al., 2011).

While the tough-on-crime approach severely disadvantages students' educational access and opportunity, it serves to politically advantage local public school officials by assuaging popular constituent concerns about school violence.[1] These concerns are ongoing despite the fact that public schools are relatively safe, and incidents of school violence exceedingly rare. Statistically, schools are among the safest places for children to be in terms of risk to life (White House, Office of the Press Secretary, 1998). In each of the years between 1992 and 2010, less than 2 percent of all youth homicides have been school-related (NCES, 2011; James & McCallion, 2013). School spaces are also statistically safer than nonschool spaces with regard to serious violent victimization, and for both youths at school and those away from school, the rate of serious violent youth victimization is extremely low at 0.3 and 0.7 percent, respectively (National Center for Education Statistics, 2014a).[2] Given the absence of a grave school violence problem, the correlated difficulty of showing a dramatic decline in violence, and the practical impossibility of guaranteeing absolute safety, administrators show their mettle in tough-on-crime policies, technologies, and fortifications, which now respond to a larger set of disciplinary offenses, many of them nonviolent (Kupchik, 2010; Kim et al., 2010).

Nationwide, many students have been suspended from public schools for the vague offense of "disrupting" or "disturbing" instruction (Kim et al., 2010;

Sundius & Farneth, 2008; UCLA-IDEA, 2006). In California schools, disruption constituted by "a willful defiance of authority" was the leading trigger for expulsion in 2003–04 (UCLA-IDEA, 2006). "Disturbing school" was the single largest offense leading to court referral in 2007–08 for juveniles in South Carolina (Kim et al., 2010). A report by the Open Society Institute documents that a majority—37 percent—of disciplinary offenses were categorized as "disrespect/insubordination/disruption" in Baltimore Public Schools in 2006–07 (Sundius & Farneth, 2008). Four times more students were suspended out-of-school in Baltimore for tardiness (at 8 percent) than for weapons possession (at 2 percent) (Sundius & Farneth, 2008).

Though the trend is national, black students have been affected by subjective disciplinary assessments more regularly and severely than youths in other racial groups (Johnson et al., 2001; Skiba, 2001; Skiba & Leone, 2001; Skiba et al., 2002). A study of nineteen large urban middle schools in the Midwest in 1994–95 reveals that black students more frequently experienced office referrals for "disrespect, excessive noise, threat, and loitering," whereas white students were more often disciplined for "an objective event" such as smoking, profanity, or vandalism (Skiba et al., 2002). Despite racial disparities in disciplinary action, there is no evidence, in this study of schools in the Midwest or elsewhere, that black students are, in fact, committing more serious offenses or engaging in more disruptive behavior (Shaw & Braden, 1990; Skiba et al., 2002). Another study by Russell Skiba and colleagues shows that among the strongest predictors of racial disparities in school discipline are the attitudes of principals and administrators (Skiba et al., 2012).

Through the legal doctrine of in loco parentis, courts have historically trusted schools to discipline students, and school administrators are allowed to exercise discretion in determining what reasonably constitutes disorder (Stuart, 2010). School administrators, though, have increasingly relied on an expanding staff of School Resource Officers (SROs) to do the policing, which has changed the nature of these determinations—and the nature of schooling itself—enabling new and more forceful expressions of disciplinary authority (Devine, 1996; Hirschfield & Celinska, 2011). SROs are full-time law-enforcement officers who are trained by and report to local police departments and sheriff's offices (Kupchik & Bracy, 2010; James & McCallion, 2013).[3] In the late 1970s, there were fewer than 100 of these officers in public schools across the country; in 1997, there were 12,500; and by 2007, the police force in public schools was nearly 20,000 strong, making this the fastest-growing segment of law enforcement (Kupchik & Monahan, 2006; Hirschfield, 2008; Hirschfield & Celinska, 2011; James & McCallion, 2013).

Aaron Kupchik and Nicole Bracy, who spent six months studying policing in four public high schools, argue that "the introduction of police officers into schools very clearly represents an area of convergence between schools and formal criminal justice systems" (Kupchik & Bracy, 2010). The daily presence of law enforcement ups the ante for student misbehavior, such that disruptive students are now threatened not only with suspension and expulsion, but with arrest and court referral as well (Rimer, 2004; Hirschfield & Celinska, 2011). In their book *The School-to-Prison Pipeline*, legal scholars Catherine Kim, Daniel Losen, and Damon Hewitt claim that school and law enforcement officials have abandoned a reasonable practice of discretion, which has led to routine arrests "for minor and entirely predictable childish misbehavior" (Kim et al., 2010). At their worst, school-based arrests are attended by physical abuse (Mukherjee, 2007; Kupchik & Bracy, 2010). Poor training in education and youth development combined with a policing mentality is the perfect storm for school-based youth criminalization (Mukherjee, 2007; Kupchik & Bracy, 2010). Officers are taught in the police academy to compel quick compliance by subjugating individuals with a commanding voice of authority as well as physical dominance (Skolnick & Fyfe, 1993). Videos circulating on the Internet show various schoolchildren, often African American, being thrown by law enforcement officers against school lockers or onto classroom floors, prior to being arrested for disruptions; these are among the most extreme examples of what excessive police force can look like in public schools (Austria, 2015; Lacour, 2015; Greenfield, 2016). The extreme examples are instructive, for it is difficult to imagine a teacher in any era going to such lengths to manipulate and physically dominate a student.

In May 2009, fifteen-year-old Marshawn Pitts, an African American male special-needs student in Illinois, was injuriously attacked by a uniformed, school-based police officer for walking down a school corridor with a flapping shirt tail and for failing to obey the officer's command to comply with the school dress code.[4] In a video of the incident that was posted on YouTube, the officer charged Pitts like a bull, twice ramming him into the wall of a school corridor and forcing him to the ground in a takedown hold that can be fatal (Giroux, 2011a, 2011b). Pitts survived the attack with a broken nose and other injuries.

In October 2015, a white police officer in Columbia, South Carolina, entered a high school classroom, grabbed a sixteen-year-old female African

American student by the neck, flipped her over backward in her desk chair, and threw her across the classroom floor, prior to arresting her (Fausset & Southall, 2015). She had violated the disciplinary code by having a cell phone in class, by refusing to excuse herself from classroom instruction, and by not standing up when commanded to do so by the officer (Fausset & Southall, 2015). The event was recorded on video and circulated by other students in the class who also had cell phones. In one recording the officer is heard threatening another student, saying, "I'll put you in jail next" (Fausset & Southall, 2015).

SOCIAL DIFFERENCE AND DISCIPLINE

In his book on surveillance titled *The Electronic Eye*, sociologist David Lyon argues that "the more marginal or nonconforming we are, the stronger the web of constraint-by-surveillance becomes" (Lyon, 1994). In schools, certain populations are more vulnerable to supervision, control, discipline, and punishment than others, and similar student behaviors are labeled and penalized differently (Ferguson, 2000; Skiba, 2001). They divide along race, class, and gender lines, with low-income male students of color bearing the most deleterious consequences. The designation of "problem student" or "youth at risk," like the designation of the "criminal," is socially constructed and determined by subjective measures in which race is a significant factor (Ferguson, 2000; Casella, 2003b). In this way, the perception and penalization of student behavior is embedded in a constellation of social, economic, and political conditions. Extreme marginalization along any or all of these axes renders students more susceptible to correctional influences in their public education, and concurrently less prepared to defend against them.

Issues of race continue to inform school security, though there have been changes over time. Stringent school security was, in the past, a phenomenon most visible in urban schools serving youths of color (National School Boards Association, 1994). After Columbine and other suburban high school shootings, the market for high-tech school security expanded, and metal detectors and surveillance cameras were more broadly established and visible in nonurban school settings. While high-tech security became more widely installed across public schools serving urban and nonurban populations, somewhat narrowing a very large gap, the stringency of disciplinary policies grew more intense in urban schools specifically, reifying patterns of extreme disproportionality in carceral treatment along the lines of race and class (Gordon et al., 2001).

The result was that urban low-income minority students were more harshly punished for their infractions than they had ever been. So, while all students are increasingly likely to experience some carceral technologies in their schools, minority students, particularly males, are much more likely to experience the carceral system by way of school discipline. Ultimately, minority students are still far more punitively managed than white students. Even as school shootings in the late nineties became statistically less of an urban issue and more of a suburban one, and perpetrators were primarily white males in suburban schools, minority males in urban schools were still targeted most frequently as "problem students" and shouldered a highly disproportionate share of school punishment. Even when controlling for other socioeconomic factors, such as class, race remains a major predictor for suspension and expulsion (Skiba et al., 2012). High rates of racial disproportion are consistent in the national suspension data. One in every six African Americans experienced school suspension at least once in the 2009–10 school year, whereas for whites, the ratio was one in twenty (Losen & Gillespie, 2012).

Highly punitive schools can't be understood as responding to an authentic crisis of school crime. Rather, acting from a fear of crisis, they are attempting to preempt risk by negatively evaluating certain behaviors committed by people of certain social groups, who are deemed a threat because of race, class, gender, and other differences (Mora & Christianakis, 2013). Punitive schools tend to punish alienated people more than they punish truly alien behavior. What, really, does it mean to be disrespectful? What is at stake in enforcing (policing) respect, other than maintaining exclusionary hierarchies of power? After all, the demand for respect from young black males reflects the power arrangements and rhetorical demands of a racial state in the pre–civil rights era, the civil rights era, and every period since.

Disciplinary arrangements can also be understood from the perspective of economic and political gain (Mora & Christianakis, 2013). At the school level, for example, there are incentives to suspend low-performing students at test time and shift the standardized-testing population toward high achievement, because under the No Child Left Behind (NCLB) law, federal funds are potentially withheld from state systems and, in turn, from schools and school staff, when adequate yearly progress (AYP) is not made (Braden & Schroeder, 2004; Carroll, 2008). Schools that fail to show adequate AYP year after year face harsh sanctions, whereby the school district is required to take "corrective action," revealing yet another layer of the punitive education model (Carroll, 2008).

A large study of Florida schools by David Figlio provides compelling evidence that school administrators in the state tried to meet the stringent demands of NCLB and bolster test scores by using harsh discipline to shift the demographics of the student population (Figlio, 2006). Schools regularly mete out harsher sanctions, such as suspension and expulsion that push youths out of school, to low-performing students than to those who are high-performing, but Figlio's study shows a greater level of discrepancy in the test-taking window (Figlio, 2006).[5] He concludes that school discipline is a tool used to manipulate and maximize test scores, or "game the test." Speaking about his findings at the University of Florida, Figlio said that at test time, schools may "hope to have more low-performing students stay home" (Keen, 2006). A report by the Advancement Project explains that minority students are on the losing end of this "numbers game" (Advancement Project, 2010). In the eight years prior to the passage of NCLB, 68 percent of the hundred largest public school districts in the country, which serve about 40 percent of the country's African American, Latino, and Native American students, had rising graduation rates: 24 percent were rising in the double digits, while only 4 percent lagged. In the eight years after the passage of NCLB, 73 percent of these schools showed declining graduation rates; 17 percent had double-digit declines; and 2 percent had double-digit increases (Advancement Project, 2010). These statistics describe what the Advancement Project report calls a "rampant student pushout problem" whereby "students are treated as if they are disposable" (Advancement Project, 2010).

PUSHED OUT

In taking a correctional approach to students, schools lead youths in the direction of the criminal justice system. The exercise of punitive school discipline in the context of systemic educational failure pushes students away from educational tracks at the same time that the criminal justice system draws them near. In this way, punitive schools generate and/or reproduce many of the conditions underlying mass incarceration and, consequently, shape a new wave of the African American migration leading from urban America to prison.

The correctional risk associated with disciplinary punishment and poor educational attainment warrants a thorough examination of the school "push-out" phenomenon. How do students arrive at the point of academic departure, and what is the role of school disciplinary policies in shaping these trajectories? Are tough-on-crime punishments at school necessary and effective? Do punitive security measures effectively combat school crime and create safe learning environments? What kinds of disciplinary violations lead to student suspension or expulsion? Is the price paid by the "pushout" a reasonable trade-off for the overall safety of the larger student body? First, schools are not immune to violence, but they are among the safest places for children to be (White House, Office of the Press Secretary, 1998; Noguera, 2008a; National Center for Education Statistics, 2011; James & McCallion, 2013). Second, the ramping up of school discipline has not delivered actual safety and has, in fact, created environments that are antagonistic to both positive social relationships and academic learning (Noguera, 1995; Skiba & Peterson, 1999). Third, many students who are turned away from school for disciplinary reasons are guilty of minor, nonviolent offenses that could be handled by school officials with discretion and diplomacy rather than by officers of the law who rely primarily on adversarial models of engagement. Furthermore, students who disrupt school often do so out of social or academic frustration. Their disciplinary issues may be symptoms of socioeconomic or educational disenfranchisement, which are initially elided and finally reproduced by punitive treatments. If there is a benefit to public schools in excising these students, it could be that punishment individualizes and masks a systemic problem of educational failure that is difficult to address without full-scale institutional change.

Public schools in the War on Crime era have reflected the political and economic expediency of being tough on crime, with heavy concentrations of school security that capture behavioral aberrations and new disciplinary polices that punish them (Nolan, 2011; Casella, 2001). Complex school-security networks support police work, and these technologies run the gamut from metal detectors and surveillance cameras to face-recognition systems and intrusion sensors (Casella, 2006). Many of the new policies, such as three-strikes rules and "zero tolerance," were adapted for schools from their origins in the criminal justice system. For example, zero tolerance was formulated as a defense against drug importation at U.S. borders.[6] School zero-tolerance policies enable school officials to decisively push out any student who offends (Casella, 2001), imposing strict penalties on even minor violations of the school's disciplinary code such as insubordination, now frequently categorized as "willful defiance."

The enforcement of zero tolerance in schools led to out-of-school suspension and expulsion and had the effect of pushing school-aged youths out of the classroom and away from an academic path (Gordon et al., 2001; Ayers et al., 2001). The most punitive school disciplinary policies were instituted in under-resourced and low-performing urban schools serving primarily low-income youths of color (Skiba et al., 2012; Losen & Skiba, 2010). Aggressive disciplinary policies thus compounded urban students' academic challenges, which were underpinned by socioeconomic marginalization and educational disenfranchisement. They simultaneously catalyzed correctional vulnerability by formalizing educational exclusion. A large longitudinal study in Texas shows that the punishments of school suspension and expulsion for discretionary violations almost triple a student's risk of having contact with the juvenile justice system within the year (Fabelo et al., 2011).

Punitive school discipline is touted as a way to close the doors on misbehavior and criminal opportunity in schools, but it has had the effect, instead, of closing the doors on opportunity altogether, especially for African American male students (Losen & Gillespie, 2012; Skiba et al., 2002; Ayers et al., 2001; Skiba & Leone, 2001). As public schools and offices of justice have become formal and informal collaborators in punishment, the ideologies of the War on Crime have gained traction, rates of African American student suspension and expulsion have soared, and incarceration has exploded (Losen & Gillespie, 2012; Pettit, 2012; Kim et al., 2010; Nolan, 2011). It is very difficult to know exactly how many students have experienced school suspension and expulsion, because the statistical data are collected inconsistently and inconclusively, which leads to inaccuracies and underreporting (Civil Rights Project & Advancement Project, 2000; Forte, 1996). The most recent figures suggest that nationally, 1.7 million K–12 public school students were suspended out of school in 1974, and in 1998–99 that figure rose to 3.2 million (Losen & Edley, 2001; Losen & Gillespie, 2012). By 2011–12, there were 3.5 million in-school suspensions, 1.9 million single out-of-school suspensions, and 1.5 million multiple out-of-school suspensions, for a total of 6.95 million suspensions in and out of school annually, in addition to 130,000 students who were expelled (U.S. Department of Education, Office for Civil Rights, 2014). The increased reliance on suspension is also revealed in localized data. In cities like New York and Boston, suspension rates and expulsion rates rose 40 percent over a few years in the late 1990s and early 2000s (Monahan, 2010; Sundius and Farneth, 2008). The total number of expulsions from Chicago Public Schools rose from 81 in 1995 to 612 in 2009, marking an 800 percent increase (Gordon et al., 2001; Karp, 2010).

When data from urban school districts are disaggregated by race, African American students are shown to be at a severe disciplinary disadvantage (Ayers et al., 2001; Gordon et al., 2001; Skiba et al., 2002). Schools with large African American student populations have the highest student-to-police ratios, the greatest implementation of high-security technologies, and the harshest punishments under zero-tolerance policies (Ayers et al., 2001; Gordon et al., 2001; Skiba et al., 2002). School districts serving large minority populations also have higher rates of school-based arrests (Contractor and Staats, 2014). A recent study found that African American students were suspended and expelled disproportionately in each of twelve large U.S. cities (Gordon et al., 2001). In some metropolitan areas, African American students were punished out of school at ratios double their percentage of the student population. This was the case in Austin, Texas, where African American students made up 18 percent of the student body but experienced 36 percent of suspensions and expulsions in 1999 (Gordon et al., 2001). From 2000 to 2003 in Texas, 83 percent of African American male students statewide were charged with at least one disciplinary offense between seventh and twelfth grades, which is disproportionately higher than all other race and gender groups in the state (Fabelo et al., 2011). Over 94 percent of these students had their first encounter with school discipline for the discretionary offense of breaking their school's code of conduct (Fabelo et al., 2011). In other words, the punitive experience for African American males in school begins with harsh treatment for minor infractions.

The growing dependence on the criminal justice system and on suspension and expulsion in school disciplinary punishments in the late 1990s and early 2000s has created a new category of student, the school pushout—a student forced by school administrators to leave school for disciplinary reasons (Arum & Beattie, 1999). There are very few ways for a public school to customize their student population, but disciplinary policy is one of them (Figlio, 2006). Students who break the school disciplinary code may be pushed out of school for days, weeks, or months—enough time to fall behind, or further behind, academically (Losen & Gillespie, 2012). Pushouts who never return to school become categorized as "dropouts," which masks the role that the schools had in pushing them toward this terminus (Lehr et al., 2004).

In 2009, there were 6.2 million school dropouts counted in America (Sum et al., 2009). There is a well-documented link between abbreviated schooling and a narrowing of adult prospects. Academic attainment is both a bellwether for economic stability—represented by earning power, wage growth, labor security, and home ownership—and an indicator of psychological and physical health (Sum et al., 2009). Statistics also show that students who have lost educational affiliation are highly vulnerable to incarceration: nearly 10 percent of all male dropouts are in juvenile custody, and the lifetime incarceration rate among African American male dropouts is 25 percent (Sum et al., 2009).

SCHOOL DISCIPLINE AS A MANAGEMENT STRATEGY

The educational context for the phenomena of racially disproportionate school failure and prison expansion in America is a severely troubled urban public school system. The punitive shift in education has had the effect of simultaneously masking egregious academic conditions in urban public schools and reproducing them. In their book *Punishing Schools*, Lyons and Drew argue that in this dynamic we are "punishing our inner city schools for the challenges they face as if their decaying buildings [and] decades of disinvestment . . . stand as evidence of parental neglect and uncontrollable youth" (Lyons & Drew, 2006). In critiquing this arrangement, they point to Ira Katznelson's notion of a "politics of dependency." When governments are overwhelmed by the responsibilities of governance and unable to solve large-scale social problems, the meting out of harsh punishment can reproduce old and generate new dependencies, thereby reframing systemic social problems as matters of individual failure (Katznelson, 1976; Lyons & Drew, 2006). Under the politics of dependency, students who don't learn in failing urban schools can be portrayed as part of a correctional solution. Educational problems are masked by this "solution," however, and they remain in situ.

Punitive school discipline makes educational inequality disappear at the institutional level by taking a lack of student engagement and "fixing" it with discipline rather than with expansive educational opportunities. As has been said of mass incarceration, school discipline uses punishment to manage large-scale social problems such as poverty, hunger, homelessness, and youth protective custody (Beckett & Herbert, 2010; Giroux, 2011b; Skiba, 2000). Thus, youth criminalization at school becomes a mode of governance that conceals a real need for robust educational experiences (Simon, 2007; Giroux, 2003; Pettit, 2012).

School discipline as a management strategy also works to alleviate the administrative problem of accommodating individual learning differences in an authentic way. There is strong evidence of this in the data on disciplinary actions against special-needs students.[7] Students with disabilities are suspended at far higher rates than students without disabilities (Losen & Gillespie, 2012). Over 6 percent of all students with disabilities were suspended at least once during the 2009–10 school year, compared to around 4 percent for students without disabilities. Students with disabilities are also far more likely to be suspended multiple times in a single school year: 6.6 percent versus 2.7 percent. When disability is conflated with minority racial status, the disparities are significant. In the 2009–10 school year, 25 percent of black students with disabilities were suspended out of school, whereas for white students with disabilities the suspension rate was 9 percent (Losen & Gillespie, 2012). Pedro Noguera has argued that a disciplinary approach that pushes students out of school for their problems suggests either an institutional unwillingness to help students or a belief that they can't be helped (Noguera, 2008a). Noguera claims that "school officials are generally aware that students on an educational path that leads to nowhere will cause more trouble and will therefore have to be subjected to more extreme forms of control," but that "the fixation on control tends to override all other educational objectives and concerns" (Noguera, 2008a).

THE STAKES OF EDUCATIONAL OPPORTUNITY

The focus on punitive educational relations brings vast disparities in education to light and thus casts doubt on the strength of the larger democratic project of the public school system, which is charged with easing social differences in order to buttress democratic aims. From its very beginnings in the middle of the nineteenth century, the American public school system was intended to provide a level playing field so that even those of humble birth could have the chance to participate in democratic government, enjoy the nation's cultural life, and compete in the marketplace. It is largely because public schools offer a mechanism for individual achievement and advancement that the United States preserves its status as a meritocratic and non-caste society. The effort to maintain this democratic status underlies the extension of educational rights to minority groups, including women and non-whites. This expansive and egalitarian view of education is clearly proffered in the *Brown v. Board of Education* decision, in which Chief Justice Earl Warren wrote:

> Today, education is perhaps the most important function of state and local governments. Compulsory school attendance laws and the great expenditures for education both demonstrate our recognition of the importance of education to our democratic society. It is required in the performance of our most basic public responsibilities. . . . It is the very foundation of good citizenship. Today it is a principal instrument in awakening a child to cultural values, in preparing him for later professional training, and in helping him adjust normally to his environment. In these days, it is doubtful that any child may reasonably be expected to succeed in life if he is denied the opportunity of an education. Such an opportunity, where the state has undertaken to provide it, is a right which must be made available to all on equal terms.

Centrally, schools serve as the starting point for social and economic opportunity and advancement in our society and, as the linchpin of democracy, are significant contexts for any degree of inequality. As a consequence, when inequalities in schools undermine the right to education, we witness a failure of democracy itself.

Though the sociopolitical stakes of inequality are high, educational opportunities remain deficient for many students, and the brunt of this marginalization is borne by poor, minority youths. The court order to desegregate schools in *Brown v. Board of Education*, for example, did not eliminate racial disparities in educational opportunity, but only mitigated racial disparities in educational access. This is to say little more than what most Americans know, which is that any child can go to a local public school, but good educational opportunities are more likely in prosperous communities. In the aftermath of the integration order, many white Americans with financial resources simply moved out of the cities and into the suburbs to establish racial separatism by geography. Consequently, many modern urban public schools are still essentially segregated (Orfield & Eaton, 1996). The *Brown* decision reversed the "separate but equal" legal doctrine, but it did little to legislate what African American students would have access to in the public schools that were now open to them (Street, 2005). Even in racially diverse schools, minority students, more so than white students, are undermined and ill served by inexperienced teachers, remedial curricula, and the pall of low expectations (Noguera, 2003a, 2003b, 2008a). In schools serving primarily minority students, the educational conditions tend to be far more marginal, often in ways that are visible in the infrastructure: poor lighting, broken windows, and weed-strewn lots (Noguera, 2008a). In *Ghetto Schooling*, Jean Anyon writes of inner-city classrooms that "smell of urine" and classroom doors that are boarded up (Anyon, 1997).

While public schools have a revered place in our society (and reasonably so) as primary sites for realizing individual agency within a democracy, they are simultaneously central sites of youth criminalization, generating opportunity while also reproducing inequality. Analyses that show the role of public schooling in reproducing inequality with regard to race, class, gender, and sexuality are quite familiar (Bowles & Gintis, 1976; Carnoy & Levin, 1985; Oakes, 1985; Apple, 1990/2004; Bourdieu & Passeron, 1977; Kirp, 1982; Weis & Fine, 1993). In the War on Crime era, schools exacerbated these primary disparities by reproducing correctional inequality.

The ramifications of a hard-edged public school system are multiple and multilayered. For students, tough-on-crime policies at school establish a tone of mistrust that belies a cynicism about the promise of youth, and when discipline produces school suspension or expulsion, it directly impinges upon young people's potential by circumscribing opportunity sets (Noguera, 2008a). School suspension and expulsion are exclusionary and may have the effect of prematurely ending an educational career while catalyzing an adult trajectory of dispossession and correctional vulnerability (Losen & Gillespie, 2012). When aggressive punitive arrangements are geographically concentrated, as they are in urban public schools serving minority students, they mark a disinvestment in human capital, which has a destabilizing effect on a larger community of relations by pressuring social ties, curbing economic development, and contracting political power (Noguera, 1995). On a societal scale, punitive public schools play a role in reshaping achievement ideologies, limiting meritocratic trajectories, and reconfiguring the basis of the democratic state itself (MacLeod, 1987; Bowles & Gintis, 1976). In this turn to the punitive, public schools also play into much larger patterns of state power relocation and ironically participate in the erosion of the social welfare state of which they have traditionally been considered a centerpiece.

As the next chapter explores, punitive schooling plays a significant role in large-scale economic, political, and social formations. Harsh discipline makes an economic impact by emboldening neoliberal strategies that privatize the public sector for the benefit of corporate profit (Wacquant, 2009; Casella,

2010; Mora & Christianakis, 2013). Schools that mete out harsh punishments carry ideological sway by normalizing severe disciplinary policies and practices, which help to underwrite the logic of criminal justice expansion and enable greater opportunities for profit within the larger network surrounding the correctional system. The penal state also absorbs and obscures seven million of the most disenfranchised Americans, who are primarily undereducated, underemployed, impoverished, and disproportionately African American and male (Wacquant, 2009).[8] Were these populations visible in their home communities, they would reveal an urban America with socioeconomic disparities so vast as to call into question the public education system as a democratic mechanism and to undermine the nation's larger political and economic schemes.

CHAPTER 2

The "At-Risk Youth Industry"

Our prison intake is fifteen thousand a year. Our high school dropout rate is fifteen thousand a year. I mean, that tells you the story of what is happening to us. They're coming out of these schools and coming to prison.

—Jimmy LeBlanc, Louisiana Secretary of Corrections

In this chapter, I expose the workings of the school security market and the "at-risk youth industry." The burden of harsh school discipline, which is borne disproportionately by African American male students, is a boon to industries designed to capitalize on youth educational and disciplinary disenfranchisement. Public schools criminalize these students, catalyze and rationalize their correctionalization, and, in doing so, build the base for neoliberal disciplinary and correctional markets. The term *at-risk youth industry* is used by leaders in these markets to describe the business of running youth disciplinary programs, treatment programs, and juvenile correctional institutions. Here, I show how school security investments and disciplinary practices contribute significantly to that economy. In this vein, the at-risk youth industry encodes the larger phenomenon of correctional embeddedness well. It is not simply that youths are pushed into juvenile or adult correctional institutions as a result of school failure on educational and disciplinary grounds, but that correctional ideologies are embedded in their experiences in schools along the way (Rodriguez, 2010; Noguera, 2008a; Giroux, 2011a). I conclude the chapter by moving toward the case study of this book, a public school at the Orleans Parish Prison in New Orleans, Louisiana, that serves as a local instantiation of correctional encroachment.

As public schools have become oriented toward punitive disciplinary modes and criminalized more and more students, they have both legitimized the War on Crime and reproduced its influence. In this era, highly disadvantaged students were exposed to the criminal justice system at an earlier age and rendered more vulnerable to criminal justice custody (Nolan, 2011). Marginalized students encountered heavy concentrations of law enforcement and traversed secured and surveilled educational spaces on a daily basis (Nolan, 2011; Monahan, 2006b; Kupchik, 2010). This hard-line approach to students reproduced many of the same experiences that youths were having beyond school campuses (Rios, 2011; Goffman, 2014). Minority males, in particular, were under constant scrutiny by the police in their home communities (Rios, 2011; Goffman, 2014). Day and night, their routine activities were generally viewed with actionable suspicion (Rios, 2011; Goffman, 2014). There was, however, a significant difference in the exercise of social control in school and in community spaces. School staff and security officers are given far more latitude than traditional law enforcement to exercise speedy retribution for juvenile missteps. School administrators, for example, don't need to obtain a warrant to conduct searches and don't require probable cause (U.S. Department of Education, 1996).

The Supreme Court has ruled that "reasonable suspicion" is just cause for student searches, even if it is not sufficient grounds for searches of adults (U.S. Department of Education, 1996; Packaged Facts, 2000). The Constitutional standard for reasonable suspicion is largely established in the case of *New Jersey v. T.L.O.*, and legal scholars have interpreted the ruling in this case to mean that reasonable suspicion could be warranted by mere presence, gesture, or gaze. The following describes what legal scholars have identified as possible scenarios for reasonable suspicion: "student makes a furtive glance to his pocket as the teacher approaches; . . . the student flees as the teacher approaches; . . . the student is present in an area where drug dealing is known to occur; . . . the student is observed placing something in a sock or shoe" (Jones and Semler as cited in Yudof et al., 2002). Since the standards of reasonable suspicion are weaker than the traditional standards of probable cause, students may be subjected to school-based agents of a correctional system whose power exceeds that of traditional justice officers (Yudof et al., 2002). The exceptional powers bestowed on school officials and school-based security officers are derived from the understanding that schools are protected sites (Giroux, 2011a). The Supreme Court has suggested that because the public school has a great interest "in maintaining security and order in the classroom and on school grounds," traditional protections of privacy are not upheld for youths as they are for adults (U.S. Department of Education, 1996).

School shootings at sites like Columbine and Sandy Hook made it seem that this tough approach was prudent and even necessary, although statistically, youth homicide at school was an exceptionally rare event (National Center for Education Statistics [NCES], 2011). There is a 98 percent chance that youths who fall victim to homicide are not at school when it happens; they are at home or on the street or elsewhere (NCES, 2011; James & McCallion, 2013). In the 1998–99 school year, the year of the Columbine massacre, there were a total of thirty-three youth homicides at schools nationally, twelve of which were at Columbine, and 2,407 youth homicides away from school (NCES, 2011).[1] In terms of risk to life, schools are generally getting safer for youths and have been trending that way since 1992 (Centers for Disease Control and Prevention, 2014; James & McCallion, 2013).

Schools have also been getting safer, rather than more dangerous, in terms of theft and nonlethal violence (NCES, 2011). At a glance, these declines in youth victimization appear to map onto the tough-on-crime period, suggesting that the crackdown on students worked to lower school-based crime. Comparable declines in youth victimization outside of school suggest otherwise (U.S. Department of Education, 2007; Western, 2006). Crime rates dropped across the nation in general, and schools reflected that shift, such that the decline of crime in schools cannot reasonably be attributed to the success of tough-on-crime measures (Zimring, 2007).

Scholars in the sociology of punishment have made much of the fact that Americans continued to be "tough on crime" in the general population even as crime rates fell through the 1980s and '90s. This generated a phenomenon of punitive excess and catalyzed the prison boom (Zimring, 2007; Western, 2006; Pettit, 2012). Simultaneously, in American public schools, a similar dynamic occurred. Schools became tough on kids without much evidence to support the approach, and students were pushed out of school in large numbers (Sundius & Farneth, 2008; NCES, 2011; Losen et al., 2015).

Schools have always been social control institutions, but historically American public schools have leaned toward *implicit* social control models (Noguera, 2008a). School authority was arranged in physical space and maintained through testing, grading, and ranking of students (Bowles & Gintis, 1976; Foucault, 1979/1995; Spring, 2000; Simmons, 2009a). Teachers inculcated preferred social values with hegemonic instruction and normative evaluation (Foucault, 1979/1995; Spring, 2000; Noguera, 2008a). A hidden curriculum of unspoken routines, rules, dispositions, expectations, and perspectives—aligning, for example, with the needs of capitalism—were transmitted tacitly in the course of instruction (Jackson, 1968/1990; Bowles & Gintis, 1976; Apple, 1990/2004). These socialization processes endure, but the rapid shift toward a law enforcement presence in public schools has radically reshaped student management strategies toward more explicit social control models. This shift isn't explained by skyrocketing crime rates in school, since that dynamic did not exist. The explanation emerges with a broader sociocultural analysis of the War on Crime itself, revealing both the social substrates of fear and the political economy of punishment.

SECURITY MARKET EXPANSION IN PUBLIC EDUCATION

As school administrators nationwide were groping for a solution to a security problem they did not have, security manufacturers were capitalizing on their burgeoning interest. At the time of Columbine, school security was a small percentage of the $16 billion security market overall, and a relatively untapped niche market. In the context produced by a culture of fear, the market was poised for expansion. The chief financial officer of Comverse Technology, Inc., a surveillance supplier, explained: "In the last couple of years these incidents have awakened the security industry to present more emphasis on solutions geared to managing the interests of school systems. You're going to find we're working very hard to make our systems compatible to the needs of school systems" (Packaged Facts, 2000). Security companies responded to Columbine and other school shootings in the 1990s as an opportunity for greater sales, and industry operators began to report exponential market growth (Packaged Facts, 2000; Chaddock, 1999). Some companies donated emergency security products to schools in hopes of spurring future investments in company products, a bet that was likely to pay off in a booming market (Packaged Facts, 2000).

The greatest beneficiaries of the clamor were metal detector manufacturers, which claimed about 35 percent of all security spending (Packaged Facts, 2000). Another 30 percent of school security spending was on surveillance, and 25 percent was on controlled-access technologies. Significantly, the first surge in metal detector use by schools was recorded before the 1999 Columbine shooting. Garrett Metal Detectors began selling their products to schools in 1993; in 1996, a company spokesman said that "schools became our largest target market segment, more than corrections facilities and airports" (Pitts,

1999). John Devine verifies the early trend, explaining in his book *Maximum Security*, which was published before Columbine, that metal detectors have long been the standard response to school violence (Devine, 1996). Even in districts for which school violence was not a big concern, metal detectors were becoming part of the educational landscape. Devine quotes a superintendent who said, after a school stabbing, "I can't say that violence is the order of the day in our schools. But I'm sure going to look again at the issue of metal detectors."

As the market for school security products grew, companies expanded their product catalogs and offered a device for every imaginable school-security purpose. Sales of high technologies included metal detectors, surveillance cameras, face-recognition systems, and intrusion sensors. Smart cards could be used for school entry, lunchroom access, and library checkout (Packaged Facts, 2000). These mechanisms were supplemented by X-ray scanning machines, burglar alarms, badges, and bulletproof wipeboards (Molnar, 2013). Antitheft tagging systems protected schools from burglary; anti-graffiti products protected facilities from vandalism; and radios, pagers, and phones aided in general control efforts (Packaged Facts, 2000; Chaddock, 1999; Casella, 2006).

The market for low technologies also grew and further sponsored industrial growth in the school security industry. Transparent lockers and backpacks were positioned in the market to facilitate search-and-seizure practices. Security services provided on-site police, guards, canine forces, and drug searching and testing tools (Casella, 2006; Monahan, 2006a). As each of these services expanded, there was an industrial ripple effect. For example, many school security guards reported to duty in uniform and contributed to the market sales for uniform attire, which rose from $900 million in 1998 to $1.4 billion in 2000 (Packaged Facts, 2000). Ronnie Casella (2006), the author of *Selling Us the Fortress*, explains that the school security industry provided business opportunities to roughly thirteen thousand private American security firms. Members of this workforce, in turn, supported a publishing industry that produced periodicals about school security issues with names like *Security Management* and *American Schools and Universities* (the latter devoted entirely to school safety). Security workers also held memberships in professional organizations such as the National Association of School Resource Officers, American Society for Industrial Security, International Association of Professional Security Consultants, and National Association of School Safety and Law Enforcement Officers. They sponsored conferences and annual meetings

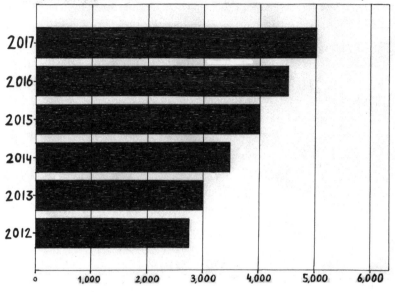

SECURiTY SYSTEMS iNTEGRATiON iN EDUCATiON
(A U.S. MARKET FORECAST iN MiLLiONS OF U.S. DOLLARS)

FIGURE 2. Security systems integration in education (a U.S. market forecast in millions of U.S. dollars). Source: IHS Research, 2013. Graphics courtesy of Rigo 23.

across the nation to discuss school security matters and bring tourist dollars to the conference host cities.

Public schools that engaged this industry did not always have the resources needed to fund their high-tech security strategies; to raise the funds, they could apply for federal grant money or cut the instructional budget (Noguera, 2001, 2003). Data gathered through market research show just how wedded schools were to the idea of advancing their security operations in the late 1990s and early 2000s and how much money they shifted in that direction.[2]

In 1996, the security market for public and private K–12 schools reached $328 million in sales. The school security market expanded so rapidly from there that sales reached $3 billion in 2013 (figure 2). Industry experts project that sales will reach nearly $5 billion by 2017 (IHS Research, 2013). By contrast, the Corrections Corporation of America (CCA), the nation's largest private prison company, reported $1.7 billion in revenue in 2011 (Lee, 2012).[3] The Geo Group, which operates the second-largest private detention company in the nation, had revenue of $1.6 billion. At its current rate of growth, the school security market will soon approach the size of the entire private corrections market, dominated by just four large companies and estimated at $6 billion (Wacquant, 2010). If we are to size up the correctional markets within the frame of the punishment industry, the vast school security market should be taken into consideration. It is projected to double the market share of the punishment industry. If we are to imagine the punishment industry as a potentially significant share of the gross domestic product, the analytical parameters could be extended further.

School-based crime and crime-control efforts interest media markets, and in this realm the network of correctional relations expands again. Media companies may be positioned in large conglomerates, with affiliates directly engaged in security sales (Monahan, 2006b). Until 2013, for example, General Electric (GE) owned a 49 percent share of the National Broadcasting Company (NBC). The parent company has been deeply involved in the War on Crime through such engagements as port security and container scanning as well as school security and surveillance (Monahan, 2006b). GE is also a large Pentagon contractor and is, therefore, entrenched in the military industrial complex. The company also supplies security technologies to the correctional system and has directly invested in private prisons (Goldberg & Evans, 1997). Given these sorts of relations, not exclusive to the GE conglomerate, there is a fiscal logic to the sensationalism of real or perceived school crime and to the War on Crime more generally.

The criminal justice system was already providing global security conglomerates with large correctional contracts, but criminal justice is highly restrictive in terms of market expansion. Growth in this sphere is dependent on determinations of criminality. When the public grew panicked about violence in schools, security corporations gained a new market share. These corporations sold crime control as a preemptive measure in schools and worked to secure some of the safest institutions in America. Their new market included nearly a hundred thousand public schools and fifty million public school students, all before tapping private resources (Center for Education Reform, 2012). Security corporations would secure their own future in this venture as new generations came to see and accept advanced security technologies as fixtures of American life. This, according to the sociologist David Lyon, is the "surveillance society," in which security technologies become ubiquitous to the point of invisibility (Lyon, 1994).

THE POLITICAL ECONOMY OF SCHOOL SECURITY

With a school security market on the rise and approaching $5 billion in annual sales, an obvious question emerges. Where is the money coming from to pay for it all? Even well-funded public school districts don't typically have great budgetary surpluses, and first-year costs for a well-rounded security system in a single school can reach three-quarters of a million dollars. Installation costs are highly dependent on the size of the school campus and the depth of the security detail, but the cost of a surveillance network for a large high school was $200,000 in 2006 (Lohman & Shepard, 2006). A scan card system potentially adds an additional $250,000 to the security budget, and effective portal metal detectors can be purchased for up to $35,000 each (Lohman & Shepard, 2006). To enable efficient school entry and reduce lines, portal detectors are often installed in multiples, and handheld metal detectors are paired with them to more specifically locate metal on a student's body for $200 to $400 each (Lohman & Shepard, 2006). A duress alarm and remote-access entry system both add $10,000 to the cost (Lohman & Shepard, 2006). School administrators who install this equipment are also committing budgetary funds to annual staffing and maintenance. The annual salary of security staff costs upwards of $25,000, and two or three officers are needed to supervise entry points and operate the equipment. Maintenance costs are ongoing, and most security mechanisms are vulnerable to vandalism and theft, which may prompt total-replacement costs. In big urban public school systems, security costs have soared with these annual investments. In 2015, the Chicago Public Schools system approved a budget of more than $100 million to employ security guards and police officers and equip them with training, safety plans, and technologies (Board of Education of the City of Chicago, 2015–2016). This figure nearly triples the $35 million Chicago Public Schools security budget of 2001–02 (Casella, 2003a).[4]

Some state budgets include funds for school security costs, but the largest source of all this school security funding is the federal government.[5] Rita Homer, working as a marketing communications manager for Inovonics Corporation, a producer of panic alarms, explains the process: "Schools can . . . apply for a grant to fund security measures . . . from the federal government" (Packaged Facts, 2000). With those funds, schools gain access to Inovonics products. The vast share of school security monies can be traced to the U.S. Departments of Education, Justice, and Homeland Security. Their interagency collaborations demonstrate how the public education system and the justice system were bound by design in the War on Crime era. Federal legislation and funding linked these agencies, and public schools became sites for fighting both the War on Crime and the War on Terror. This made them politically expedient initiatives on the national stage, but they were also advantageous for their political sponsors, who were working to secure election and reelection by tapping into civilian concerns, advancing corporate interests and neoliberal policies in their states, and building campaign coffers (Tonry, 2004).

There are a large number of federal initiatives to fund school security and link public schools to law enforcement. In 2002, for example, the Department of Justice funded the Community Oriented Policing Services (COPS) Secure Our Schools (SOS) Grant Program. The acronyms reference both "cops" and SOS, the radio code for "distress," thereby declaring school violence to be an emergency requiring law enforcement. The program is described as "encouraging law enforcement agencies and school districts to partner together to advance school security and safety through the prevention of school violence" primarily by funding surveillance systems, metal detectors, and scanning devices, including those used for fingerprinting (U.S. Department of Justice, 2008, 2013a). A review of award recipients in 2007 reveals that $15 million was distributed for school security; with the exception of two school districts, the funds were directed to city offices and city police departments (U.S. Department of Justice, 2007). In 2011, nine years into the program, the COPS initiative had invested $70 million in the SOS program, but this is ultimately a small part of COPS, which also runs the Safe Schools Initiative, the COPS in Schools program, and the School-Based Partnerships program. Including the SOS program, COPS has made a combined investment in school security totaling $900 million (U.S. Department of Justice, 2011c).

The Department of Homeland Security also funds school security, which links the cause of school security to the rhetoric of terrorism. The U.S. Office of Homeland Security was established in 2001, eleven days after the terrorist attacks of September 11. In 2002 the office was named a cabinet department and integrated twenty-two federal agencies under one administrative roof. With the mission of protecting the "homeland" of the United States, the department sponsors investments in school security and pays for equipment as well as training (U.S. Department of Homeland Security, 2013).

Perhaps the most explicit attempt to model school security tactics on correctional and military strategies was presented in the Safe Schools Security

Act of 1999 (U.S. Congress, 1999). The initiative, which was federally funded in 2002, established the School Security Technology and Resource Center at Sandia National Labs (Cornell University Law School, 2002). Sandia is a privately owned national security facility that is managed by the defense contractor Lockheed Martin and funded by the U.S. Department of Energy (Sandia National Laboratories, 1999; S. Res. 638, 1999). The National Law Enforcement and Corrections Technology Center and the National Center for Rural Law Enforcement were named as Sandia's partners in the new center, and they were authorized to provide resources for "school security assessments, and security technology development" (S. Res. 638, 1999). Urging fellow legislators to vote for the bill, Senator Jeff Bingaman (Democrat, New Mexico) explained: "Because of Sandia's expertise in evaluating and designing security for our Nation's nuclear sites, Sandia is well suited to evaluate the security of our schools and advise school administrators on how to create safer learning facilities" (U.S. Congressional Record, 2001). A review of campaign contributions reveals that Lockheed Martin was the second-largest benefactor of Senator Bingaman, and Sandia National Labs was the senator's seventh-largest campaign contributor (Pitts, 1999). Senator Bingaman, like other members of Congress, thus had a significant political motive for backing the neoliberal plan to privatize school security. Tenure in political office was tied to a congressional capacity to imagine new ways of being tough on crime and respond to public concerns about safety in the post-9/11 and post-Columbine era (Tonry, 2004).

YOUTH CORRECTIONS ON A MASS PRODUCTION MODEL

The tight link between educational failure and incarceration was not lost on private youth correctional firms. These corporations sought to capitalize on youths who had been disenfranchised by educational inadequacy and disciplinary severity prior to actual incarceration. The capacity of youth correctional institutions to reach youths and profit from them in advance of incarceration shows just how limited the rubric of the school-to-prison pipeline is in describing the dimensions of correctional influence in children's lives.

In a detailed, forty-five-page market report to potential investors in 1997, SunTrust Equitable Securities described "at-risk youth" in terms of "A Growth Industry." The leading investment firm calculated that it was "poised to capitalize on an estimated $50 billion . . . in annual public spending on youth services"

(SunTrust Equitable Securities, 1997; Press & Washburn, 2002). In their "corrections index performance" graph for 1995–98, SunTrust portrays correctional securities as outperforming the S&P 500 and NASDAQ. SunTrust Equitable Securities is a publicly traded corporation of the parent company, SunTrust Bank, with a mission to "preserve and enhance client wealth" with "unique and/or proprietary products or services," researching and identifying corporations that yield high returns on client investments and managing assets valued at $1 billion. SunTrust also underwrites equity offerings for private companies that are going public. SunTrust's own stock values are linked to its effectiveness in securing profit, which helps explain the interest of SunTrust Equitable Securities in for-profit corrections (Equitable Trust, 2014).

Private youth corrections was actually new terrain for investors in 1997. Only a year before, the federal government passed the 1996 Welfare Reform Act, which enabled the privatization of government youth services. As a component of larger neoliberal shifts, government funds for youth services, which had been primarily restricted to nonprofit agencies, were opened to for-profit management. A few years later, in 2005, President George W. Bush would push unsuccessfully for the privatization of Social Security.

The rosy predictions in SunTrust's report are buttressed by an account of U.S. demographic trends. The authors predict that the fourteen- to twenty-four-year-old cohort will grow over fifteen years, and they equate this population growth to rising crime rates. If this prediction and the assumption held true, the at-risk youth industry would, by their estimation, deliver vast opportunity for correctional profit. The logic is that more impoverished youths mean more offenders, and more offenders mean more treatment and higher demand for juvenile-justice-facility beds. The report claims that youth offenders will be generated within this cohort by a rise in child abuse and neglect, considerable increases in single-parent and working-poor families, and increased juvenile drug use. In other words, the hardships faced by low-income youths are made over as a well of profit.

According to the report, "The combination of these severe social problems has directly led to an increased number of at-risk youth and, in turn, to growth in crimes committed by the youth population." A series of charts depicts the highlighted socioeconomic indices and graphs rising murder rates in the youth category from roughly 1984 to 1991. However, the data don't deliver on the predictions. The SunTrust claim about rising youth drug use, for example, ultimately proved inaccurate. From 2002 to 2008, drug use among youths held constant (National Substance Abuse and Mental Health Services Administration, 2008). The charted upward trend in youth homicide commission was also short-lived. Between 1994 and 2003, murders involving juvenile offenders dropped by 65 percent (U.S. Department of Justice, 2011b). Relying on limited data through 1997, however, the SunTrust authors mapped the conditions for a crime wave by youth offenders that didn't come to pass. There is no attempt in the report to strategize about addressing any of the social problems identified. While there is attention to class dynamics in the report, there is no consideration of race or gender, despite the fact that African American males were captured by this correctional profiteering strategy in high disproportion.

The overarching suggestion of the SunTrust report is that hikes in child abuse, childhood poverty, youth drug use, and juvenile crime—even murder—will be advantageous for the correctional economy. Eyal Press and Jennifer Washburn, in an exceptionally thoughtful and broad-reaching piece for *The Atlantic*, offer this critique of the report:

> In August of 2000 the National Center for Children in Poverty, at Columbia University, released a study showing that despite the country's recent economic boom, 13 million American children were living in poverty—three million more than in 1979. For most Americans that was unsettling news, but for a small group of publicly traded companies it represented an opportunity. As the ranks of children living in poverty have grown during the past two decades, so have the ranks of juveniles filing through the nation's dependency and delinquency courts, typically landing in special-education programs, psychiatric-treatment centers, orphanages, and juvenile prisons. These were formerly run almost exclusively by nonprofit and public agencies. In the mid-1990s, however, a number of large, multistate for-profit companies emerged to form what Wall Street soon termed the "at-risk-youth industry." (Press & Washburn, 2002)

They note that SunTrust makes severe social problems sound like a good thing. For example, as if excited by the prospect, the authors of the SunTrust report claim that "Not only has the raw number of abused and neglected children increased ... but ... the rate of children reported as abused and neglected has increased from 28 per 1,000 children in 1984 to 43 per 1,000 in 1993" (Press & Washburn, 2002). This is framed as an investment boon rather than a social disaster.

Delving further into juvenile corrections as a market opportunity, the SunTrust authors chart an anticipated acceleration in the juvenile correctional population. For one thing, federal funding for juvenile justice facilities grew

through the 1980s, and SunTrust records the increase at an annual compounded rate of more than 13 percent, with expected increases of 7 to 8 percent
over a decade. The kinds of "dramatic growth" seen in juvenile incarceration
from 1988 to 1995 will continue to benefit the "industry landscape," according
to the report, and the youth population in residential detention settings will
nearly double, from 52,000 in 1995 to 90,000 in 2004. The report indicates
that the number of youths in nonresidential correctional programs will more
than double, from 51,000 in 1995 to 107,000 by 2004. They expect the number
of facility beds to increase as the juvenile corrections population grows, referring to numbers of youth beds as "slots." In 1996, they explain, there were "1,993
bed/slots" and in 1997 there were "5,033 bed/slots." They write that "We look
forward to the significant growth achieved in 1997 to continue in 1998."

The enthusiastic perspective on correctional market growth continues
throughout the report as if it is summarizing an industry for automobile sales
or housing starts rather than prison cells for children. The primacy of fiscal
concerns in youth corrections is corroborated by Luis Lamela, the president
and CEO of Ramsay Youth Services, which runs youth psychiatric hospitals.
Lamela explains that youth corrections *is* mass production, saying that "It's a
product-to-market approach. . . . We view everything as a product. . . . What
we look for is the achievement of economies of scale" (Press & Washburn,
2002). Similarly, Florence Simcoe, who directed services for mentally disturbed children at Century HealthCare, explained that at-risk children were
simply "bodies that we got $300 a day for" (Press & Washburn, 2002).

The political economy of youth correctional privatization is shaped both
by public pressure to cut government budgets in corrections and continued
public support for longer sentences and mandatory incarceration for repeat
offenders. The SunTrust authors write that "Private correctional/youth services companies have been able to enter the market and alleviate some of this
pressure by providing efficient, cost-effective facilities." The profit in corrections is primarily found in cutting costs, which is what Angola Prison Warden
Burl Cain has called "feeding them with a thimble." Tax loopholes provide
another avenue for savings. SunTrust explains that for-profit corporations can
access tax exemption for facility capital needs.

With the aim of helping clients seize capital opportunity at every stage,
SunTrust Equitable Securities touts its ability to lead investors in charting
the juvenile corrections "Privatization Spectrum—from Schoolhouse to
Jailhouse," indexing the youth disenfranchisement process and showing how

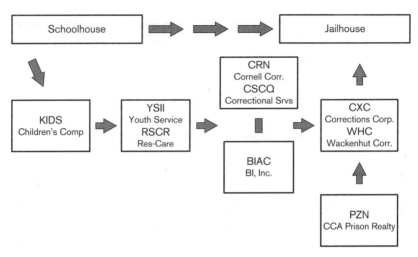

FIGURE 3. SunTrust's overview of the at-risk youth industry. Source: SunTrust Equitable Securities, 1997, *Youth Services/Juvenile Corrections Industry*.

for-profit corporations build on each other to achieve total custody. Youths are pushed out of school and cycled through the correctional corporations like products in a mass-production enterprise. Press and Washburn write that on their way from the schoolhouse to the jailhouse, "children . . . pass through one publicly funded, privately run facility after another" while corporations profit (Press & Washburn, 2002). SunTrust narrates the continuum this way:

> Our privatization spectrum encompasses companies in three areas of the correctional services industry: adult detention services, community corrections, and at-risk youth services. The services provided by these companies are (i) adult prison and jail management; (ii) electronic monitoring, day reporting, probation and parole services, and the management of halfway houses; and (iii) educational treatment, and detention services to the rapidly expanding at-risk youth population.

This overview articulates SunTrust's entrenched position in their report on the at-risk youth industry, and figure 3 shows how it is visualized in the report.

In SunTrust's depiction, schools are positioned as the starting point for all correctional investment. From that point on, the arrangement of for-profit youth corrections is a matter of stepping-stones leading from schools to KIDS (Children's Comprehensive Services) to YSII (Youth Services International) and RSCR (Res-Care, Inc.) to CRN (Cornell Corrections, Inc.) and CSCQ (Correctional Services Corporation) or to BIAC (BI, Inc.), to CXC (Corrections Corporation) and WHC (Wackenhut Correctional Corporation), to the Jailhouse, with an alternative pathway through PZN (CCA Prison Realty Trust). The implication is that SunTrust will walk investors through the opportunities of the correctional continuum from start to finish. In actuality, these transitions are an embodied experience for disenfranchised and primarily African American male youths. From the corporate perspective, however, their bodies are merely vessels of capital.

THE ECONOMY OF YOUTH SERVICES IN THE CORRECTIONAL MATRIX

SunTrust Equitable Securities refers to the network of privately managed corrections companies as a "matrix" of businesses, which charts private correctional entities and their horizontal diversification in the carceral arena. The entities shift within the matrix as corporations change names to reflect new priorities, protect liabilities, and participate in mergers and acquisitions, the latter of which can be managed by SunTrust. In the spectrum of private youth corrections, several entities are designated as "aggressive players," including Children's Comprehensive and Youth Services International for their acquisition histories. These corporations have their own securities through which they raise capital, and SunTrust has helped manage their public equity offerings. The 1996 secondary offering for Children's Comprehensive Services was a $36.8 million deal for SunTrust.

Many of these corporations had, like CCA, experience in running private adult correctional facilities before entering the juvenile corrections market. They were lured into the youth market in the 1990s by large pools of federal funds and juvenile per diem correctional payments, which were higher than those for adults, with the idea that they would help cover the costs of education and mental health services (Press & Washburn, 2002). Private youth correctional agencies routinely got no-bid contracts to provide services (Press & Washburn, 2002). Press and Washburn report that powerful government lobbies were instrumental in arranging the transfer of federal and state funds (Press & Washburn, 2002).

SunTrust presented a financially appealing correctional marketplace in 1997 and spurred facility expansion, but a great deal of the reported promise was never realized. While Correctional Services Corporation (CSC) opened a 350-bed facility for juveniles in Florida, and Children's Comprehensive Services (CCS) leveraged opportunities to reach revenues of $115 million annually by 1999, the private youth services industry became mired in concerns over capital and human management. Private correctional corporations were not as successful in trimming operational budgets as was thought, and the bare-bones approach to youth services had a cost to human life.

Few resources were available to manage these human concerns, and administrators were arriving on the job with "no background in treatment or education" (CCS as cited in Press & Washburn, 2002). Barry Krisberg, the president of the National Council on Crime and Delinquency, claims that delivery in private juvenile corrections is to the bottom line, with very little oversight for social programming. In his words, "We have less regulation of the interstate commerce in troubled kids than of meat products" (Press & Washburn, 2002). As in public schools, privatization and pseudo-public configurations of education have fractured the delivery of services and sacrificed accountability structures. Once youths are pushed out of the public sector into new spaces of supervision, it is difficult to know what their experiences are, or even how they might align with the experiences of others. Michel Foucault argues in *Discipline and Punish* that isolation disaggregates power and disbands cabals (Foucault, 1979/1995). The arrangement benefits corporations acting in the shadows and under various auspices while compromising the collective capacities of the youths, their families, and the communities from which they come to demand change.

The primary objective of the corporate officers, trained in business management, was to keep correctional facilities full. An inside report from CSC revealed that ten juveniles had their institutional release days delayed for the sole purpose of keeping occupancy up and maintaining per diem government funding based on head count (Press & Washburn, 2002). Delaying release dates is an egregious way to ensure financial solvency in private youth corrections. It could point to greed or to financial trouble. Market analyses do reveal that the youth corrections industry has fared less well financially than expected. It is a far less compelling market to investors than SunTrust once reported.

Despite a tougher economy for the at-risk youth industry in the late 1990s and early 2000s, many for-profit correctional corporations have endured, and public money continues to fund their private enterprises (Press & Washburn, 2002). Companies like Youth Services International continued to expand what has been described as a juvenile jail empire (Goodman & González, 2013, 2014). The top brass at Youth Services International entered the private sector in the mainstream hotel business and transitioned in the 1980s to "welfare hotels," which were publicly funded but privately run housing projects for homeless populations. Many of these were ultimately closed for excessive code violations and incidents of resident death. The next big privatization scheme in the Reagan era was corrections, and juvenile jails followed on the "welfare hotel" idea. For twenty-five years, operating under various names (including Correctional Services Corporation), the owners of Youth Services International have operated juvenile jails in sixteen states and have incarcerated more than forty thousand juveniles. The company motto is "Preparing Troubled Youth for the Future," though it is unclear which future they mean (Youth Services International, 2016). In an exposé on the corporation, reporter Chris Markham found that government contracts with Youth Services International have been secured with little regard for the company's sordid past. Their service record has been stained by allegations of bribery for government contracts, charges of inmate neglect, and abuses that were fatal. These charges did not seem, however, to affect their ability to get government contracts (Goodman & Gonzaléz, 2013, 2014; Ferriss, 2012).

Across the nation, many juvenile correctional corporations have closed facilities in the past decade. News reports tell stories of juvenile jails run amok with scandal and abuse, and Youth Services International is included among them. If we have passed the heyday of private youth jails, it is not because the structural forces and ideologies that produced them have changed. These forces are expressed in one scheme or another, and the schemes themselves can fail even as their underlying structure gains momentum. Correctional ideologies are intricately bound to the hegemonic social, economic, and political forces that shape our world, and there is very little evidence that we are shifting away from the fear-based, neoliberal, profiteering, and lobbying practices that gain their footing by stepping on the backs of America's most dispossessed. As scholars like Michelle Alexander have argued, the impact of these ideological arrangements strikes a very familiar chord and can be traced to slavery, the convict lease system, and Jim Crow.

THE YOUTH SERVICES TARGET

In the tapering of juvenile correctional populations since 1999, corporate goals of correctional production have likely affected economies of scale. Nationally, there were 76,222 juveniles in public facilities and 31,271 juveniles in private facilities in 1999. In 2011, public correctional facilities held 42,584 youths and private facilities held 18,830 (U.S. Department of Justice, 2011a). Measured in percentages, the ratio remains constant: 63 percent public and 26 percent private in 1999, compared to 62 percent public and 27 percent private in 2011 (U.S. Department of Justice, 2011a). Florida is an exception; in that state, private facilities hold 100 percent of the juvenile correctional population (Goodman & Gonzaléz, 2013).

Almost all youths held in public institutions are in custody for law violations—96 percent are delinquent and 3 percent are status offenders—but at private correctional institutions, law offenders are a remarkably lower percentage of the population (U.S. Department of Justice, 2011a). They make up 59 percent of the youths in private facilities; 45 percent of these are delinquent and 14 percent are status offenders. The remaining 41 percent of youths in private juvenile facilities are non-offenders. The significance of these statistics is that private youth correctional institutions have been contracted to serve the bulk of non-offenders as well as the majority of status offenders. They target neglected, abused, disturbed, and disabled youths, as well as youths who commit quasi-crimes and can be referred to the institutions by schools, parents, and juvenile courts (U.S. Department of Justice, 2011a). This is a high-needs but law-abiding population, which is exactly the population that would be well served by robust social welfare services, especially if provided in their homes and communities. Social services are expensive, however, and their budgets are often cut first when for-profit correctional facilities are looking at the bottom line.

Social welfare services are also a good match for status offenders. The Vera Institute of Justice (2014) describes status offenders as "disobedient but not delinquent"; these youths have behaved in ways that are disallowed by law only because of their status as youths. Adults cannot be criminalized for skipping school or violating curfew laws or running away, but youths can because these behaviors create problems for the adults who supervise them. Status offenses are a primary mechanism for juvenile justice entry, and school administrators are leading actors in staging the transition of youths to custody. In the interest of further articulating the disciplinary collaborations between schools and the criminal justice system, I turn now to the case of New Orleans.

GETTING TOUGH IN FAILING SCHOOLS: NEW ORLEANS

In the context of the systemic educational failure that followed on decades of racialized divestment, Orleans Parish Schools grew tough on crime and on behaviors that could be analogized to crime. Fifty percent of all disciplinary

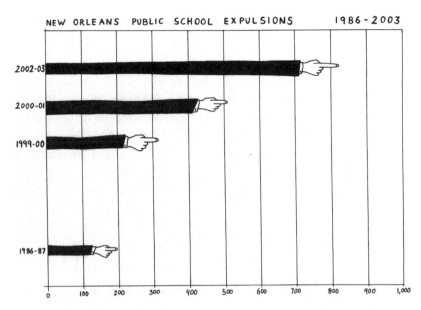

FIGURE 4. New Orleans public school expulsions, 1986–2003. Sources: Louisiana Department of Education, 2003, 2005; Tuzzolo & Hewitt, 2006. Graphics courtesy of Rigo 23.

punishments in 2006 were triggered by status offenses. Heavy security was not ubiquitous in the Orleans Parish Schools, as it was becoming in other parts of the country. For example, in the New York City school sites that John Devine studied for his book *Maximum Security* in the late 1980s, there were twelve to eighteen school security officers on duty at each school, and the New York Board of Education hired a security force of 3,200 uniformed officers that was larger than all but eight police departments in the United States (Devine, 1996). By comparison, there were a total of approximately two hundred security officers stationed at 123 district schools in New Orleans in the early 2000s (Juvenile Justice Project of Louisiana [JJPL], 2008). Just under $3 million was spent on school security in Orleans Parish in the 2004–05 school year, which meant that, on average, each school invested approximately $23,000 in security (JJPL, 2008). In the 2002–03 school year, however, almost fourteen thousand students were suspended at least once and 829 students were expelled, as shown in figure 4 (JJPL, 2008). This was a marked increase in suspension and expulsion rates from previous years.

Data on disciplinary occurrences by infraction type for the fall of 2006 show that half of all suspensions and expulsions were for minor conduct offenses, such as disrespect, profanity, and cutting class (JJPL, 2008). Twenty percent of expelled students in April of 2007 were assigned to alternative schools (JJPL, 2008).

Schools with the toughest approach to students have tended to be academically failing institutions serving minority populations. The New Orleans Public Schools are a quintessential example of this apposition. The schools have been ranked among the worst in the nation in terms of scholastic achievement. By the 2004–05 school year, 63 percent of the district schools had been deemed "academically unacceptable" by the State of Louisiana, which itself had some of the nation's lowest academic standards (Morgan Quitno Press, 2003; Vaughan et al., 2011). Louisiana also had the nation's highest high school dropout rate. Approximately fifteen thousand, or 17 percent, of all Louisiana high school freshmen failed to complete high school (WWLTV, 2011).

A large number of factors shaped school failure in New Orleans. White flight in the post–civil rights era meant that the public schools increasingly served the black population. Until 1950, when school integration efforts began, whites outnumbered blacks in the public schools of New Orleans. By the time blacks constituted a racial majority in the system in the late 1960s, whites had fled New Orleans public schools or left New Orleans proper, taking their tax base with them. By the 2004–05 school year, the city of New Orleans itself was 65 percent African American, and African Americans made up 94 percent of the public school population (Cowen Institute, 2010).

African Americans, having been denied equality in socioeconomic opportunity for generations, constituted a majority of the city's poor and lived in historically segregated neighborhoods, which were tenuously located in the lowlands of a swamp basin. This meant that the New Orleans Public Schools were serving the most dispossessed population in the city. Almost three-quarters of the student population qualified for free lunch because their family income was near the poverty line, and the federal poverty line in 2005 for a two-person family was $12,830 (U.S. Department of Health and Human Services, 2005).[6] Discussing white flight, poverty, and school failure in New Orleans, one local put it this way: "Most people who have the means do not stay in the public schools." New Orleans Public Schools became the educational institutions of last resort. Academically, the parish schools and their students suffered from this divestment. In 1997, per pupil spending in New Orleans Public Schools was $4,800, which was 26 percent lower than the national average that year of $6,060 (Bureau of Governmental Research, 1998).

White flight also diverted social and human capital away from the public schools in New Orleans, which meant that families with resources stopped fighting for these institutions.

Occasional scandals on the Orleans Parish School Board suggested that some school administrators had also given up on the institutions they were managing. In 2004, the school district administration was deemed so ineffective and corrupt that state officials called for help from the Federal Bureau of Investigation (Vaughan et al., 2011). With the public school system of New Orleans at a point of educational and administrative collapse, the State of Louisiana began takeover proceedings. A group of the lowest-performing schools were turned over to the newly created Recovery School District and reopened as charter schools.

LOUISIANA GOLD RUSH

While public schools in New Orleans and in other parts of Louisiana were faltering from divestment, the correctional system was growing stronger. Tough-on-crime sensibilities were sponsoring vast correctional growth. This phenomenon was not generated solely by a simple shift of resources from the left hand of the state to the right. Rather, Louisiana's correctional ascent was based in large part on a local control scheme with a potentially positive profit margin. Under the plan, the state authorized Louisiana sheriffs to expand local prisons with state inmates and paid them for custodial services based on their daily head count. This arrangement released the state from the burden of a federal mandate to reduce the state's incarcerated population, while handing the sheriffs a great deal of power as well as an opportunity for profit. Ultimately, this opportunity for correctional growth would monetarily incentivize the tough-on-crime approach, turning the Achilles heel of New Orleans's failed public schools into a source of correctional capital.

The state's dropout numbers and its incarceration numbers were reported by Secretary of Corrections Jimmy LeBlanc as an exact match annually: fifteen thousand high school dropouts and fifteen thousand prison intakes. These are not necessarily the same bodies—out of school and into prison in the same year in some hyper-actualized and apocalyptic version of the school-to-prison pipeline—but the ratio of undereducation and overincarceration is one to one. As LeBlanc explains, "That tells you the story of what is happening to us.

They're coming out of these schools and coming to prison" (Georgia Public Radio, 2013).

The profit motive raised the stakes of educational failure in New Orleans and transformed the role and status of Louisiana sheriffs. No longer a mere officer of justice, the sheriff was now an entrepreneur with a financial incentive from the state to build bigger prisons and lock up more people (Chang, 2013). Punitive profit helps explain why Louisiana gained the highest incarceration rate in the world. In the early 1990s, tough-on-crime laws in Louisiana meant that more people were given correctional sentences, those sentences were longer, and the prison population was soaring. There were fewer than twenty thousand inmates in the state in 1990; fifteen years later, in 2005, there were forty thousand. According to Lucky Severson, a news correspondent on the subject, "the state prison system simply couldn't keep up." The institutions were so overcrowded, unhealthy, and ultimately unconstitutional that the federal government ordered an overall reduction in the state's prison population (Chang, 2012a).

To comply with the federal ruling, the Louisiana Department of Corrections convinced local sheriffs to house state inmates by building their own prisons. By 2009, the local sheriffs in Louisiana held a larger percentage of state inmates than the state did (Chang, 2013). The blueprint of the plan was as follows. The Department of Corrections paid local sheriffs $24.39 per day for every inmate they held in confinement (Chang, 2013). The sum paid for inmate costs like food but also covered the sheriff's building and personnel costs. If the budget could be trimmed and expenses covered cheaply, a fraction would remain for the sheriff to skim off the top. With the potential for profit as a motivating factor, the bargain was struck with sheriffs across the state. Once the financial arrangement was in place, however, sheriffs found themselves forced to keep the local prisons full. A reduction in the inmate rolls meant a reduction in inmate expenses, but building and personnel costs remained roughly the same. This made the economics of incarceration in Louisiana quite a bit like innkeeping. Cindy Chang, a reporter for the local *Times-Picayune*, explains: "The prisons function just like hotels—that they get a payment per person per day, and if they don't keep the beds full they're going to lose money" (Chang, 2013). A sheriff with empty inmate beds lacked income to pay capital prison expenses and, thus, faced bankruptcy, but for a sheriff with all beds full and a tight budget, excess funds were suddenly available. The sum of $24.39 wasn't large, but the fractional profit would add up if the heads multiplied. It made for a devil's bargain. Louisiana sheriffs were incentivized to put large numbers of individuals in jail and keep them there as long as possible (Chang, 2013). The profit motive accounts for why one correctional official in Louisiana referred to local prisons in the state as "honey holes" (Blow, 2012).

When there was no vacancy in a local prison, the sheriff could simply ship inmates to sheriffs in other parts of the state, spreading the honey around. The favor could be returned when the tide changed. These logistics radically changed the nature of the job. Increasingly, sheriffs in Louisiana spent their days on the phone, orchestrating a never-ending game of shuffle. Inmates were known to get lost in this cycle, and family members of the incarcerated were led on wild goose chases to find them. This shell game may partly explain why Orleans Parish Prison officials did not know who was in their prison when it flooded after Hurricane Katrina. The lack of accountability is also why Warden Marlin Gusman could claim in the aftermath of the storm that there were no deaths at Orleans Parish Prison, even as traumatized guards reported stories of lifeless floating bodies. If missing individuals weren't known to have been in the prison, they could not be said to have necessarily died there.[7] A month after the storm, however, over five hundred inmates in the larger system remained unaccounted for (Goodman, 2005).

These Louisiana correctional machinations also unlocked opportunities for private investment. Cindy Chang writes: "In rural, impoverished north Louisiana, the deal was particularly alluring, not only for sheriffs but for private investors, who knocked on sheriffs' doors, dangling financing and profit-sharing deals. Low, cinder-block buildings ringed with barbed wire sprouted along country highways across the state" (Chang, 2012b). With these incentives, local sheriffs expanded their prisons until they held half of the inmates in the state. They also ran for-profit jails for private entities, which increased their profit share, or gave their inmates to private corporations that attempted to run carceral facilities under budget. Correctional profit sharing became so preferred in Louisiana that these institutions now hold a majority of the state's inmate population. The correctional population itself grew so large that Louisiana doubled its prison population in twenty years and became known as the world's correctional capital (National Public Radio, 2012).

The sheriffs could use the correctional profits to update their department, funding squad cars, weapons, and bulletproof vests, but the arrangement secured something even more important to local sheriffs than profit:

patronage. Local sheriffs used funds to expand their staff. In rural Jackson Parish, a department of fifty staff members tripled to a hundred and fifty; these were good jobs with benefits, which meant strong local support and the kind of patronage that translated into reelection (National Public Radio, 2012). Taking advantage of these opportunities, Orleans Parish Sheriff Charles Foti expanded his prison population from eight hundred inmates in 1974 to eighty-five hundred in 2004 (ACLU National Prison Project, 2006; Gerharz & Hong, 2006). He was well liked by locals for providing good jobs, was reelected seven times, and served as the criminal sheriff for almost thirty years. In 1999, he had enough political capital to open a public school inside his prison, with money from the Orleans Parish School Board attached to each pupil. In 2003, he successfully ran for Louisiana Attorney General.

THE ETHICS OF THE CORRECTIONAL BOTTOM LINE

Years in, this profit-seeking correctional scheme has its detractors, and some of Louisiana's most powerful correctional officials are among them. Incentivized incarceration crosses ethical boundaries because it turns the inmate into a commodity. The more cheaply that commodity can be produced, warehoused, and transported, the higher the profit margin will be. Produced on a mass scale, fractional profit adds up like thousands of good bets on a set of penny stocks. Burl Cain, the warden of Angola State Prison, objects to this kind of profiteering. He explains:

> The profit motive bothers me when the profit motive is the motive to not provide the necessary essentials for the inmate. You feed them with a thimble, is a term I use. You try to cut them to eighteen hundred calories a day, and so those things bother me, and they do that in the private sector more than the public, because they measure every little thing they give you. They're cutting costs, they're cutting dollars, and when they cut your quality of life by doing that, that's wrong. (Georgia Public Radio, 2013)

Trimming the production budget for a commodity, when that commodity is an inmate, means trimming the basics, like food and health services, and cutting social welfare programs—such as education, job training, reentry programming, and psychological or substance-abuse counseling—altogether. Longer sentences that help secure the prison's profit-making capacity also mean that inmates are denied these resources for longer. Richard Crane, the former chief counsel to the Louisiana Correctional Department, frames the ethical problem with a rhetorical question: "Is that the way to finance those things, you know, by increasing sentences for the sole purpose of filling up local jails? Is it ethical to incarcerate people for the sole purpose of making money?" (Georgia Public Radio, 2013).

Louisiana's leading correctional figures offered a second critique of prison profiteering that involved public education in the state. Arguing that the state both undereducates and overincarcerates, Burl Cain, the Warden of Angola Prison, said: "You shouldn't pay more for corrections than you do for education ... but you are, and you're keeping the wrong people in prison because you're keeping everybody" (Georgia Public Radio, 2013). The demographics of the Louisiana prison population prove his points. A third of all Louisiana inmates read below the level of an average fifth-grader, and two-thirds of the inmates in the state are incarcerated for nonviolent offenses (Chang, 2012a; Blow, 2012).

CONCLUSION

This chapter documents how and why public schools became so punitive in the War on Crime era and situates their disciplinary practices within a larger set of social, economic, and political forces shaping the War on Crime and the at-risk youth industry. The ideologies and practices of the era arranged power relations and leveraged authority even in the absence of criminal activity. As the legal scholar Jonathan Simon has argued, crime-control tactics were extended in their application to metaphors of crime to create "new opportunities for governance," but they were also opportunities for reproducing social, economic, and political hegemony (Simon, 2007). Punitive practices in schools preempted crime and were attached to perceptions of criminal potential, which were inevitably linked to expressions of difference. Many African American male students eventually found themselves in prison—the ratio is one in three—but they had been punished for years before ever committing a crime (Rios, 2011).

The punitive shift in education serves larger political, economic, and social needs in schools by catering to public demands for safe schools and meeting testing standards and their related funding thresholds by gerrymandering the student population. Investments in discipline cater to larger interests by supporting neoliberal strategies while managing marginalized populations who aren't easily absorbed by the service and high-tech workforce of the postindustrial state. As a political strategy, punitive practices capitalize on tough-on-crime ideologies while sponsoring economic growth to pave the way for reelection as well as potential political ascendancy. In the chapters that follow, these dynamics are further revealed in an ethnographic case study of a coordinated educational and correctional enterprise at the Orleans Parish Prison with Criminal Sheriff Charles Foti at its helm.

CHAPTER 3

Undereducated and Overcriminalized in New Orleans

Throughout the United States, schools tend disproportionately to punish the students who have the greatest academic, social, economic, and emotional needs.

—Pedro Noguera, 2003

When Hurricane Katrina slammed into the Louisiana coast in late August 2005 and the water rose in New Orleans, the city's public school system was virtually destroyed. The event was called a natural disaster, but it was a sociological disaster first. For generations, African Americans had been clinging on the edge of survival in a swamp of racial discrimination, unemployment, poverty, and systemic educational failure. The flooding from Katrina brought this desperation to the surface and the whole world could see it. W. E. B. Du Bois famously proclaimed in 1903 that "the problem of the Twentieth Century is the problem of the color line," but images from New Orleans in the aftermath of Katrina suggested that the color line would be the problem of the twenty-first century, too (Du Bois, 1903/2007). The refusal to see the collapse of New Orleans as a story of the nation's enduring racial inequality—and the willingness to see it solely in terms of geography and climate change—shows not how faint the color line has become but how willing Americans are to call it by another name.

No one could have accurately predicted the exceptional events of August 2005, but there was ample evidence in the early 2000s that New Orleans was on the verge of collapse. I initially traveled to New Orleans for a national educational conference, but I stayed to understand how locals could possibly subsist on the city's meager educational opportunities and how, on a larger level, egalitarianism, meritocracy, and democracy could be taken seriously in a country with such abundant and extreme expressions of inequality. I learned, in fact, that most locals only barely survive in New Orleans, and that many are incarcerated in the process.

From his living room where he sat with me, Spider complained to his mother, who was lying in bed in the next room, about having only one shirt to wear. "Momma! I need some kind of *shirt* to wear!" "You wearing it!" she yelled back. "I *been* wearing it!" he said, shaking his head in disgust. I studied the thin fabric of Spider's shirt, which resembled once-white gauze. Like the veil in Du Bois's *Souls of Black Folk*, it served as a metaphor for the color line as Spider experienced it (Du Bois, 1903/2007). The shirt only barely covered the dark brown skin on his lithe adolescent frame, but it seemed to yoke Spider with the weight of the poverty it represented. On school days, which held the promise of equally thin educational opportunities, he carried this freight forward and was often punished for being late.

For Du Bois, the veil is a figure of "double consciousness" that conceptualizes the African American experience of striving in the context of racism. Du Bois describes double consciousness as the "sense of always looking at one's self through the eyes of others, of measuring one's soul by the tape of a world that looks on in amused contempt and pity. One ever feels his two-ness, an American, a Negro" (Du Bois, 1903/2007). The divide is made, Du Bois claims, when the doors of American opportunity are closed to African Americans, which suggests that one cannot be both of African descent and American. Striving under those cloven and irreconcilable conditions has almost no reasonable or authentic realization other than rage. It builds with a steady accretion to encompass generations of small and large indignities (Winant, 2004). In this chapter, I trace the color line through the educational experiences of Chui, Jamal, and Spider—two generations of men in New Orleans—to show what lies beneath the cover of limited opportunity. Their life experiences offer a lens for viewing racialized oppression in New Orleans as it functions through historical and contemporary processes of undereducation and overcriminalization. By way of New Orleans, the chapter deals centrally with dilemmas in black urban America and points to the experience of young black males who are in the liminal state of losing educational affiliation while being caught in the net of correctional control.

FAILING SCHOOLS

From the outside, it is unclear whether this school is abandoned or in use. The lot is strewn with weeds and surrounded by a chain-link fence. Windows hold a grid of panes in various translucencies. Some doors are chained shut. Paint is fading and/or falling in strips from the structure, and graffiti is washed over the exterior walls. To determine the present status of things, I look for an opening to the interior and find none. I wait to see if school busses line up on the street outside at the end of the school day. The ghostly aspect of these institutions is heightened by the fact that a great many schools have literally been abandoned and loom on street corners as empty masonry shells. (ethnographic field note)

When I toured New Orleans in the spring of 2002, I found schools so dilap-idated that I could not easily tell which ones were abandoned and which were in use. I looked hard for any signs of life. Even the schools that opened their doors to students on weekdays were clad in anachronism. Stepping inside felt like a step back in time. The typical school followed Henry Barnard's blue-prints for school architecture; it was a three-story square structure, with each floor connected by bulky wooden staircases with massive newel posts. Sound echoed through the stairwells and down the long central corridors that linked the classrooms. While it is true that disinvestment in New Orleans as a whole has uniquely preserved the details of the city's architectural history in quaint dilapidation, the charm of an outdated school is easily displaced by its inher-ent limitations as an educational building in the twenty-first century. Many of the buildings were approaching a century in age and could not physically accommodate recent technological developments, such as Internet wiring.

The inferior infrastructure of the typical New Orleans public school was indicative of the educational failure rampant within the school system. In 2002, the city's public schools were the second-worst in all of Louisiana, a state with the second-worst school system in the nation (Louisiana Department of Education, 2002; Morgan Quinto Press, 2003). In 2002, the Louisiana Depart-ment of Education determined that 92 of Orleans Parish's 108 schools were either below the state average or altogether unacceptable to state standards (Louisiana Department of Education, 2001–2002). Given the context of edu-cational poverty in the state as a whole, these determinations pointed to extreme academic destitution. The city had basically botched the job of edu-cating its citizens.

The burden of the city's systemic education failure was borne overwhelm-ing by low-income African Americans. Although Orleans Parish was 70 percent African American in 2002, the public school system was 93 percent African American and 3 percent white (Louisiana Schools, 2002). Eighty percent of the parish's public school population received a subsidized lunch, which was offered as a way to marginally address the depths of the students' indigence and curb the kind of hunger that severely compromises academic learning (Louisiana Schools, 2002). Families with more resources could pay for a one-way ticket out, sending their children to private or parochial schools or leaving the school district altogether. The students who remained in the public schools were the "have-nots," as Orissa Arendt, a local reporter and youth advocate, put it in our first meeting; they had no other choice.

Local residents decried the poor educational conditions in New Orleans and spoke of how the system had "betrayed" them for generations. In studying the public schools in New Orleans for nearly three years, I found no one who could vouch for them. Chui Clark grieved for the loss of educational opportunity in his community, saying: "We are exhausted by not having excellent public schools in our city to offer our children. And we decry the current conditions of many of our public schools, which do not nurture and empower our students, because of their lack of appropriate funding from the school board to refurbish or replace buildings, pay competitive teacher salaries, and offer more on-campus after-school tutoring, mentoring, and extracurricular programs for our cherished young ones." The African American community depended on the public schools as their primary vehicle for socioeconomic advancement, and many, like Chui, refused to give up on them no matter how bad they got. So tied were their fortunes to educational opportunity that surrendering the schools would have meant surrendering their own lives.

The problem with the local schools was not simply that they were academically inferior, but that their educational climates were hostile and had been that way for generations. "Our youth were (and are still) labeled recalcitrant," said Chui, who led antiracist campaigns in the city. As students navigated school corridors, they were perceived as suspects for crimes not yet committed. Slight deviations from the established codes of conduct, such as fractional tardiness, were criminalized, especially among males. Harsh disciplinary practices like this were standard in the New Orleans public schools, and the rates of suspension and expulsion were astronomical—as high as 60 percent in some schools—which meant that large numbers of students lost time in the classroom (Williams, 2012). Even though instruction in New Orleans classrooms was marginal at best, educational exclusion disenfranchised students further. In the context of abject poverty, high unemployment, poor health-care systems, and an extremely precarious set of housing conditions, related to the position of the city at the mouth of the Mississippi River, locals needed a public school system that worked and that offered some hope for social mobility.

Many members of the New Orleans community saw the experience of substandard and punitive public education in the city as the antecedent for state incarceration. Louisiana, which has one of the worst track records in the nation for educating youths, also has the world's highest incarceration rate (Chang, 2012a). This is often regarded as the school-to-prison pipeline: youths who begin school at a disadvantage are not given the academic resources they would need to catch up and are simultaneously criminalized by harsh disciplinary policies at school (Kim, Losen & Hewitt, 2010; Wald & Losen, 2003; Losen & Edley, 2001). While I have critiqued the pipeline metaphor for its oversimplification of the relationship between schools and prisons, it does the work of describing how all too often, these youths find themselves adjudicated by the correctional system, where they are further distanced from any slim chance they had to overcome the confounding obstacles of their birth. The structure of the problem preexists schooling and builds on extant societal race, class, and gender inequalities, but the problem expands in schools. This is a paradoxical condition, because public schools were designed to be an institutional common ground that could ameliorate socioeconomic disparities among Americans in the interest of a democratic order. Because schools reinscribe the axis of marginalization horizontally, they play a role in leading youths further away from any hope of vertical socioeconomic ascent. In the War on Crime era, it has become increasingly hard to see the role that schools play in educational failure and in larger social problems, because educational dysfunction at the institutional and district levels is hidden by disciplinary mechanisms that construct the problem as individual and behavioral. The arrangement closely mimics the way in which the War on Crime pathologizes and criminalizes racialized poverty. This is not to say that individuals have no agency in directing the course of their lives, but that as agents, individuals are responsive to larger structural forces and constraints, which require examination and remediation. In the three accounts that follow, Chui, Jamal, and Spider point to their individual weaknesses but establish them in the larger context of the color line as it is drawn by undereducation and overcriminalization.

Albert "Chui" Clark

In the late 1960s, Albert Clark was a poor and illiterate young black man, living in New Orleans in segregated public housing and attending segregated public schools. The civil rights and black liberation movements were growing all around him, and the Black Panthers were organizing against racism in the housing projects where Albert lived. They put him in charge of their art collection; he could understand images if not words, and they named him "Chui," Kiswahili for "Panther." In school, however, Chui Clark's limitations were not so creatively addressed, nor were they mitigated, and as a poor young man of color in the segregated South without any academic skills, the odds were stacked against him.

As Chui explains it, extreme social, economic, and educational conditions set the stage for his path to prison. On a large scale, he suggests that "[it was] the discriminatory nature of the whole system. You know . . . I came up during the Jim Crow period. I was born in that period. In 1953, Jim Crow was alive and well." Racial discrimination combined with other factors to further marginalize Chui and make him vulnerable to the justice system. As he explains, "it was race, class, and gender . . . as a youth" and "[my] being functionally illiterate, not, in a sense, acquiring a decent education [that] played a role in [my] going to prison." Compared to peers in his school age group, he says, "I was way off."

Chui's disenfranchisement was further impressed on him by the police who patrolled his neighborhood. They made him aware of their authority even before he had committed any crime. He remembers his introduction to police authorities: "Every day as a young person . . . the police would stop me, practically every day. When they patrolled our community, they put us on the side. That was just a way of life." The police demonstrated Chui's vulnerability to correctional authority by targeting him and interrogating him on the street, regardless of reasonable suspicion. As Chui understood it, he was treated as a suspicious character by virtue of his marginalization, which was, in turn, further exacerbated by these negative confrontations.

Despite this frequent, informal association with the police in his neighborhood, his formal relationship with the criminal justice system began as a surprise to him. When friends of his stole money from the lunchroom cash box at their elementary school, Chui was accused as a party to the crime. Chui was actually in a school classroom at the time of the incident, but his teacher did not speak up on his behalf, and a local merchant who frequently saw Chui at his store with friends on other days said that he was with them on the day a group entered the store with an unusual amount of spending money. Subsequently, Chui was charged with burglary, denied a trial, and sent to a reformatory for colored boys. He was fourteen years old and had been retained in school so many times that he had failed to progress beyond the fifth grade. Consequently, Chui entered the youth reformatory unable to read and write. As an adult, Chui lamented the fact that the punishment took him away from his mother.

Reform school did more to cement Chui's path to prison than to prevent it. "Spending four years inside the reformatory, in a sense, prepared me for adult facilities," he said. "It tends to steer you to, rather than away. . . . That is why I wound up all the way from youth reformatory to the Parish Prison to Angola." Though he returned home from reform school to enroll in eighth grade at a local high school, he still could not read or write, and he dropped out. He was eventually arrested for willfully defying law enforcement; as Chui explains it, he was arrested for a "slow walk." This kind of arrest, which continues to be legislated in some cities through "manner of walking" laws, has been at the center of contemporary conversations about racialized police harassment and brutality in cities like Ferguson, Missouri, where a police officer shot and killed Michael Brown, an unarmed eighteen-year-old African American, in 2014. An investigative report by the U.S. Department of Justice reveals that officers in Ferguson conducted regular but unconstitutional "ped checks" in which they stopped African Americans who were "wandering around" without reasonable suspicion and arrested them without probable cause, thus violating the Fourth and Fourteenth Amendments (U.S. Department of Justice, 2015).

After his arrest for a slow walk, Chui spent two years in the Orleans Parish Prison with Sheriff Charles Foti as his warden, and by age twenty-two he was serving eighteen years in the Louisiana State Penitentiary at Angola. Chui asserts that everything he knows he learned while at Angola. There was no education program at the prison, but with arduous self-study he taught himself to read and write by working with whatever materials he could get his hands on. Chui left prison for the last time in 1993 and dedicated himself to the cause of racial justice. In the beginning of his work out in the streets, Chui was interested in organizing for large-scale community change and not partial to the cause of school reform.

> [Schools] really [weren't] my interest, in a sense. I always thought about when I
> get out what was I going to do to try give back to the community. To make up for
> the years I lived in the streets as an outlaw. I had made a change in prison. I was
> pretty confident that this was the life that I wanted to live. I thought about a

variety of things, but that wasn't my primary focus. I wanted to get out and join some political groups, particularly some revolutionary groups, and uh, and pursue it on another front, and you know, really think about changing the whole structure and condition of the community, but, you know, things don't ever turn out the way you wanted them to, [the way] you dream they are going to turn out.

With guidance from other activists, he began to see education as a powerful antidote to the oppression that concerned his community, and he concentrated his efforts there. He explains that "School's important because that is where our kids are."

Chui recognized education as a remedy to the prison path, partly because, as an uneducated youth himself, he felt a "lack of genuine opportunities to consider other things—aside from crime." Chui had assumed that the path of education would lead youths away from the criminal justice system, but in truth it hadn't—not for him in the 1960s, and not for the young boys in his community forty years later. In part, he blamed the historical collaboration of officials in public schools, police departments, and prisons. In a protest flier, Chui wrote: "Historically, the New Orleans School Board . . . has always collaborated with the New Orleans Police Department and/or the Department of Corrections in targeting Afrikan youths for harassment, detention, and imprisonment, under the pretense of addressing the problem of juvenile delinquency." These collaborations, which sent many African American boys like Chui to reformatories, thus ending their formal educational experiences, were part of what civil rights leaders were fighting against. The fact of their continued collaboration spurred Chui to think about racial inequalities in school discipline as a major civil rights issue. When Criminal Sheriff Charles Foti, Chui's former warden, tried to open his own public school at the Orleans Parish Prison in 2002, Chui fiercely opposed it.

Since Chui's resistance of the Sheriff's Prison School was framed by his experiences of the civil rights movement as a member of the local Black Panther Party, Chui took me to visit leaders in those struggles. His friend Robert Hillary King was a member of the famous Angola 3 and had served time in solitary confinement at Angola. Chui called him "King," and the three of us hung out in King's living room enjoying his now famous prison pralines. King's recipe for these sugary treats used purloined butter, sugar, and pecans; during his time in prison, he cooked the ingredients in a pot over a soda-can chimney with toilet paper for fuel. As we ate pralines, King told me the story of his incarceration.

King first went to jail in 1970 at the Orleans Parish Prison, the complex that would later house the Prison School. He was serving a sentence for armed robbery; he maintains that he was innocent of the crime. His codefendant had chosen King out of a lineup after he had been beaten by police and forced to pick an accomplice. In 1972, King entered the Louisiana State Penitentiary and joined inmates Albert Woodfox and Herman Wallace, who had started a Black Panther Party inside. The three men, who later became known as the Angola 3, galvanized inmates around the cause of justice, worked to end abusive labor practices, and fought against the most egregious conditions in the prison, including sexual assault and rape. Their campaign for justice ended, however, when prison officials committed Woodfox, Wallace, and King to solitary confinement for murders that had occurred inside the correctional facility. Woodfox and Wallace were charged and convicted of the murder of a prison guard, but there was no forensic or physical evidence linking them to it, and there was evidence that prison officials had incentivized the testimony against them (Robertson, 2016). King was eventually charged with the murder of another inmate, but he spent nineteen years in solitary confinement at Angola before the prison board gave him their first explanation for his isolation. In total, King spent twenty-nine years in solitary confinement; Woodfox and Wallace would each spend over forty. Claiming to have been framed and punished for their political affiliations and their organizing capacities, the Angola 3 became known as political prisoners.[1] In a radio interview, King explained the political motivations of his incarceration:

> The Angola 3 are three members of the Black Panther Party, or former members of the Black Panther Party—Albert Woodfox, Herman Wallace, and myself. . . . Herman and Albert, they preceded my going to prison. . . . They begun a chapter of the Black Panther Party and in the process of organizing this chapter . . . [they] become targets. Um, there was an issue went down where an officer was killed. Prior to all of this, or prior to Herman and Albert's organizing skills, Angola as you know, uh you may have heard, that Angola it was the bloodiest prison in the nation. And it was segregated. There were inmate guards who were running the prison. They engaged in rape, extortion and all other kind of activities with regards to other prisoners—black prisoners, [guards and prisoners]. And prisoners were victimizing themselves as well. Herman and Albert kind of brought the Black Panther Party ideology into the prison, and they began politicizing the prisoners there both black and white. And [it] started as a threat. (Valrey, 2006)

After King told me this story in his living room, Chui learned forward with his arms resting on his knees and said, "You see why we don't want a criminal sheriff and warden of the Orleans Parish Prison educating our young people?" With this visit to King's house, Chui situated the Prison School and his protest of it in a broad historical context of race relations in the city itself. The Prison School, as Chui talked about it, was emblematic of the racialized oppression that led to King's life behind bars as a political prisoner.

"IT IS CRAZY OVER THERE AT THAT SCHOOL"

Jamal and Spider grew up in an impoverished, undereducated, and segregated African American neighborhood in New Orleans, on the south side of the Mississippi River, not very far from where Chui was a child forty years earlier. And in many ways, they lived with the same rampant poverty, the same racial disparity, and the same failing public schools. In 2000, in their immediate neighborhood, 93 percent of residents were African American (U.S. Census Bureau, 2000). The median reported family income was $16,974, while the per capita income was $7,441. Among males in the immediate vicinity, 15 percent had less than a ninth-grade education, and another 54 percent had no college experience (U.S. Census Bureau, 2000a).

As middle school students, Jamal and Spider went to a failing public school, where teachers were underprepared, classrooms were overcrowded, and students ranked substantially below the norms on state and national standardized tests, including the Louisiana Educational Assessment Program (LEAP) and the Iowa tests (Louisiana Department of Education, 2003). "It is crazy over there at that school," said Spider's dad, shaking his head. The dysfunction Spider's father perceived was corroborated by the state statistical assessments. Only 63 percent of teachers at Jamal and Spider's middle school were certified, compared with 82 percent at the district level and 90 percent at the state level (Louisiana Department of Education, 2003). More than 86 percent of all classes were as large as twenty-seven to thirty-three students, compared with 65 percent in other district middle schools and 27 percent in other middle schools at the state level. On standardized tests, the students at Jamal and Spider's middle school were far behind their peers in the state and nation (Louisiana Department of Education, 2003). On the LEAP, a statewide test used to assess student skills, one percent or fewer of the students at Jamal and Spider's school demonstrated mastery in English Language Arts, Mathematics, Science, or Social Studies. In these core subjects, over 75 percent of the students at their school failed to demonstrate even basic academic skills

(Louisiana School Report Card, 2002–2003). When compared with state percentages, the school was far below the average in these assessments. Nationally, the school ranked in the bottom 25 percent on the Iowa tests.

At the end of the 2001–02 school year, very low standardized test scores had serious consequences for the students in Jamal and Spider's middle school. The teachers and administrators judged, on the basis of these scores, that most of the eighth-graders did not meet the requirements to enter ninth grade. As a result, over 40 percent of the eighth-grade class was retained in a single year (Louisiana Department of Education, 2003). In the previous year, over 50 percent of the eighth-grade class had been retained, so statistically this was a significant improvement. In the academic environment of extreme failure at Jamal and Spider's school, there was also a significant emphasis on discipline. In the 2001–02 school year, over 30 percent of students at the school were suspended out of school (Louisiana Department of Education, 2003). In taking them out of the classroom, suspension increased the chances that these students, who were already academically behind, would not catch up.

Jamal

I first met Jamal in front of a small house on a wide uncurbed street south of downtown New Orleans, across the Mississippi River. His house and those around it were very modest bungalows, with no similarity to the elaborate homes of the French Quarter. The houses each had low rooflines and exterior walls in faded pastel paints. Small porches extended along the front entry of many of the homes, and they seemed to be well used, especially on this Saturday. Up and down the street I saw movement and heard adults and children talking and playing together outside their homes. Everyone I saw was African American.

A low chain-link fence surrounded Jamal's house and enclosed a small grassy yard. It was a very hot day and the sun was so intense that the visual landscape of the neighborhood broke apart into a shimmering dot-matrix pattern of light. I squinted and walked through the gate, across the yard, and toward the front door of the house. A small group of young people were sitting in the shade of Jamal's porch, but Jamal was inside. He was a sturdy-looking teenager in black jeans and a thin white undershirt. His face was round and his eyes were clear as he focused on me intently and invited me into his home.

Inside I met Jamal's mother. I learned later that this was one of the rare occasions that she was with her family. Her job on a cruise ship took her up and down the Mississippi River to significant Civil War ports and kept her away from home for more than half of every month. She was a tall woman with a strong build, and her features matched those of her son. Her skin was dark, and her face was gently curved and expressive. She invited me to sit down with her and her son and her own mother, who was Jamal's guardian when she was away for work. We sat together at a small table in their dining room and began to talk. (ethnographic field notes)

At the age of fourteen, Jamal was a student at a low-performing public middle school within walking distance from his home. According to his mother, the conditions at his middle school were so marginal that Jamal's chances of academic success were significantly compromised. "I think the school system kind of failed him," she said, referring to large classes as one of the most significant problems. "As long as they keep building the classes up—'cause some classes have thirty to thirty-five students—it is hard for one teacher to go around to each student to make sure that they are doing the right work. It was several times [that Jamal] would come home to me and say like, 'I can't get it. I don't know what she is talking about.'"

The teachers at Jamal's middle school were asked to serve large numbers of students in their classes and were consequently unable to provide any individual attention to specific students. Given that more than 99 percent of the eighth-grade students at the school were deemed by standardized tests to have basic or less than basic skills in every core academic subject, practically the entire student population needed extra help. In classrooms as large as thirty or thirty-five students, however, it is difficult to imagine how one teacher could meet this challenge, especially if that teacher is not certified as an expert in his or her subject area. There are potentially steep consequences for learning in overcrowded environments, especially when students have high needs and can't get help in addressing them. Recent studies by the sociologists Richard Arum and Gary LaFree have suggested that districts with high levels of classroom overcrowding are also the districts with excessive levels of correctional control. They found that school districts with high student-to-teacher ratios produce adults who face higher risks of incarceration (Arum and LaFree, 2008).

When Jamal couldn't get support from his classroom teachers, he tried on his own to stop his free fall into school failure. The problem was that he could not understand what was going on around him. He was lost at school and painfully aware of it. The data on school performance in New Orleans suggest that Jamal was not alone. With 40 to 50 percent of students being retained in a single academic year, the problem is clearly systemic. Even so, individual students like Jamal were made to feel that they were the problem.

Jamal's school records reveal that his academic problems began as early as second grade. When he was eight years old, he had D's in Language, Reading, and Spelling and an F in Science. For several years he managed to maintain C's in Arithmetic, but by his sixth-grade year he had D's and F's in all subjects. Jamal barely passed sixth grade the second time around, and when he took the Iowa Test of Basic Skills that year, his composite score ranked him in the eleventh percentile. He had no more success in eighth grade.

Despite his academic difficulties, Jamal explained to me that he was gifted in certain areas and wanted to pursue studies to advance those innate abilities. He felt naturally inclined toward engineering and recognized math as an academic area in which he had strengths.

> J: I like to mess with computers and stuff like that, like going on the inside of them, like I can mess around with stuff like that.
>
> L: If something is broken can you . . .
>
> J: Fix it? Probably.
>
> L: What are you good at in school?
>
> J: Math. Math is my favorite subject. I like math. That is really easy to me, but not to other people. Math and science.
>
> L: What kind of math?
>
> J: Algebra. Well, I just got good at that, I ain't gonna lie.

Jamal spoke positively about his abilities in math and science, and he further testified to his true love of school in general. He even professed that he had dreams of one day being a teacher.

> J: I like school. I love school really.
>
> L: What do you love about it?
>
> J: I love to be around people. I am a people's person, but at the same time, I really like math. At one time, I wanted to be a math teacher.
>
> L: Do you still want to do that?
>
> J: Mmmm . . . mmm [shaking head no].

Even in the most marginal contexts of education, Jamal found something in the instruction that he felt was worthy of his respect and emulation. His dream of being a teacher faded, however, as he continued to struggle academically.

In narrative comments on Jamal's performance, several of his teachers acknowledged his keen social orientation—and indicated that it was a detriment to his academic focus. One elementary teacher described him as "playful," while another admonished him. It is, of course, difficult to determine whether Jamal's grades dropped as a result of his socializing or whether his participation in the social life of the classroom increased as it became more and more difficult for him to participate academically. His mother said he couldn't escape the label attached to him. "They would be so used to him being the class clown or a follower that when he *was* trying to do his work, they wouldn't take him serious." Midway through his second year of eighth grade, Jamal was in disciplinary trouble.

As Jamal explained, he went to school—because he admittedly loved it— but he did not always go to class. When asked about this discrepancy, he explained that peer pressure had gotten him off his true path.

> L: You said to me that you really liked school, that, in fact, you loved school, so what kept you from being . . .
>
> J: Knuckleheads. Following behind knuckleheads. That is the truth. I was a big ol' follower. At that time, I was young. I wasn't thinking.

Perhaps without a clear understanding of the consequences of tardiness, Jamal spent some of his class time hanging out in the hallways of his school. "I wasn't going to class," he said. "It was in my mind to go to class, but I just didn't go." He received several suspensions in a row for this behavior and was sent home and told not come to school at all for several days. By January of the 2001–02 school year, he was cutting four hours or so a week. Ultimately the school's administration "got tired" of his consistent tardiness, he said, "and they didn't let me back in school." Expelled, he stayed at home with only his grandmother to care for him for weeks at a time. His mother was away at work, and his father was altogether absent.

Jamal did not want to sit at home waiting for the next academic year when he could start school again. The easiest option was to declare himself a dropout, but he refused that, because he wanted to go back to class. There was only one other offer on the table. To be accepted back into public schools after a long history of absenteeism, he would first have to spend time in a new public school at the Orleans Parish Prison. Absenteeism in Louisiana was, after all, a status offense, a kind of offense that only juveniles can be charged with. In the eyes of the law, children who arrive late to school may be treated as offenders.

Spider

> I got to Spider's house by crossing the Mississippi River driving away from downtown New Orleans. After several minutes, I turned onto Spider's street, which was a broad empty boulevard with a wide overgrown median. The late summer

air felt hotter here than on the other side of the river, and the lack of shade was noticeable. Brick duplexes of various shapes lined the road. The small plots of grass in front of each one did little to soften the hard façade of the structures as they squared to the street, and this was especially true for the buildings with boarded up windows.

I parked in proximity to Spider's address on a side street so that I could walk through his neighborhood on my way to find him. A car was on cement blocks, just in front of mine, but otherwise there were few automobiles. A couple hundred feet off the main boulevard was a two-story structure so densely covered in kudzu that it took on a strange otherworldly aspect. It seemed to be shaped like a two-story apartment building made entirely of plant material. In the other direction, two older African American women were walking down a sidewalk in church clothes; one African American man was crossing the street. In such a large flat space, however, their bodies and movements seemed to be in miniature.

In the distance I saw Spider's street address, and I approached the front door and knocked; no one answered. I knocked again, and stepped back to look around. The building was an unembellished 1950s stucco four-plex in a dingy light brown with metal windows. The bottom floor apartment still had Christmas decorations on display, now dusty 8 months past the holiday. Still I waited, and after some time, I used my cell phone to call Spider to say that I had arrived. Spider came down a metal stairway at the rear of the building to find me. He was tall and lanky with dark skin, and he wore a bright white jersey with an Atlanta Braves cap. A smile crossed his narrow face and his voice lilted a subtle southern drawl as he greeted me and led me up the back stairs to his mother's second-floor apartment. "Yeahhhhhhhhh," he said, "we can talk here."

Spider and I entered his apartment through the kitchen door. His mother was home, but not feeling well, so I spoke with her only briefly before sitting down with Spider for the first time. The television was on in the living room, and while Spider waited for me, he sat on a brown L-shaped sectional sofa watching a Sunday gospel show. When I came into the room and sat down beside him, he turned the television off and focused on our conversation. (ethnographic field notes)

I asked Spider to tell me about himself. "Let me get a sense of who you are. Tell me what you like to do," I said. Spider looked at me and said quizzically, "What I like to do? I can say what I want to do!" I nodded encouragingly. "What I want to do," he said "is go to college." There was no hesitation in his voice.

Spider might have hoped to make a good impression on me and suggest that he was interested in the same things I care about. That he seemed to wear his best white shirt, or possibly his best borrowed shirt, to our first interview substantiated this notion. When we hung out on subsequent days, he wore a threadbare tank top. He also wanted to see me as someone who could fix his educational problems and, possibly, to be seen as someone potentially deserving. When Spider introduced me to his father, who lived elsewhere, he said, "This lady is going to get me into a good school." In that moment I reexplained my role as a researcher to Spider and his father, saying that I was trying to understand how and why he and his peers were pushed out of their neighborhood schools. That I did not possess the power to help him as he imagined proved to be a significant methodological dilemma. I struggled over the ethics of ethnography and what it meant to be a participant observer. What did it mean to participate in Spider's life and produce written accounts of my observations in order to share them more widely, when what he needed was a good school?

It is difficult to know how Spider's interest in education translated into actual academic achievement, since his public school records were transferred to a church basement and eventually lost. On the institutional level Spider was an invisible entity, a degraded status that reproduced his social, economic, political, and academic disenfranchisement as a young African American man living within a highly impoverished and segregated neighborhood of New Orleans. The only record I ever found of Spider's academic performance came from a nonprofit educational organization in the city that had, at one point, taken Spider and his brother on as part of a school-to-work program. Under their auspices, in what would have been his sophomore year in high school, Spider took a standardized educational test. The results showed that his reading was at a third-grade level, seven years below grade. In math he was four years behind. Pushing students like Spider and their records of failure out of the system meant a kind of absolution for the schools—that's the only way that keeping public school records in a church made sense.

In conversation with me, Spider always claimed that his main problem in school was related to discipline and not academics. His offenses, never violent, ranged from public displays of affection to tardiness. His very first suspension was punishment for kissing a girl during recess in fifth grade.

L: Tell me about the first time you got in trouble at school?

S: First time?

L: Yeah. If you could say that there was a first time.

S: Like in middle school? Or what?

L: Yes. As early as you want to go.

S: Mmm. I'd say when I was in the fifth grade, and I kissed a girl, and the teacher saw it. And the teacher didn't like it or whatever, and referred it to the principal. Even though the girl wasn't really worrying about it, 'cause the girl wanted me to kiss her, but the teacher saw it and thought that we weren't supposed to be doing that. On that premises.

L: So, what happened?

S: They suspended me. They were about to expel me for doing that.

L: Why were they going to expel you for that?

S: I can't remember too much. But I know they called the girl's mom and all that, and so her mom came to school and talked to me or whatever and so the girl, like she was alright with it, but you know like on that premises, that wasn't supposed to be happening on that premises.

L: So, they suspended you?

S: Yeah.

L: Did you get a hearing?

S: No.

L: How long did they suspend you?

S: Two days.

L: And that was fifth grade?

S: Mmmm ... mm [yes].

L: When did that happen? Was it in class?

S: It was in recess.

L: Was that your first suspension?

S: Yeah. Yeah it was.

In retelling the incident, Spider suggested that he and the girl were consenting participants in the kiss, but that only he was reprimanded with school suspension. This scenario raises questions about uneven vulnerabilities to school punishments. Spider was disciplined and the girl was not when they engaged in the same behavior. The consequence for him was school suspension and two lost days of classroom instruction.

Spider was given a second suspension two years later, in seventh grade. Spider and his mother were scheduled to come to school together for a parent conference. The meeting, however, conflicted with his mother's work as a parking attendant and she was unable to go. Instead of staying at home alone, Spider chose to go to school alone. As he explained, though, he was not supposed to go to school without his mother, and for this the school suspended him for three days.

L: What was your second suspension?

S: I had a parent conference, and they had to bring my mom in.

L: When was that?

S: Seventh grade.

L: Seventh grade. Did you get suspended?

S: Yeah, I got suspended.

L: What was that for?

S: For not attending, going to the parent conference.

L: For not attending? Did your mom go?

S: No, she was at work, and I told her but I came to school that day.

L: Your mom was at work and you . . .

S: I wasn't supposed to go to school, but I went to school.

L: You weren't supposed to go to school . . .

S: Yeah.

L: Why not?

S: Because I had a parent conference, and I couldn't come to school without my momma.

L: And so she didn't show up, and then they suspended you?

S: Yeah.

L: For how long?

S: Three days.

In this scenario, Spider's experience with school discipline seems to be inflected with socioeconomic meaning. While it is not clear from Spider's story what precipitated the need for a parent conference—whether it was a routine meeting or a meeting scheduled in response to a problem Spider was having at school—his story suggests that he was, in part, disciplined for the fact he had a working mother who was unavailable during the daytime for a meeting.

In addition to these first two suspensions, Spider was suspended on at least three other occasions for tardiness. He said he regularly had a difficult time getting to school for the homeroom period before classes began and was harshly punished for it. I asked him to describe the circumstances under which he was deemed tardy.

L: So, tell me what made it hard for you to get there on time.

S: I would be tired at night. I'd take my shower in the morning, and be lazy.

L: Do you feel like there is any particular reason why you were really tired?

S: Probably because I used to be on the phone till like twelve o'clock.

L: Did you have a job?

S: No.

L: If you had to guess, how many days a week would you say you were late to school?

S: Out of five, I would say three.

L: Three out of five? And how late?

S: Fifteen ... twenty minutes.

L: So, what did you miss when you showed up late?

S: Not really nothing.

L: What was your first period?

S: No, just to go in there and wait till the bell rings for nine o'clock when school started ... Well, check-in was at eight-thirty, but we'd go to our first-period class at nine o'clock.

L: So you were never late to your first-period class?

S. Mm–mm [no, shaking his head no].

L: Oh, So what did students do from eight-thirty to nine?

S: They'd just be in the cafeteria, and wait until the teacher comes to get the classes.

L: So, you were just supposed to sit there?

S: Yeahhhhhh.

By his own account, Spider was late to school on most days, but not so late that he missed any classroom instruction time. By arriving at school late he missed part of the check-in period from 8:30 to 9:00 A.M. On days when Spider was twenty minutes late to school, he arrived at 8:50, still ten minutes before his first class. Spider's repeated failure to arrive at school by 8:30 prompted the school administrators to take disciplinary action against him.

I found Spider's tardiness curious, since he said he was a student who wanted, more than anything else, to get an education and go to college. There was a discrepancy between his self-avowed devotion to education and his consistent tardiness, so I asked if there was any particular reason why he didn't want to be at school on time. "I wanted to be there. It is just that I just used to come late, and that was a problem, and I let laziness just took over me as the standard problem in my life." Spider's problem with tardiness began simply enough—he "used to come late"—but then it developed into something much larger—something that "took over." He was surprised by what happened next. For arriving late to school, he was told not to come at all, as if no school time would fix a problem of less school time. In his mind, Spider made a positive, albeit marginal, effort to attend school. Plenty of his peers, he said, didn't try to make it to school at all.

I felt bad because I know that they have *so* many people around here that I know, and that they *don't* go to school and that they don't *attempt* to go to school, *and I attempt to go to school every day*, and you sending me home sometimes. And you know. Some people don't want no education. I want my education. You are stop-ping me from getting it. Even though I am having a little bit of problems that I need to work on, you know. They got people every day out here saying, "I'm not going to school. I'm not going. School is stupid." I want to go to school but they are giv-ing me hard problems not to go.

As he spoke, Spider's tone was inflected with anger. Certain words and phrases—those in italics—were spoken with great force. What was the logic in sending him home after he had made a sincere attempt to show up? And once he got home, what was he to do other than join the company of neighbor-hood peers who didn't make the effort to go at all? Spider felt superior to his peers who shirked their education and did not appreciate being lumped in with them. If he had truly not wanted to go to school, he argued, he would have just stayed home in the first place.

Spider's lateness to school could be understood as simple self-sabotage, but race theory offers another way of conceptualizing it as a problem of traction in the context of the color line. This is unlike Jay MacLeod's argument, in his book *Ain't No Makin' It*, that disadvantaged students will have no use for schooling if they have no clear sense that it's a sure way out of the hole they are in (MacLeod, 1987). MacLeod's "hallway hangers" didn't buy into what he calls the "achievement ideology." They believed they weren't going to rise in the world anyway. By contrast, Spider had the sense that education would pay off and would distinguish him from his family and peers, but others' expecta-tions of him were low, and within his impoverished community there were virtually no models of achievement to emulate. He trod on that shaky founda-tion when he went to his failing public school, wearing the veil of the color line on his back. Playing out the double consciousness of blackness, he arrived late to a party he wanted to attend but wasn't formally invited to.

A positive orientation to schooling and earnest avowal of achievement ide-ologies set students like Jamal and Spider apart from MacLeod's hallway hang-ers and from the school-aged "lads" in Paul Willis's *Learning to Labor* (1977). In the school studied by Willis, the lads distanced themselves from achievement models and formed a "counter-school culture" by resisting rules and regulations. Willis argues that young males accept oppressive conditions in school and in society and see their marginal condition as a product of their own choices. Jamal and Spider, on the other hand, believed in the ideals of education and refused to accept the ways in which that ideal had been sacrificed for discipline, such that their own life chances were compromised. It is not that Jamal and Spider had oppositional identities, but that they were presumed to. They broke the rules at school by arriving late, but they were not active resisters. Both claimed that their school had not given them anything to show up for.

Spider was eventually left with only one educational option, and it was the same as the one offered to Jamal. Spider could go to the new public school at the Orleans Parish Prison, under the supervision of law enforcement and Criminal Sheriff Charles Foti. Not understanding the official rationale linking Spider's tardiness to correctional supervision, I pressed for clarification: "*How* did you get to Sheriff Foti's program?" "Oh," said Spider, as if there were some embedded logic, "because by . . . they were looking at my record and saying that I would be tardy. They were saying that I needed to improve in that and that I need like to stop being tardy. . . . They sent me to Foti's program to work on my tardiness."

As it turned out, the criminal sheriff's van would pick Spider and Jamal up at their homes, drive them across the city and across a wide Mississippi River to their new public school at the prison, and bring them home almost twelve hours later. The scheduled pickup and drop-off and the distance meant that there was never an opportunity for either student to work on tardiness or absenteeism. The correctional environment didn't, in fact, support them in correcting much of anything—neither the problems for which they were ostensibly being punished nor their academic deficiencies. The school touted its ability to provide superior opportunities for rehabilitation, but it offered classrooms in correctional spaces with inexperienced and uncertified teachers and provided remedial instruction without textbooks, where students accrued no credits toward high school graduation. In the larger correctional system, claims to rehabilitation have also proved farcical. Rather, the retributive nature of the criminal justice system has reproduced extant disenfranchisement along multiple lines of marginalization—including race, class, gender, sexuality, and disability—and magnified their significance.

Hanging out with Spider one day, I said, "Let me ask you something. Could you have just dropped out?"

S: Yeah.

L: But you chose not to drop out?

S: I chose not to.

L: Tell me why you chose not to drop out.

S: Because I felt that a lot of people in my family . . . they didn't really go nowhere. . . .

Spider explained that he needed an education to survive (Murphy & Dingwall, 2001). "I got an example as a brother," he said. "He is still staying with us. He is twenty-three years old. He dropped out in tenth grade, so I am always looking at him like I want to be better than that."

THE PUSH TOWARD PRISON

It was a Hearing Commission judge who informed Spider of his two options. Either he could work on his tardiness at the Prison School or he could stay home and work on nothing. Spider's mother explained that if he did well in the Prison School, he might stand a chance of getting back into a regular public school at a later date. In Spider's words, it was a no-win situation that he "couldn't really do too much about. Because it was either that as I couldn't really get back in the public school. I had to go to the alternative school, 'cause I had to work on my tardiness. To not be tardy I had to work on that. Until I could get into another school." The choice of attending Foti's program was not, then, a real choice. It was just the only way Spider could pursue a high school diploma and get to college. Jamal's mother explained her son's dilemma similarly:

Mother: In order for him to get back into regular school, he had to go to Foti's program and complete the eighth grade, and then they'd let him back into public school, regular school.

L: So, did you then see it as a choice?

M: I think he had no choice.

J: I had no choice. It wasn't a choice. I'd have been sitting at home.

M: He'd either have either been . . .

J: Sit at home. Sit at home.

L: So, your choice was to sit at home . . .

M: And do nothing

L: Or?

M: Go to Foti's program.

Believing that the Prison School was his only hope for reentry into the regular public school and, thus, his only hope for obtaining a high school diploma, Jamal enrolled. In his mind, there was really no decision to make; in essence, the system made the decision for him.

A PRISON SCHOOL

Criminal Sheriff Foti's proposal to open a public school at the Orleans Parish Prison was no doubt informed by his experience and authority in the criminal justice system itself. Foti, a white man born and raised in New Orleans, held the honor of being the only "criminal sheriff" in the country, and he held it for nearly thirty years.[2] The criminal and civil duties of the sheriff's office were separated in New Orleans during Reconstruction (1863–77) and weren't reorganized until the early 2000s. The fact that political appointments in twenty-first-century New Orleans remained marked by the hierarchies of the Reconstruction era was evidence, in Chui Clark's mind, that race continued to be the primary axis around which power in the city was organized. Reconstruction began at the end of the Civil War with the freeing of Southern slaves, so the criminal sheriff's office, which was established as part of Reconstruction, put a tool of racialized control in a box that Southerners bemoaned as having been emptied. The criminal sheriff's division in Orleans Parish became responsible at that time for the custody and supervision of all Orleans Parish inmates, and Charles Foti is the longest-serving criminal sheriff in the city's history.

Sheriff Foti maintained strong support from the local community during his tenure, and in his 2002 election he received nearly 75 percent of the parish vote. He was known inside and outside of the prison as an innovator, with an entrepreneurial spirit and a knack for getting his way. A local professor I interviewed referred to him as "the most innovative penologist God has ever created." Proponents and opponents agreed that the dimensions of his power were unusually extensive. In addition to controlling one of the nation's largest jails, he controlled a large sector of industry. Along with the local universities, Sheriff Foti's office was among the largest employers in the parish. Foti's work, however, extended beyond direct correctional services. Inside the prison, he established a hydroponics laboratory and a tilapia fish farm; he sold the fish in a local market under his name. He also bid on painting contracts for private businesses outside the prison, and even outside the parish, and supplied prison labor for the work. Chui claimed that "literally every day Orleans Parish Prison 'inmates' are sent to private job sites throughout the city of New Orleans. [This] slave labor is a lethal threat to wage labor." For Chui, these arrangements were examples of the prison industrial state and neoliberal practices that seek profit from the privatization of public institutions. Among other locals, these enterprises were cited as evidence of Foti's resourcefulness. Whites and African Americans spoke with reverence about several training programs that Foti started inside the Orleans Parish Prison for elders and for women, which were transferable for later employment there. With these and other programs, he developed his authority in the public sector, even as it extended into the public schools (Katz & Columbus, 2012).

In January 2002, with the consent of the parish school superintendent, the help of a career military man named Al Davis, and the support of a few professors at two local universities, Sheriff Foti decided to apply his resources to an intervention strategy aimed at the link between school failure and mass incarceration. In an interview, Sheriff Foti outlined his rationale: "The basic problem, and some of it is not their fault, is that these youth are not getting sufficient education. They become problem makers. Then they drop out of the system and then become prime candidates for anything going through the system." What Foti proposed was an alternative education program at the Orleans Parish Prison for "at-risk" public school youth. Foti would lead the school, and his prison deputies would help staff it. The plan was developed among a small circle of associates for many months before it was introduced to the public. In the fall of 2001, a contract was negotiated and approved, allowing Sheriff Foti to serve New Orleans Public School students at his correctional site. The school board paid Foti $316,622 to run the school, which took much-needed funds away from traditional public schools. Early in 2002, approximately fourteen students, all African American boys, were enrolled.[3]

The story of this new project at the Orleans Parish Prison broke in an editorial by Sheriff Foti that ran in two local papers, titled "Let's Save the Children" (Foti, 2001). In it, Foti explained that his program could turn troubled kids around by tapping into their innate potential. Anticipating questions about why his office of criminal justice was becoming involved in a public school issue, he outlined both his intent and the public need. "[Our] program is intended to save these children," and it is necessary, he wrote, because "we know from our experience in law enforcement that if nothing changes in the lives of these young people, they will be . . . without an education, no job skills, no personal skills, and filled with resentment of the hopeless situations they find themselves in. As we know, this is a recipe for disaster, not only for the individuals involved but also for anyone who happens to cross their path" (Foti, 2001). In an interview with me, the sheriff said that he believed he could "reach out to these kids; help them solve their problems; show them that they can learn." He also believed that he could reach these youths before it was too late. "I don't want to see kids wind up in the juvenile justice system or the criminal justice system," he said. "We can work with them after or prior," indicating that incarceration was inevitable unless someone stepped in to redirect the youths. The sheriff's primary assistant reiterated this point, saying that the sheriff's program was designed "to keep these kids out of jail where they were sure to end up."

The sheriff explained that it was his knowledge of corrections that enabled him to understand the dimensions of the school-to-prison pipeline, but that it was his experience in prison education that gave him the credentials to address it. Prior to opening the Prison School, Sheriff Foti started a General Equivalency Diploma (GED) program inside the Orleans Parish Prison for youths who had been convicted of crimes and were serving time. With this, his associates argue, his experience as an educator deepened and his plans grew bigger. In an interview, his assistant claimed that this program awarded more GED degrees than any other institution in New Orleans. It was proof, she said, that the sheriff "knows how to educate." The Prison School was a logical next step; his goal was to reach non-adjudicated youths before they reached him.

SAVING THE CHILDREN

Sheriff Foti's project and the characterization of him as God's most innovative penologist bear striking similarities to the "child-saving movement" of the mid-1800s. Anthony Platt (1970), in his book on the subject, characterizes the child-saving movement as "a moral crusade" fixated on treating the ills of industrialization, urban living, and large-scale immigration. These reformers believed that children born into these conditions would inevitably devolve into criminality. With a religious fervor, the child-savers sought to mitigate the ills of impoverishment and simultaneously prevent crime by extricating youths who were perceived as delinquent, neglected, or simply poor from their urban communities (Platt, 1969). The philosophy of the child-savers is uniquely captured by the penologist Enoch Wines, who in 1880 wrote of such children,

"They are born into crime, brought up for it. They must be saved" (Platt, 1969). In houses of refuge, these children were introduced to Puritanical values of hard labor. Other children were boarded on "orphan trains" headed for the farmlands of the West, where they were installed in families that were new and strange to them. Some of the orphan-train children were taken from the streets or from orphanages, while others were taken from their biological families with the idea that a rural village could provide what their urban immigrant communities and families could not.

The doctrine of *parens patriae* ("state as parent") that underlies the child-saving movement is based on the idea that the government has the right to make decisions for a child whose welfare is in question, and can even take the child away from its family for what is perceived to be a better alternative. It was not often asked what the children would inevitably lose in an arrangement that took them away from their families. Child-saving was seen as God's work and was, therefore, beyond reproach. Significantly, the threat of familial separation was precisely what worried Spider. When Sheriff Foti assigned him to a public school in the Orleans Parish Prison, he went. If he didn't go, he said, they'd "probably put me in a group home or . . . take me away from my momma." That was a risk he was unwilling to take, saying, "My momma and me, we have a *good* relationship!"

While Sheriff Foti was reinvigorating the purchase of the nineteenth-century child-saving movement for modern youths whom he perceived as delinquent, Chui Clark was publicly charging Foti with racism. "This is racism. . . . [It is] so typical for white people to have some kind of 'savior' complex" (Foti, 2001; Furness, 2002b). To Chui's pronouncement, Foti responded, "It has nothing to do with black and white. It has to do with kids," and defended his "child-saving" agenda with the rhetoric of color-blind benevolence (Furness, 2002a). Foti's simple, outright denial is a powerful defense against the charge of racism. Sociologists have argued that "As long as racism is denied, there is no need for official measures against it, for stricter laws, regulations, or institutions to combat discrimination, or moral campaigns to change the biased attitudes of whites. By selectively attributing 'racism' only to the extreme right, the mainstream parties and institutions at the same time define themselves as being 'not racists'" (Van Dijk et al., 2002).

Foti's populist approach to the issue of race also aligns with the myth of state impartiality, whereby the state and its agents are held to act in good faith, in the interests of the larger political community, and without discrimination toward any particular group within the society. A stance of impartiality is also preferred in modern New Orleans over an outwardly supremacist logic, even if the wielding of power and the effect of power resemble the latter. The expressed rationale in dodging a charge of racism inevitably involves a recollection of slavery and Jim Crow, to suggest that late-modern examples of racial discrimination are weak by comparison (Wilson, 1987; Simmons, 2009b). In New Orleans, the cultural reference for historical racism draws out an exceedingly dark past. It looks quite a bit like what is portrayed in 12 *Years a Slave*, the first feature film to deal with slavery as its central narrative, which is set on plantations outside New Orleans. In denying or dodging the contemporary charge, however, the daily experience of racism is elided and racism itself is reproduced.

Foti's claim of color-blindness dismisses race as irrelevant even when there is a great deal of evidence to the contrary. Further, he accepts the role of child-saver to a group of young men but rejects the fact that they are all black. Sociologist Eduardo Bonilla-Silva calls this kind of color-blindness a "sincere fiction." He argues that "whites have developed powerful explanations—which have ultimately become justifications—for contemporary racial inequality that exculpate them from any responsibility for the status of people of color" (Bonilla-Silva, 2006). "Regardless of whites' 'sincere fictions,'" he claims, "racial considerations shade almost everything in America. Black and dark-skinned racial minorities lag well behind whites in virtually every area of social life" (Bonilla-Silva, 2006). This was Chui's argument precisely:

> When you see a significant number of black babies die compared to white babies. When you see a significant number of black schools that are failures. When you see a significant number of individuals that are being arrested and hauled off to jail, are black. When you see a significant number of individuals on death row are dying or go to the death chamber are black. . . . When you see a disproportionate number of black males or females that are unable to find a job. It is racism. It is genocide. That is basically what it is.

Naming the failures of the health system, the education system, the criminal justice system, and the economic system, Chui explained that racism is the racially disproportional experience of inferior public services and systems. He saw the Prison School as epitomizing the inferior operation of public services and systems for African Americans. He said that "The responsibility of the school district, the education department, the education system, is to educate, nothing else."

CONCLUSION

Close relations between the New Orleans public school system and the local criminal justice system meant that law enforcement officers had access to "at-risk" youths like Jamal and Spider, and had the capacity to engage them in punitive arrangements. Though Jamal was excessively tardy to class and Spider was continually tardy to school, both did make individual efforts to go to school. They weren't highly oppositional or defiant students, like MacLeod's hallway hangers or Willis's lads, and their stories can't easily be framed by the prominent theories of youth resistance within the sociology of education. Spider suggested that what they really faced was institutional resistance: "There are a lot of people who want the education, but in certain ways they go through a lot of things that they feel that, you know, it is hard to get it."

Many students in urban schools are low-income minority youths living in single-family homes in impoverished neighborhoods, attending public schools that are segregated de facto and failing abysmally by state and national standards. They are surrounded by peers for whom schooling is a fruitless enterprise; even if they graduate from high school, they are hard pressed to find legitimate local employment. These students have to overcome significant obstacles in order to get to school at all. Sending such a student home for being twenty minutes late to the check-in period, or late to class, overlooks these potential obstacles and denies education to students who are already disenfranchised socially, economically, and academically. Students like Jamal and Spider know that they need more education, not less, and they know that meaningful school disciplinary policies can only be born from this recognition.

Disciplinary policies that suspend or expel students for nonviolent offenses effectively interrupt or terminate educational opportunities that are already hard to get, while expanding carceral vulnerability. In this chapter, African American men from two successive generations articulate the primary role of school discipline in their departure from the academic track and in their correctional arrival. Their educational experiences help explain how Louisiana gained the highest incarceration rate in the world. In Louisiana and nationally, the correctional system is filled with individuals who have dropped out of school. In 1997, almost 75 percent of state inmates lacked a high school diploma (Harlow, 2003). Extreme school disciplinary policies have the effect of adding to that group students who have been pushed out of school (Harlow, 2003).

As Jamal and Spider expressed, however, school was the one site where they had a chance to overcome stark social and economic barriers and achieve some sort of mobility. They needed greater academic support and more positive discipline in a school system that believed in them at least as much as they believed in it.

CHAPTER 4

The Prison School

The new prisons would overflow, to be followed with a cry to build more, more, absorbing the lifeblood of the downtrodden.

—Robert Hillary King, 2012

> I followed one of the protestors today to . . . the "Prison School" [that] the activists were talking about. . . . The building itself was located within the Sheriff's "city within a city," a roughly 20 square block tract of land controlled by the Sheriff that contained one of the largest jails in the country. At the site for the school, many of the old prison fortifications were visible from the outside as vestiges of its former carceral function. It was a small building tucked behind the Orleans Parish Prison, and it looked just like the building pictured on the protestors' pickets. . . . Almost the entire structure of the building was hidden below the roofline behind a tall fence that surrounded the property. Only the tops of the windows and the surveillance cameras mounted on the upper corners of the building were unobscured. The most striking physical fortification at the site was the bars on the windows—so bulky that little light could have passed into the interior spaces. (ethnographic field notes)

Charles C. Foti came to power as the criminal sheriff of New Orleans and warden of the Orleans Parish Prison in 1974, and he served in that office until 2004, with a tenure that spanned what is now recognized as the nation's War on Crime era. Under his leadership, the criminal justice system in New Orleans bore the central hallmarks of the War on Crime by way of its massive expansion project. The Orleans Parish Prison's facilities mushroomed, the inmate population exploded, and law enforcement pushed into new territories of influence, including the local public school system. In 1974, Criminal Sheriff Foti controlled only one property in New Orleans, but he gradually incorporated the contiguous lots in the Mid-City area. With expanded facilities holding adults and children in Central Lockup, the Community Correctional Center, the House of Detention, and Templeman buildings I–IV, Sheriff Foti's compound eventually spread over twenty square city blocks. The inmate population rose nearly a thousand percent—eight hundred inmates in 1974 and eighty-five hundred by 2004—helping New Orleans reach the highest incarceration rate in the world (ACLU National Prison Project, 2006; Gerharz & Hong, 2006).[1] Locals called the new carceral landscape "the sheriff's city-within-a-city," which suggests the sheer magnitude of the complex as well as the absolute authority vested in the sheriff himself. By 2002, the sheriff's city-within-a-city included a new public school with Criminal Sheriff Foti at its helm.

A "Prison School" is what Chui Clark called Sheriff Foti's educational program. Standing in front of the school together, Chui directed my attention to the institution's correctional signature. He pointed first to a sign emblazoned with the sheriff's badge and the name "Sheriff C. Foti," and then turned his eyes toward the school building, which stood in the foreground of the larger prison complex that rose several stories high in the distance. A tall fence marked the edge of the property and was topped by barbed wire. Surveillance cameras were mounted on the building corners, and thick bars covered the windows vertically and horizontally, making the entire building look like a cross between a small train depot and a large cage. Flying above the pitched roof was an American flag. There was a single entry at the front and center of the building. Gesturing to it, Chui repeated a claim I had often heard him make: "It is literally a youth penal fortress." He later added, "I've done been in prisons. I have been in prisons since I was a little boy," and "I know a prison when I see one. There is one way in and one way out."

The Prison School opened with fourteen African American boys between the ages of twelve and seventeen who were labeled "at-risk."[2] The state defines at-risk students as youths who qualify for free or reduced lunch in school, but the sheriff and the superintendent who collaborated with him intended this program for students who were considered disruptive in the classroom. They had not been involved in crime, beyond status offenses, and had not been expelled from school (Louisiana Schools, 2002; Foti, 2001; Bell, 2001). Since proof of criminal activity was not a prerequisite for matriculation, assignments to the Prison School depended on the logic of preemption. A law enforcement officer who volunteered at the school explained, "You need to do something to catch them before they do get in trouble," thereby suggesting that the sheriff could help children avoid the snare of prison by incorporating them in the criminal justice system earlier and before their problems became real (Furness, 2002b). In approaching candidates for the Prison School, Sheriff Foti extended the long arm of law enforcement into the traditional public school population. He captured students who were already pushed to the margins of their traditional schools because of their socioeconomic status as low-income African American boys, their poor academic performance, and—though based on minor and nonviolent infractions—their histories of school disciplinary trouble.

New Orleans began to suspend students at high rates during the War on Crime era, and the punishment effectively pushed students out of school and into spaces at the fringes of mainstream society. As in cities nationwide, African American males in New Orleans bore the brunt of the corrective and suffered the impact of the consequent educational exclusion most severely (Johnson et al., 2001; Skiba, 2001; Skiba & Leone, 2001; Skiba et al., 2002). One-quarter of all black male students in New Orleans Public Schools were suspended at least once during the 2002–03 academic year (Louisiana Department of Education, 2003). Suspended students are largely left to their own devices while serving their sentence, and suspensions can last for days or months (Sullivan & Morgan, 2010). Many sit at home while their parents (often single mothers) are at work, or hang out on the street supervised only by other school "pushouts," neighbors, and law enforcement. In his book on school punishment, Ronnie Casella argues that expulsion and suspension put kids "in greater contact with the individuals in their lives who may be central to their problems in the first place" (Casella, 2001).

Sheriff Foti took school pushouts and, with the complicity of the Orleans Parish School Board and the local juvenile courts, denied them other local public educational outlets. As schools have taken a correctional approach to discipline, meting out harsh punishments for minor offenses, students like Spider and Jamal—and 3.5 million like them nationally—have been pushed away from academic opportunity and pulled toward the criminal justice system in a black prison diaspora (Losen et al., 2015). Harsh school disciplinary policies that stem from the War on Crime have legitimized racialized educational exclusion in the post–civil rights era and led to the kind of socioeconomic marginalization that increases criminal justice exposure and ultimately exacerbates incarceration risk.

Chapter 3 described undereducation and overincarceration in New Orleans as coordinated phenomena by showing how students experience school conditions that engage the criminal justice system and push them to the margins of educational opportunity. In this chapter, I delve further into the case of the Prison School to document the pull of the criminal justice system on innocent youth.

HELLHOLE

We would be unable to paint the dolorous impression that we received when, on examining the prison of New Orleans, we saw there men thrown in pell-mell with swine, in the midst of excrement and filth. In locking up criminals, no thought is given to making them better but simply to taming their wickedness; they are chained like wild beasts; they are not refined but brutalized.

—Beaumont & Tocqueville, 1833/1979

The conditions of confinement in Orleans Parish Prison so shock the conscience as a matter of elemental decency and are so much more cruel than is necessary to achieve a legitimate penal aim that such confinement constitutes cruel and unusual punishment in violation of the Eighth and Fourteenth Amendments of the United States Constitution. (*Hamilton v. Schiro*, 338 F. Supp. 1016 31)

—U.S. Federal Court decision, Louis Hamilton class action suit, 1970

The Prison School was sited on the edge of the Orleans Parish Prison compound in an empty correctional building that had been used to house a school for blacks in the era of formal segregation. The Mid-City neighborhood that stood beyond the correctional border presented a contrast to the Haussmann-style Parisian boulevards that provided access to the French Quarter. The side streets were narrow, and the elaborate postcard homes that showcase the Crescent City were altogether absent. Small and worn 1920s bungalows with sagging porches and peeling paint were mixed in with other buildings for light industrial use on uncurbed streets. In 2000, the median household income in the census tract including this neighborhood was $12,901 (U.S. Census Bureau, 2000b). The geographer Pierce Lewis calls the area a "derelict wasteland," built at the "lowest part of a ... swamp" and, as backswamps go, "generally odious" (Lewis, 2003). "The reasons are simple and deadly.... Mid-city [sic] is surrounded completely by natural levees, which have turned it into a shallow bowl whose center lies below sea level. At best it was wet, but after heavy rains or a flood it filled up with water, most of which stayed to form a noisome swamp" (Lewis, 2003). For centuries, this backswamp of Mid-City was considered uninhabitable—it had bad drainage, unstable building foundations, unmaintained streets, mosquito infestations, and frequent flooding—but

African Americans were pushed there for the cheapest housing possible, and the old Orleans Parish Prison was built there (Lewis, 2003).

The hellish descriptions of the neighborhood accord with published characterizations of the adjacent correctional complex. A *Mother Jones* exposé on the institution, titled "Complete Lawlessness," begins "[A]s hellholes go, there are few worse places than the Orleans Parish Prison" and continues with descriptions of the decades-long history of prison abuse in which guards have subjected inmates to sexual assault and excessive force (Ridgeway & Casella, 2012). Petitions filed for a federal consent decree highlight rampant inmate violence within the prison, including egregious corporal violations such as gang rape (Vargas, 2012). The U.S. Department of Justice found that for the most part, "inmates are left to fend for themselves in the Orleans Parish jails" (Schwartz & Miller, 2008). Sheriff Foti himself brought attention to the problem of overcrowding at the prison in 1980 when he drove 147 state inmates from the Orleans Parish Prison to a correctional center in St. Gabriel, Louisiana, and abandoned them in the parking lot (ACLU National Prison Project, 2006). In 1999 the prison was the subject of national critique when prison officials under Sheriff Foti used electroshock stun belts within the segregated prison unit for all inmates who had tested positive for HIV (Body Positive, 1999).

The most serious claims against the Orleans Parish Prison have involved cases of inmate death. Motions filed by the National Prison Project in the case of *Hamilton v. Morial* point to the "catastrophic failure of [Orleans Parish Prison] staff to use proper restraint techniques or monitor [inmate] activities and behavior" (ACLU, 2006). The motion cites the case of Shawn Duncan, who was a heavily inebriated but otherwise healthy twenty-four-year-old when he entered the prison in August 2001 on charges of public drunkenness. He died a week later, after being held for forty-two hours in five-point restraints (ACLU, 2006). In my explorations of the city, I heard stories about inmate deaths regularly, as if these events represented life as usual in New Orleans. At dinner one night at a quiet old Creole restaurant, I asked my young waitress if she was a student in the public schools. She said that she was, but she was heading to a historically black college, and eventually to law school, in order to seek justice in the case of her father, who entered the Orleans Parish Prison for unpaid parking tickets and never came home. He died in the prison, and she never saw him again. Approximately 60 percent of the inmate population at the prison consists of individuals like this man, held on minor charges such as traffic violations, public intoxication, and sleeping in public.

A report by Human Rights Watch indicates that inmates at the prison have been known to wait in jail for as long as six weeks to get a trial for such charges (ACLU National Prison Project, 2006; Human Rights Watch, 2005). That wait is riddled with peril. Once inside the "city within a city," there is a real risk of never seeing the light of day again, supporting the repeated claim that the prison is hell on earth.

There is a long history to the negative appraisal of the Orleans Parish Prison. In 1833, Tocqueville and Beaumont surveyed the prison as part of their study of American penitentiaries and were at a loss for words to describe the filth of the institution and the "dolorous impression" it left on them. To date, there is not much evidence that would revise their assessment. In a class action suit filed by the Southern Poverty Law Center in 2012, an inmate who had served time in several other prisons stated: "With God as my witness, I will testify. . . . Those guards smacked me around. They beat me. They threatened to kill me. . . . That is the scariest place I've ever been. It's hellish in there" (Webster, 2012).

Abusive conditions at the Orleans Parish Prison made national news in the aftermath of Hurricane Katrina when the prison descended into chaos (ACLU, 2006). At the time, almost 90 percent of the adult inmate population was African American and male; in the juvenile population, 95 percent were African American, and the youngest inmate was ten years old (ACLU, 2006). Prison officials put the institution on lockdown and kept inmates in their cells even as water levels rose to chest height. As officers lost access to traditional weapons and ammunition in the flooding, they began to improvise social control strategies and resorted to throwing hot water balloons to keep inmates in their cells (ACLU, 2006). Eventually, some prisoners were evacuated by boat and taken to sit in the hot sun on an interstate highway overpass, where some developed sunstroke and dehydration and were abused by guards with attack dogs. Repeating the strategy used by Sheriff Foti, a group of inmates were subsequently evacuated to a field near the neighboring St. Gabriel correctional facility and left to fend for themselves for three days without food or water (Gerharz & Hong, 2006). Back at the prison, many inmates were reported to have been left to die in their cells, and a prison deputy stated that "there were bodies floating by." Despite this testimony, Criminal Sheriff Marlin Gusman, who succeeded Charles Foti, claimed that there was "not a single fatality or serious injury" at the Orleans Parish Prison during the Katrina crisis (Editorial Board, 2010). The American Civil Liberties Union (ACLU) found it difficult to prove the sheriff's statement false, because prison officials never provided an accurate account of who was detained in the prison at the time. If individuals were confirmed as inmates, there was no easy way of arguing against the logic that the inmates had simply "escaped." The similarity to the school pushout phenomenon is striking. Administrators in both the public education system and the criminal justice system in New Orleans were practiced in the art of making people disappear.

Although Sheriff Gusman was in office when Katrina struck and storm water flooded the prison, the ACLU and the Department of Justice held Sheriff Foti responsible for the catastrophic failure of the Orleans Parish Prison in the aftermath. The ACLU argued that "the problems at [the prison] did not begin with Katrina" but that the prison "has a long history of cruelty and neglect toward its prisoners" (ACLU, 2006). "The problems that Marlin Gusman inherited, he inherited from Foti," said Marjorie Esman, head of the ACLU's New Orleans chapter (Vanacore, 2013). Forty years' worth of litigation referencing unconstitutional prison conditions and leading to a remedial decree provided abundant proof of Foti's adverse legacy.[3] According to the Department of Justice:

> The Orleans Parish jails had pervasive and long-standing problems prior to Hurricane Katrina. At the time of the hurricane, Sheriff Gusman had been in office for less than one year following a prior sheriff's administration that had been in place more than thirty years. Quite apart from the hurricane related problems, Sheriff Gusman is confronting a daunting set of challenges in changing the culture of the organization. . . . The sheriff is also dealing with the remnants of a long-standing "good old boy" system and an organization that has historically been personality driven. (Schwartz & Miller, 2008)

Sheriff Foti was the personality that drove the Orleans Parish Prison for three decades. He was known as a "controversial and colorful" character who ran the prison "with an iron fist" (Schwartz & Miller, 2008; Katz & Columbus, 2012). Though well liked among his staff, he was also known to have fits of "terrible rage and temper" and was generally obeyed with the fear of reprisal as an impetus (Katz & Columbus, 2012). On the other hand, Foti was elected by huge margins whenever he ran for office, which helps account for his tenure.

Foti was also well connected to the political elite in the state and was distantly related to the Landrieu family, which has had a dynastic presence in Louisiana politics in the second half of the twentieth century (Donze, 2012). Louisiana Senator Mary Landrieu, Judge Madeleine Landrieu, and current New Orleans Mayor Mitch Landrieu are Charles Foti's second cousins, and their father, Moon Landrieu, governed New Orleans in the civil rights era.[4] Moon and his son Mitch have been the only two white mayors of New Orleans since 1970 (Krupa & Donze, 2010). For their iconic status in Louisiana politics, some locals refer to the Landrieus as the "Cajun Kennedys" (Donze, 2012).

Foti's renowned charity work was also represented by locals as instrumental in his popularity. Jamal's mother suggested that Foti had proved himself to her over many years: "He's been around for, since I can remember. Since I was a kid." Pointing to her son, she said: "He doesn't know too much about the history of it, of Sheriff Foti, but uh, he put back into the community. . . . He does charity work. He, he gives to the poor. He has little things for elderly people for Thanksgiving and Christmas." Sheriff Foti had strong character references across the spectrum, with the exception of anyone who had actually been under his correctional supervision, such as Chui Clark, Robert Hillary King, and the students at the Prison School.

Locals like Chui incorporated critiques of the Orleans Parish Prison and its leadership into their ongoing protests about criminal justice leadership in public education, pointing to ample documentation of misconduct and poor accountability at all levels of local law enforcement in every generation of its existence. In his book *Black Rage in New Orleans*, the historian Leonard Moore presents the New Orleans Police Department as

> arguably one of the most brutal, corrupt, and incompetent police units in the United States in the postwar period. . . . At the height of its corruption in the mid-1990s, the New Orleans department had the highest number of citizen complaints of police brutality in the country, and a 1992 Justice Department study reported that New Orleans citizens had lodged more complaints with federal officials about police abuse than residents in any other city between 1984 and 1990. The majority of these complaints came from the African American community. (Moore, 2010)

Moore documents how police brutality in New Orleans spawned African American activism in the city. To protect white privilege and oppose black progress in the post–World War II era, the New Orleans Police Department endeavored on a daily basis to "let African Americans know who was in charge by utilizing any and all means of police repression" (Moore, 2010). Ordinary African American citizens across the economic spectrum felt the pressure of law enforcement's tyranny, but poor and working-class black people were instrumental in staging confrontational protests (Moore, 2010).[5] In challenging the police "at every opportunity," these groups shaped a legacy of local resistance that Chui would inherit. Moore's historical record of black protest organizations operating in New Orleans suggests the ubiquity and magnitude of the city's police violence. The organizations operated as Citizens Committee on Negro Police (CCNP), Committee to Prevent Police Brutality to Negro Citizens (CPPB), Concerned Citizens on Police Matters of Brutality and Harassment (CCPM), Citizen's Observers Committee (COC), United Front for Justice (UFJ), Ad Hoc Committee for Accountable Police (AHC), Police Brutality Committee (PBC), People's Conference on Police Brutality (PCPB), Committee for Accountable Police (CAP), Liberation League (LL), People Defense Council (PDC), Black Panther Party (BPP), Soul Patrol, Community Action Now (CAN), Community Advancement Committee (CAC), Black Police for Positive Action (BPPA), and Black Organization of Police (BOP) (Moore, 2010).

Chui Clark's own organization, Neighborhood Unity/MERGE (Mobilization to End Racism in Government and Everywhere), has sustained this history of protest into the twenty-first century, as long-standing demands to end police brutality and establish accountability remain unmet. Chui was joined by others in protest, including a Tulane University doctoral student, Jay Arena, who spoke up at a school board meeting, stating querulously: "So-called 'at-risk youth' are being placed in a 'school' . . . with barbed wire, bars on windows and surveillance . . . provided by [the] sheriff—the same force responsible for various deaths of people under custody . . . ??" For Chui, the egregious conduct of New Orleans law enforcement across the span of his lifetime explained his long-standing claim that "it is inappropriate for the sheriff's department to be involved in our public education system."

JIM CROW LIVES HERE

The past ain't past yet.
—Moon Landrieu, Mayor of New Orleans (1970–78)

Chui and I often met in or around the New Orleans Public Library on St. Charles Avenue to talk about his life in Jim Crow Louisiana and to talk about the Prison School in historical perspective. The library and the grounds were generally quiet, which helped ensure audio clarity for my recordings. Chui also spoke in a thick New Orleans accent that even I, as a southerner, had difficulty deciphering. Like many New Orleanians, he dropped his R's and packed his words with diphthongs. One afternoon in September, the library was busy with patrons, and we sat outside to talk on a concrete exterior balustrade under the canopy of an ancient oak tree. It was hot at the end of hurricane season, and the shade of the massive tree offered a dappled shield. The St. Charles streetcar rattled in the background every few minutes, much as the railcars would have a hundred and fifty years ago, traveling to plantations upriver.[6]

In the foreground, Chui looked at me and shook his head, asking, "What has changed for the better? . . . Nothing!" He considered the Prison School powerful evidence of this charge. It was a way, he said, to "maintain de facto Jim Crowism" in the post–civil rights era. Within the criminal justice system, the white domination of blacks appeared even more extreme to him. Chui compared the Prison School to the segregated reform schools of his youth: "Its windows are ironclad, and barbed wire fence and a huge wooden structure, encircles the fortress. It is no school. Its conditions are more extreme than such former youth penal 'facilities' as Milne Boys Home and [the] State Industrial School for Colored Youth [have] ever been."

The Milne Boys Home opened in 1933 on a large plot of land (far from the Orleans Parish Prison) after a merger with the Colored Waifs' Home (famous for once housing Louis Armstrong).[7] For nearly forty years at Milne, blacks were housed on the north campus and whites on the south side in colonial-styled barracks with separate dining and recreational facilities. The institution was known locally as "a home for bad boys" and a "juvenile prison" (Richard, 2012). In 1974, locals protested the punitive conditions at Milne and the institution was found to be in violation of the bequest that had originally endowed it as an orphanage (Kimball, 2012).[8] Chui also refers to the State Industrial School for Colored Youth, which was opened in 1948 as a state-run secure care facility. "Secure care" is described by the state as "the deep end of the juvenile justice system," where youths are in "locked units" and "high security" and "monitored constantly under direct supervision of staff" (State of Louisiana, Office of Juvenile Justice, 2013). In Chui's childhood, neither of these youth reformatories was fortified with bars and barbed wire, and neither was positioned on the grounds of a prison. They both functioned, in fact, to keep juvenile delinquents apart from adult facilities (Schlossman, 1995). Prior to the youth reformatory movement, which gained momentum in the early 1900s, children as young as seven were incarcerated in the United States alongside adults (Schlossman, 1995; State of Louisiana, Office of Juvenile Justice, 2013).

In many ways, Chui felt that conditions for African Americans had deterio-
rated, such that even Jim Crow racism seemed an inadequate comparison.
When the criminal justice system is understood as an industry that profits
on black custody and black labor, slavery is a tenable analogy. Angela Davis
makes an argument along these lines in her essay "The Prison of Slavery and
the Slavery of Prison," in which she reads the convict lease system of the
post–Civil War South and the crisis of modern black incarceration as forms
of enslavement (Davis, 1998). The claim that prison is slavery, however, has
older roots in the legislature. In 1871, in the legal case *Ruffin v. Commonwealth*,
a Virginia court determined that prisoners, by virtue of their crimes, forfeit
all personal rights; the prisoner is said to be "the slave of the state" (as cited in
Davis, 2012).[9]

In *Slavery by Another Name*, Douglas Blackmon declares that Jim Crow
itself was an "Age of Neo-Slavery." This Pulitzer Prize–winning book's central
argument is that slavery did not end with the Civil War, but held a firm grip
on American society as long as "governments . . . [were selling] blacks to commercial interests" (Blackmon, 2008). This accords with Frederick Douglass's
definition of slavery as "the granting of that power by which one man exercises
and enforces a right of property in the body and soul of another" (Douglass,
1846). The practice of black subjugation extends, in Blackmon's account,
through World War II and into the era of Jim Crow segregation. Significantly,
the tactics of excessive punitiveness that Blackmon records in those eras and
the practice of selling blacks to commercial interests bear a striking resem-
blance to practices in the War on Crime era, and in New Orleans in particular, as the intergenerational experiences of Chui, King, Spider, and Jamal
suggest.

> Instead of true thieves and thugs drawn into the system over decades, the records
> demonstrate the capture and imprisonment of thousands of random indigent
> citizens, almost always under the thinnest chimera of probable cause or judicial
> process. . . . Instead of evidence showing black crime waves, the original records
> of county jails indicated thousands of arrests for inconsequential charges or for
> violations of laws specifically written to intimidate blacks—charging employers
> without permission, vagrancy, riding in freight cars without a ticket, engaging in
> sexual activity—or loud talk—with white women. Repeatedly, the timing and
> scale of surges in arrests appeared more attuned to rises and dips in the need for
> cheap labor than any demonstrable acts of crime. Hundreds of forced labor camps
> came to exist scattered throughout the South. . . . These bulging slave centers
> became a primary weapon of suppression of black aspirations. (Blackmon, 2008)

Blackmon's historical account representing the criminal justice system as a "primary weapon of suppression of black aspirations" resonates with Chui's experiences, which he similarly conceptualizes through the lenses of slavery and Jim Crow. It is easy to pull the thread of that argument through to the War on Crime era, and in Louisiana, a continuity of place presents the generational fabric of oppression seamlessly. The forced-labor camps to which Blackmon refers are America's southern prison farms, of which Angola was one. The site was named after the Angolese slaves who first farmed the area as a slave plantation, and the land was purchased in 1880 by a Confederate major to function as a prison (Sturgis, 2014). The black inmates continued to work the land and were leased out to private companies to build the nearby levees in a convict leasing system (Sturgis, 2014). Angola is now a Louisiana State Penitentiary called colloquially "The Farm," which reflects its origins as a plantation under slavery (Schenwar, 2008). Inmates at Angola today are compelled to cultivate its eighteen thousand acres of farmland in twelve- to seventeen-hour shifts (rain or shine), earning four to twenty cents an hour while being supervised by armed guards (Schenwar, 2008; Segura, 2011).[10] Chui spent seventeen years of his life incarcerated at that very site, and King spent twenty-nine years there in solitary confinement. They are two of the few inmates to have been released from this state penitentiary; 90 percent of Angola inmates live and die there because of Louisiana's severe parole policies (Segura, 2011). As if to make the terminal fate of most Angola inmates clear, and to cut costs, inmates at Angola actually build coffins for prison burials while they are there (Fields, 2005).

Once released from Angola, Chui was intent on exposing racism wherever he saw it, and this charge pulled him quickly into the orbit of local public schooling, where he saw egregious racial inequalities. The Prison School became the object of one of his greatest battles, and he pointed to the building that housed it as another blatant index of Jim Crow's fluid transition to correctional control. The structure was built as a segregated school for blacks; repurposed for correctional use; and then adapted for a public school under correctional supervision.[11] In the second of these shifts, the sheriff had not attempted to remove the bars that explicitly marked the space as a correctional one. Chui suggested that the building held hostage the same population as Jim Crow—just three generations later—with the same racist and correctional intent. The Prison School was just a new iteration of an old racialized correctional scheme. In this instantiation, carceral expansion leveraged the disciplinary mechanisms of public education. Chui recognized this scheme instantly as a mechanism of racialized power: "My first thought was that they were attempting to expand the criminal justice system. You know, that they were, in a sense, really trying to, once again, talk to our kids and get them ready for the prison system."

In studying the geography of the school space myself, I was struck by the insistence of the sheriff and his staff that the transitions from Jim Crow corrections to correctional public schooling were entirely unproblematic. On the backside of the prison, however, the building and the students in it were largely hidden away. Their invisibility was facilitated, too, by prominent media outlets. The *Times-Picayune*, the city's most circulated newspaper, did not publicize Chui Clark's highly visible protests of the Prison School for six weeks. Chui called agents at three television stations, who sent film crews, but ultimately the story was left out of the evening news.[12] Publicity for the protest came only from the *Louisiana Weekly*, an African American periodical that had served the city since 1925 and through the post–civil rights era. They printed an image of Chui and fellow activist Llewelyn Soniat holding a sign in front of a school that read "Jim Crow lives here" (*Louisiana Weekly*, 2002).

Sensing editorial neglect in the mainstream press, Chui took my efforts to investigate the story of the Prison School and its sociocultural context seriously. As if to guide me to the evidence of Jim Crow's endurance, he drove me one day to see an inmate-painted mural on the roof of a correctional building in the prison complex. In preparation for this tour, Chui said, "Make sure you bring a camera." When we arrived, he pointed and asked, "Do you see what I am showing you?" Painted on the roof was an image (about twenty feet wide) of the American landmass, with the entire southern region painted as a Confederate flag. The mural was faded and the day was overcast, but I took the picture Chui wanted. In a protest flier that was distributed at demonstrations, Chui staked a claim to the New Jim Crow: "Foti's scheme represents . . . [a] continuous catering to white supremacy . . . [This is about] racism . . . [and the will] to dominate and/or eliminate people of color" (C. Clark, 2002, unpublished pamphlet, "A Treacherous Alliance").

For his claims of racism, Chui gained a reputation in New Orleans as an "extremist" and a "radical dissident" (Foti, 2002; Katz & Columbus, 2012). With a racist connotation that was difficult to overlook, Ed Morse, a university professor with links to the sheriff, referred to Chui as "Chewbacca." Morse "mistook" Mr. Clark's nickname for the name of the immense hirsute beast in *Star Wars* who is freed from slavery by Han Solo and joins the Rebel Alliance. But while he was marginalized as a local figure, Chui Clark's claims were not out of sync with a national dialogue among legal scholars like Michelle Alexander, who has claimed that the War on Crime produced a "new racial caste system" whereby African Americans are relegated to positions as second-class citizens (Alexander, 2010). Alexander argues that in the custody of the criminal justice system, African Americans are "banished to a political and social space not unlike Jim Crow, where discrimination in employment, housing and access to education was perfectly legal" (Alexander, 2010). As a consequence of racialized control mechanisms embedded within the ideologies and practices of correctional expansion, large numbers of black male youths are subjected to legalized discrimination and are as locked out of mainstream society as their grandparents and great-grandparents were (Alexander, 2010). Outside of academic circles, cultural figures like the Reverend Al Sharpton have brought the argument to a popular audience, claiming that "We've gone from plantations to penitentiaries. . . . They have tried to create a criminal justice system that particularly targets our young black men" (as cited in Alexander, 2010). Voicing similar concerns about racial targeting in law enforcement and linking it to systemic school dysfunction, Chui wrote:

> Our youth were (and are still) labeled recalcitrant, as though . . . it is appropriate . . . to maintain the system of "white" racism . . . [by] targeting Afrikan youth for harassment, detention and imprisonment, under the pretense of addressing the problem of juvenile delinquency. (Never mind that the public school systems of America do not train or encourage Afrikan youths to become entrepreneurs or to obtain the skills that would allow them to find gainful employment). (C. Clark, unpublished pamphlet)

Chui understood the New Jim Crow as a coordinated set of investments and divestments that prioritized dependency in correctional programs and deprioritized opportunity in public schooling.

"THEY GOT CAGES"

On a winter morning in 2002, Sheriff Foti's van arrived at Spider's home shortly after sunrise and drove him across the Mississippi River and to the Orleans Parish Prison, where he would start an eleven-and-a-half-hour school day. According to a counselor at the school, the 8:15 A.M. to 7:30 P.M. school schedule was designed to confine the children during the school day and beyond to cover the peak hours of juvenile crime (Furness, 2002b). In long days away from home, Spider would be with a cohort of thirteen other students, though several matriculated students managed to dodge the sheriff's van each day. When he arrived on day one, Spider stepped out of the van and found a public school unlike any school he had ever been to. "To me [it looked like] a jail. That is what I say. You can't see anything out of the windows. You can't see out. They got cages around the windows. They got like bars inside the school."

In March, Jamal joined Spider at the site and immediately felt the prison-like atmosphere. "It was like a little jailhouse. All they did was put a couple of desks in there, and some computers and that was it. They had little books, an area of books, and that was it. Otherwise it was a straight jailhouse. A straight jailhouse. . . ."

In contrast to the students, Sheriff Foti touted the facility in a local editorial as having been "beautifully renovated and furnished by our community service program" with a computer facility that "is the equal of any in the city" (Foti, 2001). Despite these advertisements, thick window bars on the exterior of the school building were highly visible to anyone who went to the backside of the prison complex to see.

A prominent surveillance system added to the facility's correctional aspect. When Spider spoke of the surveillance cameras, we were sitting in his living room at home, and I had a tape recorder on a coffee table nearby. He pointed to each corner of the room to mark the relative locations of each monitor and elaborately described the school's surveillance network. "Oh! And another way, another way I felt like it was a jail—they had cameras in there. They had a camera like see right there, see like right there and in that corner and in that corner and they had security, you know in a room with video screens watching us."

In the War on Crime era, surveillance cameras became common features of the public-school landscape and are indicative of the correctional approach that has shaped public schools nationwide. In the early 2000s, however, surveillance cameras were still uncommon in New Orleans Public Schools, and they stood out to students like Spider as remarkably "like . . . jail." The Prison School's unusually robust surveillance network summons up the image of Jeremy Bentham's famous Panopticon prison. It certainly made students conscious of their custody within the criminal justice system.

I was sitting at Jamal's dining-room table when I asked him about surveillance. "Oh, yes. They did [have surveillance cameras]. They did," he said. His mother sat across the oval table from him, and she pursed her lips and nodded slowly as she turned to look at me, as if to affirm that her son was setting the record straight. The range of the school's surveillance network had been a point of debate between the sheriff and the protestors. C. C. Campbell-Rock, who toured the school with the school board president, Ellenese Brooks-Simms, claimed that there was a bathroom with no stalls but with "a row of stainless steel toilets and a camera . . . mounted on the wall" (Campbell-Rock, 2002). Jamal's account of the surveillance network matched this published one. "[They were] everywhere," he said. "Each room."

> L: The bathroom?
>
> J: Each room. Everywhere outside. They had a little basketball court on the side like on the concrete. It wasn't a basketball court but they put a basketball goal out there. They had cameras going all on the side of like the building. They had three cameras. One right, one in the middle and one on the other end, and it was facing right down the court. And they had some on top of the building. They had a big tall red gate, and they had one facing so you could see on the sidewalk right there, and they had one where you can see the corner.
>
> L: What about inside? Tell me which rooms had . . .
>
> J: Everywhere. All of them. All of them. All of them.
>
> L: Are you sure about the bathroom?
>
> J: Positive about the bathroom.

Sheriff Foti's office responded to Campbell-Rock's article with an editorial in the local paper the following week, in which he wrote: "There is no camera in that bathroom or any bathroom in the school. Ms. Campbell-Rock is correct in saying there are no stalls in the boy's bathroom. Because the bathrooms are used by one student at a time, there is never a lack of privacy" (Morse & Glazer, 2002). But Jamal dismissed the sheriff's claims and confirmed Campbell-Rock's account:

> L: Were the bathrooms private?
>
> J: No, all of us went in there at one time.
>
> L: And there were no stalls and there were surveillance cameras inside the bathroom.
>
> J: [nods yes]

In the collection of local accounts, those stemming from the sheriff's office stood out as anomalous. Every claim the sheriff and his affiliates made about privacy at the Prison School was ultimately rejected by local students, youth advocates, and reporters.

The conflict intensified around the issue of armed guards at the Prison School. Campbell-Rock reported that the school guards were "four armed sheriff deputies sitting around watching four television monitors . . . and no principal on the premises." Spider said that all he knew was that he was to call the guards "Sarge," and Jamal's description of them matched his description of the school itself as a "straight jailhouse": The guards were wearing "black with Sheriff Foti's sign on it, 'cause they worked at the jails. That's what they was. They were, you know, security guards for Sheriff Foti at his jailhouse. I guess that was a part-time job or whatever. I don't know, but they had on their uniform . . . boots, their gun, and their handcuffs."

The sheriff's associates didn't deny staffing the school with Orleans Parish Prison deputies, but they did deny the claim that they were armed. Two of the sheriff's associates—including Ed Morse, the Tulane University professor already mentioned—published a retort on the sheriff's behalf, stating that "we can report that the deputies were not armed and are never armed when on school grounds" (Morse & Glazer, 2002).

Professor Morse met me in his office for an interview in September just as the fall semester was beginning. He sat at his desk in a tweed sport coat, surrounded by books and stacks of papers. He began by calling Sheriff Foti "God's most innovative penologist" and ended with a long answer about the debate over the guards: "He never wore a gun. He was a deputy. He wouldn't wear a gun. . . . It would be nonsensical for him to wear a gun. You don't wear guns inside a jail, not unless you want to get hurt."

The claim that the deputies in the school were unarmed because officers don't wear guns in a jail was an insinuation that the school within the prison complex was, itself, a jail and, thus, not distinct from the larger correctional complex. Realizing the inner logic of this rebuttal and the problem it posed for the sheriff who claimed to be running a school and not another instantiation of his prison, the professor abruptly added "And this was not a jail." In a quick step, the professor returned to his original logic, stating "And [that is] not the way jails are run these days." I mentioned this interview to Spider, and watched his generally relaxed composure shift toward visible irritation. "They was armed," he said incredulously. "Real guns." Spider's jaw tightened then, and his voice rose in volume, slowed, and dropped in pitch. "Now, why would they need to be armed for us?"

SCHOOL DISCIPLINE, ISOLATION, AND ACCOUNTABILITY

That local accounts of the Prison School could differ so radically from the sheriff's account reveals a weak structure of accountability and fits into the historical pattern of law-enforcement deceit. In a traditional public school, the presence or absence of surveillance cameras or guns would have been an objective fact easily determined by public observation. As traditional education is removed from public spaces under the pretense of discipline, institutions and staff are increasingly shielded from public scrutiny. The legal scholar Christopher Edley, writing alongside the educational law and policy analyst Dan Losen, has issued a warning about the risk to accountability when placing "at-risk" children in alternative disciplinary school environments. In such institutions, Edley and Losen expect to find experimentation, low standards of education, and correctional approaches to children: "As a result [of zero-tolerance policies], one can expect an increase in the likelihood that 'at-risk' minority children are isolated in separate schools, where they will receive watered-down curricula, have few positive role models, and be held to low expectations by unqualified instructors. Although some good alternative schools may exist, parents should be wary that an alternative school might be another conduit for the school-to-jail pipeline."

Edley and Losen refer to alternative disciplinary schools as possible pipelines to jail or prison because these institutions tend to limit educational opportunities that lead to positive engagements while heightening students' exposure to punitive ideologies and increasing their proximity to law enforcement. The pipeline is an effective analogy, but as I have discussed elsewhere, it fails to account for a collapsed distinction between schools and jails in the War on Crime era—indeed, a school in a prison. Bracketing this difference, Edley and Losen's warning about alternative disciplinary education ultimately reads like a description of the Prison School, as was later revealed in student and staff accounts of the curriculum. The veil of correctional supervision meant that only the sheriff, his ranks, and the students really knew what was going on inside.

Campbell-Rock revealed the concealed nature of the Prison School when she reported on her visit there with Ms. Brooks-Simms, the school board president. She states that the school principal, Mr. Delaney, who was working under Sheriff Foti to run the school on a half-time basis, "did not arrive [at the school] until called to speak with the Board President." The other 50 percent of Delaney's time was dedicated to running the GED program in the Orleans Parish Prison's Juvenile Detention, where youths with criminal convictions were held. By local accounts, Delaney was a burned-out leader who was demoted to this leadership role at the prison after failing as a principal in the traditional educational sector.

In designing the school, Sheriff Foti had negotiated directly with School Superintendent Al Davis, who had been a career military man before assuming this post in the New Orleans Public School System. Chui Clark claimed that in order to hire Davis, whose experience was limited to the military, the Louisiana State Board of Education amended their law regarding education credentials for parish school superintendents. In an edited volume titled *Education as Enforcement,* the sociologist Kenneth Saltman suggests that military leadership fosters disciplinary programs in education (Saltman & Gabbard, 2003; Saltman, 2003). Taking advantage of this alignment, Professor Morse explained that Sheriff Foti was "pretty sure" that Superintendent Davis would go along with a school in the prison, and they brought it to him with confidence. Chui believed that Foti and Davis were collaborating to breach an ethical code of care in public education and forward a mutual law-enforcement agenda: "They are not educators, nor are they concerned with public education. They have dismissed . . . [the] potential [of] young people in care of the 'criminal justice system.'"

Members of the school board, including Ms. Brooks-Simms and her colleague Cheryl Mills, later claimed that they knew very little about Sheriff Foti's program, but the school board did approve Davis's project proposal. To open a New Orleans public school on Sheriff Foti's prison grounds, they signed an interagency agreement between New Orleans Public Schools, the Office of the Criminal Sheriff, and three other local agencies, including the Louisiana State University Health Sciences Center (New Orleans Public Schools, 2001). The *Times-Picayune* published a story on the new school, calling the interagency collaboration "pioneering" (Bell, 2001). Chui asked, "What is so 'pioneering' about the treacherous collaboration of the . . . school board and the . . . sheriff?"

EDUCATION IN A NATION AT WAR

Saltman and Gabbard's edited volume *Education as Enforcement* helps make sense of the collaborations between public schools and law enforcement in the United States since the terrorist attacks on September 11, 2001. Saltman situates punitive influences in education within a global context, noting a sharp rise in the militarization of American society after 9/11 (Saltman, 2003). In his analysis, America has institutionalized a unilateral and "permanent war" in the wake of 9/11, in which even "education is becoming increasingly justified on the grounds of national security." Saltman critiques such arrangements as benefiting neoliberalism (a concept explored in chapter 2 with regard to the profits of privatized school discipline), an agenda to which the Prison School ultimately leads—while also enabling the erosion of public democratic power, which is part and parcel of the paring of accountability. In his foreword to *Education as Enforcement*, the cultural critic Henry Giroux builds on political scientist Anatole Anton's assessment that the national community is now constructed "through shared fears rather than shared responsibilities" (Giroux, 2003). Giroux assesses the political impact of fear-based rhetoric this way: "Within the rhetoric and culture of shared fears, patriotism becomes synonymous with an uncritical acceptance of governmental authority" (Giroux, 2003). Sheriff Foti's plan for a public school on the prison grounds hinged on his authority as a correctional leader, the authority vested in retired colonel Al Davis, and their shared sense of education as enforcement, with support from the Orleans Parish School Board. Beyond Chui and his associates, there was no significant and vocal opposition to the program.

The rhetoric of counter-terrorism in the post-9/11 period is conflated with the rhetoric of crime control, but legal scholar Jonathan Simon insists, in his book *Governing through Crime*, that the War on Crime came first and heralded "a generation-long pattern of political and social change," within which the "'tough' response to terrorism . . . may now be relegitimized" (Simon, 2007). At the center of Simon's "governing through crime" thesis is the notion that "crime has now become a significant strategic issue" and has "distorted American institutional priorities across a wide variety of domains," including public schools. He writes: "Across all kinds of institutional settings, people are seen as acting legitimately when they act to prevent crime or other troubling behaviors that can be closely analogized to crime" (Simon, 2007).

The Prison School was a response to the troubling behavior of disruption. In advocating for the program, Dr. Elliot Willard, an Orleans Parish School Board member, explained, "If you drive around our schools . . . walk into our school yards, restrooms, hallways, and classrooms, there's a lot of disruption. They are interfering with the progress of learning." The Prison School essentially targeted these students who weren't going to class. A consultant to the program, Dr. Gwen Jones, explained that the school district had programs for students who had been recommended for expulsion; the Prison School was a "new task initiative" for "students who have not been recommended for expulsion" (New Orleans Public Schools, 2001). It was an opportunity to be "proactive" and "get them on track before they actually get recommended for expulsion" and thus represented a preemptive strike on delinquency and crime (New Orleans Public Schools, 2001). In this rationalization and in the imperative voiced by Sheriff Foti "to catch them before they do get in trouble," the fear of black male crime preexists crime itself.

In her book *Making Crime Pay*, Katherine Beckett puts the fear of crime in the context of the civil rights era and ties the obsession with law and order to a mid-century political agenda among southern officials who aimed to undermine the civil rights movement and, later, Lyndon Johnson's "Great Society" programs by painting impoverished communities as the undeserving and criminally inclined poor (Beckett, 1997). Beckett claims that the so-called "crime problem" was constructed then to support a conservative political agenda that would maintain lines of racial stratification and rein in the social welfare state, which threatened to mitigate the structural inequalities that helped keep socioeconomic classes segregated. The argument that crime is socially constructed is supported by data showing that America became exceedingly more punitive in an era in which the crime rate was shrinking (Western, 2006).

According to Loïc Wacquant, in his book *Punishing the Poor*, "the rolling out of the penal state after the peaking of the civil rights movement responds, not to rising criminal activity, but to the wave of social insecurity that has flooded the lower tier of the class structure" (Wacquant, 2009). Social insecurity emerged from the vetting processes of a postindustrial economy, which left a large sector of the population without an economic place and role—essentially marooned on islands of poverty that were concentrated in communities of color—at a time when the state was retracting social welfare programs. The mere existence of the underclass is a state problem, an economic sore, and a source of general unpleasantness. The penal state solves the puzzle with a profit, while also unburdening the state of its welfare obligations. By punishing the poor, the state manages the dispossessed by "forcibly 'disappearing' them" through a correctional containment strategy while generating opportunities for moneymaking, both by freeing up money from state welfare budgets and by creating a correctional industry, with profits for the public and private sectors stemming from custodial contracts, building projects, transportation, communications, health care, security, food, and the profit of inmate labor. Wacquant articulates this transition from "the social safety net of the charitable state" to the "dragnet of the punitive state" as the "new politics of poverty" and "relief not to the poor but from the poor" (Wacquant, 2009). In this scheme, the individuals trapped at the bottom of the economy can be capitalized on, serving the interests of the neoliberal state by trumpeting the capacity of free-market economics and heralding the code of individual responsibility. Secondarily, incarceration transforms the city itself, as the black ghetto is reincorporated under lock and key (Wacquant, 2009).

Mass incarceration is the term David Garland has coined to describe what followed these adjustments in American "governmentality." By 2009, America had the highest incarceration rate in the world, with as many as 768 of every 100,000 Americans behind bars (Pettit, 2012). The United States once had an incarceration rate that paralleled those of other industrial nations, but in each year since 1975, the U.S. incarceration rate rose by 4 percent annually. Facing the angle that graphs the national incarceration rate's rise from the ground in 1975 to the present would be like looking up at a wall. If we accept Beckett's claim that the crime platform originated in the late 1950s as a regional political tactic, we are soon tracing the arc of a national strategy. By the late 1970s, in the early stages of the War on Crime, every state shows a rise in incarceration rates. Louisiana, however, led the nation, and the world, incarcerating 801 out of every 100,000 by 2003 (Western, 2006).

QUASI-CRIMES AND CIVIL RIGHTS

The War on Crime has had steep consequences for American civil rights, in terms of incarceration and in terms of criminalization. Almost half of the 2.3 million inmates in American prisons are African American, though they represent only 13 percent of the national population (U.S. Census Bureau, 2013). At current rates, African American males face a one-in-three lifetime chance of being incarcerated (National Association for the Advancement of Colored People, 2009–2016). These racial disparities are similarly revealed in public school discipline, where African American and Latino children are grossly overrepresented in suspension and expulsion. Between 1973 and 2006, the suspension rate for African Americans doubled from 6 percent to 15 percent, and reached 18 percent for African American males (Losen et al., 2010). Of the 3.5 million students suspended annually, as many as a million suspended and expelled students are transferred to disciplinary alternative schools each year with programs that vary widely, and African Americans represent the majority in these placements (Losen et al., 2010).[13] In some states, like Texas, nearly 50 percent of students in alternative disciplinary programs are certified as disabled (Losen et al., 2010, 2015).

Edley and Losen claim that disparities in disciplinary alternative schooling are a major civil rights issue. These environments force children of color and disabled students to encounter law enforcement and face tough disciplinary punishments that leave them isolated in marginal school spaces without a vetted curriculum, standard instruction hours, or certified teachers. They explain: "The idea of isolating 'at risk' children is generally regarded as a recipe for failure and distinctly frowned upon in the area of special education research and law. . . . Unfortunately, some politicians appear willing to commit large numbers of poor and minority children to experimental institutions" (Losen & Edley, 2001).

Typically, the data regarding these transfers to disciplinary alternative schools are collected on an annual basis, so it is difficult to know when students are being pushed out of their mainstream classrooms. The timing of the pushout event could, however, prove to be significant. The fourteen students sent to the Prison School were pushed out of their traditional schools in late winter, just before the spring season of standardized testing had begun. As well as being deemed disruptive, students like Spider and Jamal were low performers and consistently did poorly on test day. A new placement at the Prison School would remove them from the test pool, with the likely effect of raising the school's average scores and benefiting school funding that is tied directly to performance measures under the No Child Left Behind law (Figlio, 2006; Losen et al., 2010).[14]

An accelerated response to students' "quasi-crimes" and actual delinquency was a funding mandate of the Safe Schools Act of 1994. The law required schools to formalize disciplinary procedures leading to expulsion and to cooperate with police and juvenile justice agencies (Simon, 2007; Casella, 2001). For all schools in compliance, a total of $3 million was available for allocation (Casella, 2001). Also in 1994, a Gun-Free Schools Act was passed that required expulsion for the possession of a weapon on school grounds. The law was amended in 1997 to be inclusive of drugs. These monetized mechanisms of exclusion came to be known as "zero tolerance," which is a reference to President Reagan's mantra in the War on Drugs. Zero-tolerance policies were designed to deter unwanted behaviors by meting out such exceedingly harsh punishments that drugs would become seen as too risky (Kebhaj et al., 2013). This logic, however, did not pan out, and prisons expanded rapidly, with the largest share owing to drug arrests (Kebhaj et al., 2013). In schools, minor offenses led to high rates of suspension, expulsion, and alternative disciplinary placements under zero-tolerance policies. Suspension Stories is a blog that describes from a youth perspective how "zero tolerance polices [ran] amok" (Rogers Park Young Women's Action Team & NIA, 2013). The youths who publish the blog claim to "feature the most ridiculous examples of school suspensions and school based arrests that we can find." The blog includes reports on the quasi-crimes of possessing allergy nasal spray, which led to the suspension of two ten-year-olds in Gwinnett County, Georgia, and burping, which led to handcuffs and juvenile detention for a thirteen-year-old in Albuquerque, New Mexico (Rogers Park Young Women's Action Team & NIA, 2013; Willis, 2012; Clausing, 2011). In New Orleans, which has a suspension rate five times higher than the national average, students were reported to have been suspended for singing the gospel song "We Lift Our Hands in the Sanctuary" within the school cafeteria (Juvenile Justice Project of Louisiana, 2011). Ronnie Casella explains that "As an integral crackdown on kids, like other 'get tough on crime' measures, zero-tolerance strategies are often forces in schools that give impetus to rules, policies, and new abilities to justify the expulsion, exclusion, shaming, labeling, and alternative placements of students" (Casella, 2001). In short, zero-tolerance policies made it easier for school administrators to "remove students from schools" (Casella, 2001). The legal requirement of criminal justice collaboration in school disciplinary procedures means that school pushouts gain proximity to law enforcement and experience greater degrees of criminalization.

"I DON'T NEED TO BE HERE. THIS IS NOT ME."

S: Like they just treat us kind of bad. And I can say that they was like. They be like cursing at us and stuff. You can say like threatening. [Well] I ain't going to say threatening, but . . . [pause] But if one of us got mad or something, they would try to make us take time out, make us go sit in a blank room or something. You know just like in the dark with just a chair.

L: A blank room?

S: Yeah.

L: What do you mean, a blank room?

S: Like a room [with a] shut door. It don't have no light. . . . You would sit in the chair for an hour or two until they feel that you know you are ready to come outside, I mean come back into the classroom or something. [And] there were cages like running around like.

    L: A cage? What do you mean a cage?

    S: Like, I ain't going to say bars, but I can't really explain it.

    L: What kind of thing would get you put in that room?

    S: Like if you don't have no pencil or else if you are going to sleep, or else if you talk bad, like if you be fussing with one of the teachers, something like that.

Spider looked tired. He slumped on the old brown sofa in the living room as he began to tell me about the guards and the dark cages where students would sit for hours. Time in the "cage" was punishment for students who came to class without a pencil or who disrupted class by sleeping or fussing, which are behaviors that have been treated in schools and in the criminal justice system as the willful defiance of authority. The technique of sensory deprivation and solitary confinement was a common practice in the adjacent prison, and though it is typically used for the most hardcore criminals, it was also used at the school.

I studied Spider's face as he spoke. The lilting drawl in his voice seemed to slow, and I sensed that he was either resigning himself to this story of his life or to my questions about it. I quickly concluded that he was too tired and was possibly too traumatized to continue, and I reached toward my tape recorder to turn it off. Before I reached it, he sat up with urgency:

    S: I know that that that that they, um, choked a child. I ain't going to really say choke, but they like manhandled him because the child was talking bad to the teacher.

    L: Well, tell me what happened and what they did.

    S: Well, the child was fussing with the teacher, because the child felt that, um, the teacher did not even know what she was talking about or something like that, so like when the teacher got mad or whatever she would like call the security, and that is like saying . . . this is the classroom and the security is like my momma's room [pointing within his home to suggest the distance between security and the classroom within the school; the distance between the living room where we were sitting and the bedroom was about twenty feet] and like she say "security" or whatever, and security come right there and they like fussing and fussing. So, the child just start like getting mad, and so the man just like hanged him up against the wall, you know. And that, and that, was the child who had got killed, you know what I am talking about?

This was the only time I heard Spider stutter. He hesitated to find the right words to describe what he'd witnessed: a guard holding a child by his neck against a wall with enough force to suspend his body above the ground. This technique, known as a choke hold, has been deemed deadly force and has been banned in the New York Police Department and elsewhere for its potential to deprive the brain of blood and oxygen, leading to asphyxia and fatality (Fisher, 1993).

In large letters, the disciplinary handbook for the New Orleans Public Schools reads: "In no case shall corporal punishment be used in New Orleans Public Schools." As a public school, Sheriff Foti's program would have been held to this standard as well, but there was little accountability for the punitive actions of the guards, who were trained to work in a correctional environment. In telling the story of the way the guards "manhandled" a Prison School student, Spider may have had in mind a much larger context for corporal violation, since the story of this child, whose name was Harman, does end with his death. He and another boy were murdered on the street. Spider, who was friends with both victims, heard about the double murder when he read the newspaper article, which detailed the dangerous neighborhood in which they both lived.

Spider's sense of the guards as treating them "bad" by "cursing" and "threatening" and using physical force aligns with Jamal's suggestion that the guards were on a power trip. They used their handcuffs to move children in the school space and performed a facedown takedown hold to enforce their authority. For its brutality and its proven risk to life, this policing maneuver is banned in eight states (Giroux, 2011b). The tactic was used (and well publicized on YouTube) in 2009 by a school police officer who forced Marshawn Pitts, an African American special-needs student at a school in Illinois, to the floor for the disciplinary offense of having an untucked shirt. As described in chapter 1, Pitts sustained multiple injuries, including a broken nose and a bruised jaw (Giroux, 2011b). Jamal remembers a similar incident at the Prison School:

> J: [The guards were] sitting in the office watching TV. And every time the teacher called them, they like come get you and bring you to the office and handcuff you and all this and all that type of stuff.
>
> L: They would do what?
>
> J: Handcuff you.
>
> L: Did you get . . .
>
> J: Oh, I never. I was, I was a good student. I ain't had to be involved with all that, 'cause I didn't want to put myself in that position.
>
> L: Tell me about a time you saw that happen.
>
> J: Mmm . . . One day a teacher walked out of class, and the dudes was going crazy making all type of noises and all this, and the security guard came back there. He grabbed them, and the dude was trying to fight the security guard, which was

wrong, but the way the security guard grabbed him was wrong too, and you know, that made a conflict, and so therefore, security guard grabbed him and pinned him down on the ground like, you know, and handcuffed him and brought him to the principal's office. But I don't see why they had to handcuff, for what? Can't go nowhere. The school is locked down. Can't get outside unless they open the door. [pause, deep sigh]

L: What had the kid done?

J: Just . . . I don't know.

Mother: Disrupting the class.

J: Disrupting the class. That's all.

In his retelling of the incident, there was an edge to Jamal's voice and more than a mild suggestion of contempt. The guards' behavior—their use of force—was overdetermined in the lockdown context. Jamal could not even remember what kind of classroom disruption had instigated the guards' aggressive reaction, but the guards stood out as the brutal antagonists.

THE PROBLEM OF BLACK MUSCLE

All the deputies working at the school were physically imposing men as measured by height, girth, or both, and they used their muscle to dominate the students. Jamal told me about a "short fat one" and a "big tall one" and "another fat one but not fat like the first fat one I said, but he was big too." They commanded attention in the hard edge of their law-enforcement uniforms, and in their actions they were demonstrably confrontational, forceful, and dangerous. Jamal explained their use of power in the terms of punitive masculinity, saying they were "cocky with it; like muscle with it."

Wacquant has suggested that late-modern penality can itself be understood as a "'(re)masculinizing' of the state in the neoliberal age," in which the paternal state is threatened by young black men being raised in the ghetto by single mothers, who are often disparaged as "welfare moms." Under the legal tradition of *parens patriae* (Latin, translated as either "parent of the country" or "government as parent"), the state preserves a patronizing goal of "saving the children," which is how Sheriff Foti framed the Prison School (Wacquant, 2009). When the social welfare state, gendered female, is pushed aside, the punitive state, gendered male, is deployed with all its armaments. The alignment between the percentage of women receiving welfare aid and the percentage of male inmates makes it look, on the surface, like a one-to-one ratio. Over

90 percent of welfare aid goes to women, and over 90 percent of inmates are male (Wacquant, 2009). It is the task of law enforcement, in the words of Wacquant, to tame "their brothers, their boyfriends or husbands, and their sons" (Wacquant, 2009). That task is also gendered male. In 2001, three-quarters of all correctional officers were male; and over 65 percent of officers were white (Sumter, 2008).

It is striking that the gender question is so undertheorized with regard to mass incarceration, especially compared to analyses of race. Quite possibly, the narrowly conceived empowerment agenda of early feminism has paralyzed gender studies by obfuscating the gender dynamics of the criminal justice system, whereby black men are oppressed by their gender status, as conflated with race and class, with the harshest consequences imaginable. Black men face probable imprisonment and the corporeal, social, economic, and political marginalization that attends it. The latter is achieved because prison constitutes a negation of civil life in a democracy and is therefore considered civil death (Davis, 2012).

Again, the problem of black muscle preexists criminality, as the mission of the Prison School suggests, and attaches to potentiality. That the Prison School targeted black males as young as twelve—just as schools nationwide have done in their suspension and expulsion programs—suggests that the problem of black muscle is a racialized masculinity in the making. Scholars like Bourgois and Rios, both urban ethnographers, have delved into the culture of manhood and revealed the desires of young men to be respected on the street as a way of surviving the terrorizing conditions in the ghetto (Bourgois, 1996; Rios, 2011). Rios points to the expectation of young urban men to achieve a "tough persona" by "posing and acting out." As one of the boys in his study explains, "You can't act weak or you'll get taken out" (Rios, 2011). This hyper-aggressive behavior was likely to engage the police, but a passive countenance was sure to invite humiliation within the community and could lead to a disgraceful downfall involving drug use or victimization (Rios, 2011).

Bourgois and Rios's accounts of hypermasculinity are convincing and help explain the threat posed by muscle, but it is not an apt framework for thinking about Spider, Jamal, or many other young boys who are suspended from school under zealous disciplinary policies for disruptions or quasi-crimes, and who find themselves at a punitive precipice. Spider and Jamal were self-proclaimed "Momma's boys." Of his mother, Spider said, "We have a good relationship. . . . I wanted to leave [the Prison School] a lot of times, but I just didn't want to put my momma and me through a lot of things." One day when I was at Jamal's house, his mother suggested that he could go into the military if he ran out of other choices—military enlistment being another neoliberal benefit of the penal net (Saltman, 2003)—to which he replied, "I don't want to die. That's all. I don't want to go fight no war and all this. I'd rather stay home with y'all and be loved." There was a long pause, his mother and grandmother smiled, and Jamal continued, "[and] get my high school diploma" and "go to college."

According to Jamal, the actual and symbolic violence of the Prison School incited the students around him, and he wanted no part of it. The students tended to meet the low expectations set by the correctional site and its staff, and it was suffocating: "I felt like I was in jail. That is what it felt like. That is exactly what it felt like . . . I didn't like it at all." Jamal fought to rise above it and held to his belief that he did not belong in Foti's program.

> L: How did you feel about yourself when you were there?
>
> J: That I don't need to be here. This is not me. That made me get a head on my shoulders really, 'cause that wasn't me. 'Cause I was looking at the little dudes like, "Y'all showing them what they want, you know. Y'all acting the way they want you to act." That is how I felt. They was acting crazy and destructive like they needed to be there. That is how they was acting. I wasn't acting like that, 'cause I was trying to get out, 'cause I couldn't take it no more.

While none of the students had entered the Prison School with violent backgrounds, as is suggested by the fact that none had been expelled, they started "acting crazy" once they got there. These dynamics support a claim, put forth by the educational sociologist Pedro Noguera, that schools that rely on technology and physical force to control students may produce rather than prevent an institutional culture of violence (Noguera, 1995). Jamal said he simply "couldn't take it no more" and he wanted to "get out." Spider agreed that he wanted "to hurry up and get out of there."

A PRISON SCHOOL EDUCATION

We know that many of these young people read at only the second or third grade level. We also know . . . that if awakened to their own potential, [they] can double their reading level in just four or five months. . . . [O]ur staff . . . will also work with the students to help them improve their speaking skills, their social skills and their awareness of the value of being non-confrontational.

—Sheriff Charles C. Foti, "Let's Save the Children"

Officials at the Prison School heralded the program's curriculum as an innovative combination of academics and behavior management. The students received about eighteen hours of instruction per week in reading, writing, and arithmetic. None of the courses led to high school graduation. The rest of the approximately fifty-six-hour week was given over to counseling sessions and basketball on a small pad of concrete. A child psychiatrist and a social worker were described as on-call employees (Finch, 2002). The sole duty of all the staff was, as Sheriff Foti put it, "to save these children." In an interview, he described the mission of the school as "just like being a sort of a surrogate family member" (Furness, 2002b).

The small initial cohort of students meant that the program provided a favorable student-to-teacher ratio and an individualized curriculum, allowing teachers to "[address] each kid at his own level," but Chui argued that the student-to-teacher ratio was a "superficial" measure of educational quality and used to mask other inadequacies (Furness, 2002a). Chui said that students at the Prison School were simply paired more intimately with unskilled adults. Professor Ed Morse himself, who served as a consultant to Sheriff Foti on the Prison School, gave credence to this charge of incompetence and similarly rendered the touted student-to-teacher ratio a moot point:

> I don't have any blooming idea what their perception of the world was. One of them was teaching what was the area of a rectangle. That was the male teacher.... He said there is no trouble with this you just add [it] up . . . This is a four by six by four by six. Four by six is half and four by six is half. It's twenty! And I am going, I think we just set some people back a little bit. And if it had been one thing that was okay, and [another consultant] would go in the evenings and say it was just a mistake. And we would say yeah it sure was. But none of it. It didn't get any better from there.

In the instruction he refers to, the teacher mistook a lesson on the area of a rectangle and taught the equation for perimeter instead. It was an incomprehensible mistake.

As an overall assessment, Jamal said, "So, they didn't really teach. They really didn't." When the staff did teach, it was either wrong or remedial. He said, "It was stuff I knew already. Everything was." Spider spoke of the extreme monotony of the instruction, saying "same thing," "same math," and "similar to the same thing."

> We didn't really study . . . All we mostly done is go to school everyday, making sure that we are on time everyday, early in the morning, you know I've got to say,

we probably just talked . . . We almost talk about the same thing most every day . . . Like, you know the same math problems and stuff, whatever. Whatever they give us. They almost be similar to the same thing.

Thinking that this meager instruction could be par for the course in the traditional New Orleans Public Schools, which rank among the worst in the nation, I asked the students to compare the teaching at the Prison School to other public schools they had attended. They offered answers like "They wasn't nothing compared to regular school" and "It was totally different. I was learning more in regular school." They tried to explain the meaningless instruction as a feature of the context, saying that the teacher took cues from the correctional context and had exceptionally low expectations for the students. I could see Jamal devising an explanatory theory as he tipped his head back to think. When he leaned forward, he said, "They probably thought dudes that were there, they didn't know nothing. Like that. But I knew a lot. . . ." In nearly every way possible, Jamal had been misrecognized. Spider suggested that he had only been recognized as a person who came late to class and not as a student who was interested in learning something.

While poor instruction may have been integral to the criminalizing context of the Prison School, as the students suggested, it was also a predictable outcome of the staffing arrangement at the Prison School. None of the teachers had teaching certifications, and some had no previous teaching experience. There was also a total lack of investment in textbooks, which could have guided the curriculum and helped even unskilled teachers meet basic standards of instruction. Ultimately, the burden of this academic poverty was borne by the students themselves. Not only were they failing to make academic gains, but they were losing whatever marginal educational ground they had.

Every time I talked to Jamal and Spider, the Prison School emerged as a negative experience, so I eventually dug for something positive. Once I asked the question, Jamal was able to respond:

L: Can you tell me about one time that you learned something in class there?
J: Mmm . . . ?
L: Can you tell me about one thing that you learned?
J: I got better at my writing.
L: You got better at writing?
J: Mmm. Mmm [yes].

. . .

J: I kept asking about this and that, you know, and the teacher was like, "Well you're the only one who want to learn so whenever you need something ask." She'd tell me how to do it, and she'd, you know, stand by my side until, you know, I know. That's how I passed the writing part of my LEAP test.

At certain points, the low student-to-teacher ratio had a real benefit. Though the teacher was not an experienced educational practitioner, she was able to focus on Jamal's needs and offered to help him develop his skills. Spider spoke favorably of the same teacher, but indicated that her value was intrinsic to her ability to shield the children from the prison deputies. She coached the students on how to manage harassment and conflict. "Yeah she was nice. You know, she tried to look out for us—tell us right from wrong. Try to tell us [how to act with] the staff if they bother us. Like how to act when we are around staff. She was nice."

Spider's assessment of the after-school counselor, like his assessment of the teacher, was in relation to the deputies. "He ain't used to treat us too bad," Spider said. In comparison to the deputies who cracked down on the kids, the counselor and the teacher were a welcome alternative. Jamal also indicated that his hard work garnered support from the program's principal.

J: I do remember one person there. He helped me though. Mr. Delaney, he was the principal.

L: He helped you. Tell me about that.

J: He helped me to get back in regular school 'cause he was talking to me, he was like after . . . you know out of all these kids in here, I did something. I was the one to do the work and I was the one to, you know, listen and don't be going crazy while the teacher is going out of the class and you know. I always have my head down, being in good behavior, whatever, 'cause I wanted to get out, 'cause I didn't want to be there no more. He was telling me, he was like, if I pass the LEAP test, he's gonna let me go. I was like "I will. I will. Give it to me now," and he did. And I passed it and I left. So that really did help me in a way, but in another way, I couldn't wake up that early in the morning and catch no bus and have to stay out till seven o'clock—from seven-thirty to seven o'clock. I couldn't do that. That's not school; that's jail. I couldn't do it, and I didn't like it. . . . But they did do me, they did me some good by, you know, getting me to my next grade or whatever, but otherwise it wasn't nothing.

Jamal believed that he had a special status in the classroom, both because he demonstrated a desire to learn and because he had a unique maturity to "have [his] head down" and shield himself from the harsh correctional climate. Because so many other students were "going crazy" in that environment, Jamal's experience was the exception that proved the rule. Jamal's forward-thinking strategy paid off when he passed the LEAP (Louisiana Educational Assessment Program) test—the standardized test given to all eighth graders in Louisiana to determine their readiness for ninth grade—and was released from the Prison School. From the perspective of this achievement, Sheriff Foti's approach seemed to deliver. Jamal had raised his grade level and tested into high school. In Jamal's final judgment, though, no academic advancement was worth spending your days in jail.

PUNISHMENT, NEOLIBERALISM, AND PROTEST

In agreement with the students about the incongruity of a public school in a prison, Chui Clark began daily protests. He picketed at the school, but it was so hidden at the back of the Parish Prison that almost no one saw him. He made himself more visible on Canal Street at the edge of the French Quarter. Soon, he and a small group of associates were protesting nearly every day, drawing spectators as they chanted and held signs reading "Schools not Incarceration" and "Close Down Foti's Dungeon." Chui passed out a pamphlet that read, "We openly resist the encroachment of private interests, especially the prison industrial complex, upon the education of our children." He and members of the larger group voiced concerns that ran the gamut from penal impropriety to pedagogical irresponsibility. They criticized the Prison School for relying on a penal model for youths who had not committed a crime, and they questioned the qualifications of the criminal sheriff as an educational leader. Chui explained: "They are not educators, nor are they concerned with public education. They have dismissed the potential of young people in the care of the criminal justice system." The group also argued that the Prison School failed to provide a good-quality education for its students, and that it reduced the resources for all other schools by siphoning off much-needed funds. When the Prison School was green-lighted, seven other schools in the parish were being considered for closure for budgetary reasons. Amplifying these concerns was a sense that these neglects were racially charged. For Chui, the racialized nature of the Prison School was not simply a matter of racial imbalance, born of the fact that all the students initially selected for the program were African American teenage boys, but was, rather, constituted by the fact that these boys were relegated to an ill-conceived penal experiment of questionable academic merit.

Chui extended his critique when the school board began to consider a proposal for a publicly funded but privately run disciplinary program that would serve more than a thousand youths at a cost of $51 million for six years (Lewis, 2002). This development remade the Prison School in the image of a pilot project. Chui wrote: "There is [a plan] to open another prison in Algiers, on Gen. de Gaulle Drive, to be run by a for-profit company called 'Community Education Partners,' to house up to 1100 young people that are labeled 'behavior problems.' We must stop this conspiracy to incarcerate our children!!"

The plan, which the board approved in a three-to-four vote, was a contract with a Texas corporation, Community Education Partners (CEP), that specialized in disciplinary schools for students who were labeled as disruptive in their regular classrooms. "We openly resist the encroachment of private interests, especially the prison industrial complex, upon the education of our children," said Chui. To him, the neoliberal shift of public school resources to a private juvenile detention system under CEP was not only an abandonment of the public education system, but an abandonment and betrayal of the African American population that public schools in New Orleans served. In an interview, he said, "The responsibility of the school district, the education department, the education system, is to educate, nothing else."

Significantly, Chui was not joined in protest by any of the students' parents, who explained their alignment with the criminal sheriff in terms of the sheer desperation they felt in facing the odds stacked against their children. Karen Gordan was a parent who publicly vouched for Sheriff Foti and submitted a letter to the school board stating that "I am a parent of a child who attended the Sheriff's program. . . . I feel that it's a chance for a student to get a second lease, not only on an education, but life itself." For Gordan and for several other parents, the sheriff's program functioned like a tourniquet for a fatal wound. The injury that everyone, including Sheriff Foti, recognized was that the New Orleans Public School System was failing to educate and nurture the children in their care, at the risk of increasing correctional vulnerability. Gordan explained how real the risk of prison was, saying, "[I] fell short. I had to receive my education in prison." In accepting the Prison School for her son, she was intending to save him from an even greater correctional threat that she herself had experienced. Jamal's mother said, "At least that mother doesn't have to worry about their child, her child going to jail, or even being killed in the streets." I asked her what worried her most, and she said she feared that "he would have been part of the *system*."

Reports on youth incarceration in Louisiana bear out the legitimacy of these maternal concerns. In 1997, the state had the highest juvenile detention rate in the nation (State of Louisiana, Office of Juvenile Justice, 2013). Nearly 80 percent of youth inmates are African American males; nearly a quarter of the youths incarcerated in Louisiana are disabled or mentally ill; and, based on data from a national study, 15 percent are LGBT (Butterfield, 1998b; Ware, 2011). Mothers began to lose hope for their sons once they were inside the real youth prison. "You can't imagine the things they do to children at Tallulah. . . . Guards beat on the children, sell them drugs and have sex with them," said a mother whose son spent three years there (Butterfield, 1998b). Chui described the youth reformatories that he went to in the 1960s in the same terms:

> The institutions is real real strict. It's very brutal. You know, the guards they used to, I mean, literally corporal punishment was the thing. I mean, they can beat you. Literally beat you with a stick, beat you with a belt. Any time. I mean, they give you thirty licks on your butt any time they desire if they thought you violated or there's some infraction. Aside from that they had also what they called a dungeon. . . . For something real serious, like if you tried to run away or something.

So much in Chui's story about the youth reformatory is familiar, and the old narratives merge so quickly with contemporary accounts of abuse in Louisiana's juvenile detention centers that the disciplinary experiences, which were a generation apart, seem identical.

While youth prisons in Louisiana were feared in low-income African American communities, they were looked on favorably by some investors. Places like Tallulah, the most notorious of these institutions, were considered cash cows for the private corporations that held the contracts to operate the facilities. For example, Trans-American Corporation's two founders had no qualifications to operate Tallulah Youth Prison—one was a highway engineer and the other a political campaign manager—but they had close ties to a former Louisiana governor, Edwin Edwards, and got the no-bid contract. Together the founders were reported to have pocketed $8.7 million from the venture over six years by warehousing youths and cutting staff and services to the bone (Bervara, 2004; Butterfield, 1998a). The management of Tallulah was returned to the state after class action lawsuits and federal reports documented pervasive brutality against the youths.

The high rate of youth incarceration in Louisiana and the notorious brutality of the state's youth correctional facilities posed a combined risk that most mothers I spoke to could not live with. Jamal's mother ultimately saw the sheriff's Prison School as a "good thing" because of its "shock" value. Even Jamal agreed at one point that "I did need to get my head on my shoulders," but he later amended this, saying, "Really. I just need someone to talk to. That's what I think." I asked Jamal what would have happened if someone had reached out. His reply: "If somebody would have, I probably would have listened. Nobody did." Spider just wanted the public schools to accept him as a student. "I wouldn't have sent that kid away," he said. "I would let him come in, you know." I asked Spider if anyone had listened to him at school. He said, "They listened but to me it was going through one ear and out the other." I asked, "What did you say to them?" He elaborated: "I was just saying how I like school and I wanted to be there!"

CONCLUSION

Just imagine, when Foti got there, it was only the Parish Prison. And it was just one little property. It was located right on the corner of Tulane and Broad. It was just one little area and it took up just about half a block. It was a small facility. It had about eight hundred inmates, and at the time these were black and white inmates. [The] prison was segregated. . . . But anyhow when Foti got in, gradually what he began to do was buy up a lot of the property. You just have to see. He expanded from one end of Broad from Tulane all the way to the expressway—perhaps about three blocks and he went deeper.

—Chui Clark, *Exodus Live* radio broadcast

In a local radio interview Sheriff Foti claimed that "it takes a village to raise a child. You and me and your callers and all the people in this city are part of the village" (Furness, 2002a). In turning to the so-called "village" of New Orleans for its capacity to serve a social control function, and in presuming the place of the criminal justice system within that village, Sheriff Foti suggests that prisons should be as much part of child rearing as more traditional institutions such as the family, the church, and the traditional public school. The radio host (who had interviewed Chui in the preceding segment of the show, because the sheriff declined an opportunity to be interviewed alongside Chui) responded to the sheriff: "But I think maybe the concern, Sheriff Foti, is that maybe *you* are not a part of the village. I mean it seems like maybe that *is* the response—that you are not a *part* of the village" (Furness, 2002a). In that moment, the matter of the Prison School was boiled down to one question: whether or not a criminal sheriff, both revered and detested as the leader of one of the largest jails in the country, could be a positive participant in local community building or whether his work in incarceration left the community so fractured and so ultimately dispossessed, along race lines, that he was using an illegitimate alibi.

"I am going to give you a parable," said Sheriff Foti, a strong Catholic, to the radio host. "When the Shepherd finds that one of the sheep has left, he leaves the other sheep and brings him back to the flock. And now I'll end with that" (Furness, 2002a). In Luke 15, the lost sheep is returned to the fold and likened to a sinner who repents. The Shepherd who carries the sheep home is likened to a righteous figure like Jesus. In relaying the parable as a story of his work at the Prison School, Foti casts the students as sinners. He essentially casts himself as God's chosen penologist, just as he was described by his colleague, Professor Morse, in an interview with me. Chui's retort was that there was not just one lost sheep, but literally "thousands of other students [who] are having the same problems and are faced with the same difficulties as the youth in his school" because the school system was systemically flawed and failing nearly everyone (Furness, 2002a). Resources going to Foti's lost sheep, then, were extractions from the larger flock, which meant fewer resources for everybody else. Foti's solution was to expand the program for lost sheep by way of CEP and include a thousand students.

On June 24, 2002, the Orleans Parish School Board finally decided that Sheriff Foti and Superintendent Davis had gone too far in their correctional approach. The school board closed the Prison School permanently and also ended their contract with Davis (Lewis, 2002; Orleans Parish School Board, 2002). A school board representative stated that the Prison School was not the direction the school board wanted to take. Even so, the private contract with CEP was only tabled for further study and evaluation (Thevenot, 2002).

While Chui had called CEP a "racist expansion" of the "racist" Prison School, Foti defended it using post-racial logic: "It has nothing to do with black or white," he said. "It has to do with kids." Though Charles Foti began his tenure as the criminal sheriff of Orleans Parish with the explicit charge of maintaining a segregated correctional facility in New Orleans, he believed that he had transcended his role as an agent of Jim Crow oppression. Instead, he positioned himself as a religious man, in the Catholic city of New Orleans, who aimed to "save the children." Spider thought the sheriff's campaign "[was meant] to probably make himself look good," and Chui linked the sheriff's sanctimony and paternalism to racism, arguing, "[It is] so typical for white people to have some kind of savior complex" (Furness, 2002a). By wanting to save the children and putting that ideology in front of democratic ideals, Sheriff Foti sold public education and public school students in New Orleans short.

Furthermore, Foti's idea that we have moved beyond race and somehow transcended racial divisions in the aftermath of the Jim Crow era is a popular but misguided sentiment in American society. The "post-racial" assertion that race no longer plays a role as an organizing feature of our society overlooks significant markers to the contrary. In the realm of race, crime, and punishment, the opposing evidence is stark. The sociologist and African American Studies scholar Lawrence Bobo remarks that "There is at least one domain that remains a glaring exception to this narrative of hope and progress, and it involves the heavy over-representation of minorities, especially African Americans among those in our jails and prisons" (Bobo, 2011). Bobo suggests that there is a "new, subtle, indirect, less intentional, but nonetheless [a] form of racial bias that is built into the operation of our law enforcement system" and has been exercised in "deeply punitive anti-crime social policies" that sponsor mass incarceration (Bobo, 2011).

Law enforcement's punitive exercise of racial bias is all the more threatening for its extensive reach, in late-modern society, into spheres of traditional education. Public schools were fashioned as spaces for democratic opportunity, where egalitarian principles were paramount. As public schools have taken punitive approaches to classroom management, youths have been pushed out of school and pulled toward correctional control, where they are distanced from any reasonable chance of academic, social, and economic success. Untethered from the opportunity structures of the democratic enterprise, these students retreat further toward the edges of our society and toward an isolation that foreshadows their likely and more complete disappearance into the criminal justice system.

The correctional approach is a path of least resistance for public schools. It enables the boon of capital accumulation by benefiting school funding, supporting the punishment industry, and sponsoring neoliberalism, while offering a containment strategy for socioeconomically and academically marginalized populations. The key democratic challenge in America has always been about incorporating marginalized populations into the citizenry and into opportunity structures while negotiating a capitalist context. The promise of democracy resides in the potential for public schools to meet this challenge. As public schools embrace the correctional approach, we let them—and the democratic order they represent—off the hook.

In disenfranchised communities, like the ghettos of New Orleans, public schools remain the only viable vehicle for mobility. Adults and children alike are committed to these institutions and want them to work for them. This dedication to public schooling contrasts with the popular sentiment, which I have encountered so often when I have mentioned my research in brief public encounters, that kids these days "don't want to learn" or "don't recognize the value of education" and that "the problem is with the parents, who don't care." This notion of apathy could not be further from my findings, and it serves yet another convenient rationale, which only barely skirts a supremacist logic, for why low-income African Americans, especially males, continue to fail in school at high rates, why suspension and expulsion rates have exploded, and why our prisons have grown to house this population on the back end of the trajectory.

Most students across the socioeconomic spectrum compromise their chances of learning at one point or another, and the students at the Prison School were no exception. An acknowledgment of agency, however, is not also a disavowal of structural constraints. Youths negotiate a complicated social, economic, political, and cultural terrain when making decisions, as all humans do. At the lower end of the socioeconomic spectrum, youths face more challenges in these areas, which means that their individual agency is further embedded, entangled, and impossible to isolate from the constraints that also shape their world.

In very few cases is it reasonable to argue that school disciplinary problems and educational failure start and end with the youths themselves. Nor is it reasonable to place the full responsibility of school failure on public schools as institutions. There are many ways to improve public schools. I recommend that we end exclusionary punishments for students who commit quasi-crimes and make educational environments positive and productive by limiting class sizes, offering dynamic curricula, and providing resources for teachers. We need to give students something in schools to believe in. Students like Spider and Jamal also need schools that believe in them. These commitments to students must be framed by a larger ideological shift, whereby everyday Americans believe, too, in the true and intended promise of public schools and recognize their egalitarian tenets as central to the American democratic enterprise.

AFTERWORD

"My school was under water because of the hurricane," said a young African American boy named Curtis, who lengthen[ed] all his vowels and made them float too. To be seen and heard, Curtis stood in front of the podium, because at seven years old, he wasn't tall enough to see over it. A group of about forty adults and fifteen young people sat at lunch tables and looked on. We strained to hear Curtis over the hum of the large fan that cooled the school cafeteria at J.S. Clark High School where we were all gathered. It was 10 a.m. and already about 95 degrees outside, but that is typical for mid-June in New Orleans. Outside the school, a few neighbors were trying to rebuild homes, and we could hear their hammers banging and circular saw blades spinning. Inside the school cafeteria, the community was trying to figure out how to rebuild the public school system. It had been nine months since Hurricane Katrina ravaged this city of New Orleans on August 29, 2005. (ethnographic field notes)

In a city built at and below sea level, it does not take a direct hit to yield disaster. In late August 2005, Katrina missed New Orleans twice, making landfall in areas east of the city on the Louisiana coast and near the Mississippi state line. The storm was accompanied by a surge of water as high as twenty feet that could not be contained by the levee system that was the city's first line of defense (Drye, 2005). The second line of defense was a large pumping system for flushing floodwater out, but it failed too. Within thirty minutes of the hurricane's landfall, the city's first levee was breached, and the underlying neighborhoods took on water. The next morning, the second levee broke, and 80 percent of the city was submerged (Liu & Holmes, 2010). In the Ninth Ward, northeast of the city's historic French Quarter, water pushed houses off their foundations and swept them away like a hose pointed at a Monopoly board. Residents who remained in their homes were forced into their attics and onto their roofs for air. More than eighty thousand people, mostly African Americans who lived in the lowlands of the city, were trapped like a human archipelago (Think Progress, 2006). Many waited as long as five days for rescue, leading one local to say, "It was as if all of us were already pronounced dead" (Haygood & Tyson, 2005).

Rescue teams ventured out into the city over the course of a week with boats and began moving survivors to dry locations, including forty-five thousand men, women, and children relocated to the city's convention center and Superdome, and another fifty-two thousand to Red Cross shelters (Think Progress, 2006). Temperatures ranged from eighty to ninety degrees, and food and water were scarce. People foraged for whatever they could find to survive. Eventually, buses and airlines moved people nationwide, many to Texas, leaving the city virtually empty. A few resolute locals remained in the city through the fall of 2005, along with government workers who were charged with a recovery effort, but months passed before the city was deemed safe for average citizens. The estimated death toll from Katrina has ranged from 1,464 to 3,500 (Olsen, 2010).

I returned to New Orleans nine months after Katrina. The city was only half populated, and just 20 percent of the New Orleans Public Schools had reopened. During the storm, school roofs caved; windows broke; walls collapsed; floors buckled; blackboards fell; and desks, chairs, books, maps, and student files piled up like jetsam. When the water was drained two weeks after the storm, a thick mold had grown on nearly every surface, and it gave the rubble of school classrooms an ochre-colored patina. Heavy metals like arsenic had been carried by the flooding and absorbed by the local soil, leaving the city with toxic school playgrounds; this made school-aged children, who play in dirt, especially vulnerable to serious medical conditions such as cancer and to environmental illnesses such as lead poisoning (Natural Resources Defense Council, 2011). Bulldozers were used to slowly clear the rubble away, but even nine months after the storm, I couldn't get into abandoned school classrooms without pushing a mass of moldy books and desks aside.

The lack of an educational infrastructure in New Orleans slowed the return migration in the post-Katrina period. This was especially true for low-income families with young children, because there were almost no public schools in the city to serve them. Some families returned to New Orleans in the spring of 2006 to reestablish employment and simply waited for schools to serve them. McDonogh High School 35 was one of the few schools that opened its doors, and it was so overwhelmed by the local need that one thousand students were placed on the school's waiting list. The returning student population had even greater needs than before. Over half of the students in post-Katrina New Orleans showed signs of having post-traumatic stress disorder (Tuzzolo, 2007).

J.S. Clark High School also opened in the spring of 2006, and the school's cafeteria became a meeting site for the Downtown Neighborhood Improvement Association (DNIA), where the community could discuss their goals for the local public schools and imagine ways to achieve them. Amid the ruin of greater New Orleans, the meeting in the J.S. Clark cafeteria was a vision of hope. The floors of the space were clean, the walls were freshly painted, and the seats were filled with a diverse set of survivors, including young and old students, teachers, a local professor, neighbors, police, and a city councilman. The organizers opened the meeting with an icebreaker, asking each person to introduce themselves to a stranger in the room and tell them a story about their worst and best personal experiences in school. Soon the room was nearly as noisy as a school cafeteria filled with students. This is when Curtis spoke about his flooded school. Many of the people gathered in the high school lunchroom said that their worst educational experience was with school discipline. Local students and former students alike pointed to harsh treatment and in-school and out-of-school suspension as the low points of their academic careers. The best moments in school were invariably about excelling academically, athletically, or socially. People talked exuberantly about having the top score on a test, making the team, or being the most popular with peers and with staff. The exercise led to an engaged brainstorming session about what local children needed most, which was a high-quality education. The participants sought accountability structures, transparency in governance, multiple arenas for public participation, fundamental curricular resources, and less harsh discipline.

While the DNIA was advocating better public education from the ground up, state officials forwarded a plan of state-level consolidation under the umbrella of the Recovery School District (RSD). Before Katrina, the state took control of a few failing local schools in the RSD; post-Katrina, the state gained control over the majority of schools. The emboldened RSD signified a historic shift of educational power toward the state and away from local control. Parents in New Orleans were apprehensive about ceding power to state officials in Baton Rouge and feared that their needs and concerns would be lost. The RSD plan allowed for the establishment of a large number of charter schools, which also had detractors.

Members of the DNIA worried about whether a decentralized power structure would lack institutional oversight and accountability and, ultimately, leave local students in academic peril. The charter-school plan was further criticized as a pseudo-privatization scheme that siphoned off public resources, and since charter schools were free to use selective admissions, there was a chance that non-charter public schools in New Orleans would serve larger concentrations of the students with the highest needs, while having fewer resources to do so. Locals began calling these public schools the "dumping grounds" (Tuzzolo & Hewitt, 2006). That these schools were de facto racially segregated, low performing, and highly secured only added to the perception that public school students were simply being disposed of.

A youth group calling themselves the Fyre Youth Squad emerged out of the DNIA to address this very trifecta. They described the new schools in the

RSD as compromising their chances for a "world class education" by way of a "prison-like atmosphere" (Tuzzolo & Hewitt, 2006). John McDonogh High School, a non-charter school within the RSD, was one of their targets. The youths claimed that police officers and security guards outnumbered teachers at McDonogh by 50 percent. A McDonogh parent corroborated the students' assertion, saying that the heavy presence of law enforcement at the school made it look like a crime scene without the yellow tape (Tuzzolo, 2007; Tuzzolo & Hewitt, 2006). Daily, the McDonogh security staff searched students, escorted students to bathrooms, administered mandatory drug testing, and conducted "sweeps." Students who arrived late to class by a fraction of a minute were "round[ed] . . . up" in the school's auditorium for automatic school suspension. On some days, as many as fifty students were sent home for fractional tardiness (Tuzzolo and Hewitt, 2006). One student, named Darrius Jones, explained that the rules were so strict that "You had to sit in a certain way. You couldn't lean or have your chair back." At Carter Collegiate Charter School where he was a student, lines were drawn down the floors of the hallway, as they are in some prisons, to designate the only acceptable path for walking. The one time Darrius stepped off the line, he was sent to in-school suspension (Kimmett, 2015). Another student was arrested by the on-site New Orleans Police Department for trespassing when he disobeyed the terms of his suspension and returned to school to pick up a homework assignment (Tuzzolo & Hewitt, 2006). The harsh school climate at McDonogh and Carter was reproduced at schools throughout the RSD. At each of the district's twenty-two schools, almost $1 million was spent on private security contractors in a single year (Tuzzolo, 2007).

The new system of state educational control meant that the the Fyre Youth Squad had to go all the way to Baton Rouge to complain about schools that were just down the street from their homes. With the support of the Juvenile Justice Project of Louisiana, the students chartered a bus in January 2007 and took petitions for change to the Board of Elementary and Secondary Education. They demanded improved educational opportunities and diminished school security as necessary and coordinated investments. Specifically, they asked for reduced class sizes, with student-to-teacher ratios of 20:1, and for more counselors and social workers to treat problems like post-traumatic stress disorder; and they argued for a reduction in the number of school security guards, as well as new training for officers regarding youth development and strategies for conflict resolution (Downtown Neighborhood Improvement

Association and Fyre Youth Squad Position Papers, 2007). They stated these positions within protest letters, and one student wrote:

> I evacuated thinking that I would come back to a better run school. Instead, I came back to an even worse environment. My teachers were gone . . . and I felt like I was in a prison at school. . . . I used to not mind going to school, but now I dread the fact of waking up and having to go to school in the morning. . . . When school started there were at least 95 kids in a class, there were few teachers and at least 30 security guards. . . . [Now] in my largest class, there are 37 kids with only one teacher, [who] is not even certified. . . . I am doing everything in my power to keep from dropping out of school, but it is hard to do when I have non-certified teachers and some teachers that just don't care. . . . With your help, I will be able to graduate high school and move on to college. (Downtown Neighborhood Improvement Association and Fyre Youth Squad Position Papers, 2007)

Another student protested high security in the RSD by critiquing criminalization processes at John McDonogh High School as racialized and explicitly decried their negative impact on his educational opportunity. He further suggested that criminalization practices forced him to confront a correctional trajectory and the image of his own relations who are already in custody.

> I understand the need for some security, but the current number of security guards present in RSD schools is ridiculous. When John McDonogh Senior High School reopened after Hurricane Katrina . . . I felt like I was visiting one of my relatives in prison. Let's be honest. When you look at me what do you see? You see a young, black male who lives in the projects, who doesn't care about his education, who goes to school only to cause problems, who robs and kills people, who doesn't respect himself or others, who sells drugs, and who is involved in all kinds of criminal activities. BUT I'm just a person who wants to go to school to better his future. I think you should reduce the number of security guards and replace them with social workers and counselors. (Downtown Neighborhood Improvement Association and Fyre Youth Squad Position Papers, 2007)

In this student's protest, the dumping grounds of McDonogh are shaped by forces of undereducation and overcriminalization, which operate in coordination through the vector of racism. Ultimately, the student reveals a remarkable self-consciousness about his vulnerability, as an African American male, to misperception, mistrust, and ultimate disposal. Scholars in the sociology of punishment have suggested that in the mass incarceration era, prisons became warehouses for the urban underclass, but this student suggests that the warehousing begins earlier in highly punitive and academically deficient urban public schools.

The Fyre Youth Squad went back to Baton Rouge to hear the Board of Elementary and Secondary Education's decisions regarding their demands. The board ultimately agreed to reduce security forces at non-charter RSD elementary schools by one-half and security forces at high schools by one-third, but it failed to divert those investments toward curricular resources (Tuzzolo, 2007). When compared to pre-Katrina conditions, there wasn't much conciliation in this resolve. In 2004–05, the student-to-security ratio in the New Orleans Public Schools was 333:1. In the RSD in 2006–07, it was 33:1, and with the agreed-upon changes it was 54:1, still more than six times higher than the pre-Katrina levels (Juvenile Justice Project of Louisiana, 2004–2008).

In the years since, shifts have continued in the public schools of New Orleans. In 2014, New Orleans became the first city with 100 percent of its students in charter schools (Khadaroo, 2014). Early reports on the charter system were so positive that the makeover was considered a miracle (Anderson, 2010; Gabor, 2015). U.S. Secretary of Education Arne Duncan went so far as to say that "I think the best thing that happened to the education system in New Orleans was Hurricane Katrina" (Anderson, 2010). Recently, though, the positive reports on the schools are under fire. Paul Vallas, who served as superintendent of schools for the RSD during 2007–11, has been criticized for making false claims about achievement (Gabor, 2015). The Cowen Institute at Tulane University was forced to retract their published research on local school achievements in the areas of testing and graduation rates (Gabor, 2015). The Network for Public Education has shown that ten years of school reforms in New Orleans and in Louisiana more generally have failed. The state's charter school system has fared worse than traditional public schools in all other states (Heilig, 2015). Louisiana students rank at the bottom of the nation now, just as they did before Katrina. In reading, Louisiana ranked forty-sixth in the nation in 2003 and forty-seventh ten years later (Heilig, 2015). In math, Louisiana ranked forty-seventh in reading in 2003 and forty-seventh ten years later (Heilig, 2015). Judging from these figures, the miracle of the charter school system was, in fact, myth.

Educational reforms in the city have come at the expense of the most marginalized students, who are reported to have been made to "disappear from school entirely and, thus, no longer appear in the data" (Gabor, 2015). Perry, a black charter-school leader in New Orleans, explained that before Katrina, "some pretty nefarious things [were] done in the pursuit of academic gain."

While Perry says he wants to do things differently, these practices persist in the larger system. A report by Education Research Alliance claims that schools in New Orleans regularly engage in "creaming" students by "selecting, or counseling out, students based on their expected performance on standardized tests" (Gabor, 2015). Consequently, the RSD has been called a "pushout factory" that is generating a "human rights crisis" (Heilig, 2015; Sullivan & Morgan, 2010).

Local concerns about charter schools as elaborate privatization schemes have been realized over time. Educational failure in New Orleans was managed by a charter system and privatization, such that there are more private charters operating in New Orleans than in any other city in America (Mullins, 2014). This issue speaks to the core economic and political considerations of this book, in which I reveal the most egregious aspects of neoliberal profiteering in juvenile corrections as a primary conflict for a democratic order that depends on egalitarianism. The case of New Orleans, both before and after Katrina, shows in stark detail how democracy's vulnerability is rendered and exploited in the very institutions designed to preserve democracy. The answer, however, is not to be cynical, but to reinvest in public schools as such—as cornerstones of the democratic state—and recognize that they are more central than they ever have been to our political enterprise. We can't afford to hand democratic institutions over to neoliberal privatization schemes and lose sight of public education. It is a matter of democratic necessity that the public sector, which includes public education, be preserved.

Conclusion

The politics of dependency is a theory that governments, lacking in their ability to govern and to provide stability to a population by way of opportunity, manage those populations instead through dependency (Katznelson, 1976; Lyons & Drew, 2006). Both opportunity and dependency are structured around capitalist advancement, and the second is dictated by a failure in the first. The presumption that low-income African American males are at risk of failure is steeped in America's history of racism. In the aftermath of slavery, the convict lease system, Jim Crow, and the civil rights movement, many of the mechanisms for institutionalizing that risk of failure are lost. What remains to actualize both risk and failure are the tools of the criminal justice system, which are themselves tarnished by a long history of oppressive practices. As Ta-Nehisi Coates has argued, the criminal justice system in America has taught African American men for generations to fear for their bodies, to fear that at any moment their bodies are in line to be destroyed. That black bodies do sometimes destroy each other in urban America is another expression of that fear, but transposed into a desperate play to find personal power somewhere (Coates, 2015). The young man I have called Spider in this book was, in fact, shot and killed in a car near his home in May of 2008. He left behind a pregnant girlfriend who was killed a year later in a shooting at a high school graduation party, when their daughter was three months old. The child is being raised by her family members.

I have argued in this book that public schools, thin in academics and thick in discipline, have failed to provide opportunities for low-income minority students and have pushed these students out. I have shown that along the way, the criminal justice system has pulled them in by constituting practices and relations within schools and not merely beyond them. These are the push-pull factors shaping the black prison diaspora, a migration of African Americans to prison in the twenty-first century that surpasses the great migrations forced by Jim Crow, resulting in a prison population that is the largest of any nation in the world (Gates, 2014).

These push-pull factors also reflect the politics of dependency. Students who are pushed out tend to be the lowest academic performers, and they are disproportionately pushed out just as the nation would ask them to perform in high-stakes tests. The fact of their low performance is a problem that requires a fix. Both opportunity and dependency fix this problem, while generating avenues for economic growth. Dependency, though, may generate economic growth more quickly. Dependency is also a potentially more stable economic generator, in that dependency breeds more dependency. As Chui Clark argued, "It tends to steer you toward rather than away."

The sheer volume of disenfranchised youths who are steered out of school and toward disciplinary programs, juvenile detention, and adult corrections and treatment programs suggests that the dependency model has worked quite well. Were there not a dependency model in place, what would be the governmental solution to the vast numbers of under-resourced, undereducated, and underemployed Americans who would crowd the streets of urban America and everywhere in between? The very fact that a dependency model is in place means that the opportunity model is allowed to fail for a particular segment of the population. Neoliberal agendas sponsor this economy of failed opportunity, which reproduces racial hierarchies that privilege whites and expands the reach of governance by way of private funding. The acceptance of a dependency model means, as well, that discipline can be a foil for the kind of large-scale educational change that would address racialized educational inequality and the systemic failure of urban schools.

With a backup plan like long-term dependency at the ready, public schools are off the hook for developing students with the resources and skills they would need to survive on their own. When teachers can send students to the principal's office and principals can send students home or have them arrested, there is a missing academic imperative. Failure is an option, because the problem can simply be shifted elsewhere, to be construed as a different kind of success.

I am not suggesting that when teachers and school administrators send students away from the classroom or away from school entirely, they are always knowingly playing at the politics of dependency—but schools might improve for many children if teachers and staff began to see it that way. Exclusionary school discipline stacks the deck against students, especially African American males, and pushes them closer to the forces of the criminal justice system, which may be the forces they fear most in the world. If teachers and school administrators were to refuse exclusionary disciplinary measures for all behaviors except the most egregious violations, which would require other kinds of support and treatment, the educational imperative could be restored. But many educators and the larger society have, it seems, accepted an alternative conception, codified and pressured by No Child Left Behind and myriad other disciplinary measures, that we are not required to educate everyone. It is my hope that this book asks us all to question that acceptance as well as the ideologies, policies, and laws that enable and, in some cases, demand it.

We would do well to heed the example of Jose Huerta, a principal at Garfield High School in East Los Angeles, who declared that "suspensions are off the table" at his school, explaining, "I can't teach a kid if he's not in school" (Rott, 2013). Huerta came to this conclusion in the 2008–09 school year, when there were 638 suspensions in his school. In the three years that followed, there was only one. With the change in disciplinary policy at Garfield, attendance rose to 96 percent and is now higher than the district average. In 2013, more of Huerta's students were admitted to the University of California, Los Angeles, than from any other high school in the state (Rott, 2013).

The legality of suspending youths under subjective categories like willful defiance is now being challenged as a matter of racial discrimination. In 2013, Public Counsel was successful in its effort to ban school suspension for students characterized as committing "willful defiance" in Los Angeles (Rott, 2013). A similar ban on willful-defiance suspensions was passed in San Francisco and became effective in the 2014–15 school year. Michael Britt, who teaches at Burton High School in San Francisco, said that for too many years his school district had taken undue disciplinary actions, admitting that "We've been on the wrong side" (Frey, 2014).

When the State of California passed AB 420 in 2014, it was the first state in the country to recognize the enormity of its school suspension problem and its correctional consequences and to pull back on willful-defiance policies

(ACLU of Northern California, 2014). In support of AB 420, Assemblyman Roger Dickinson said: "In just a few short years, school discipline reform has become an important education policy priority in California because the stakes are very high—research has shown that even one suspension can make it five times more likely that a child will drop out of school and significantly increases the odds they will get in trouble and head into our juvenile delinquency system" (ACLU of Northern California, 2014). There are promising signs of school disciplinary reform in this legislative logic, but unfortunately, AB 420 is so limited in its scope that it is unlikely to create a major shift in how California students, outside of San Francisco and Los Angeles, experience school discipline and how they are made vulnerable to correctional control. AB 420 applies only to California public school students in grades K–3 through the year 2017, and suspension rates tend to be four to ten times higher in high schools (Losen & Martinez, 2013). Furthermore, there are twenty-four other disciplinary mechanisms in the California Education Code that can be used in place of willful defiance (State of California, Legislative Counsel, 2012; ACLU of Northern California, 2014). Nonetheless, California and its school districts are beginning to see the problems that have been created by harsh school punishments and are piecing together reforms.

There are also signs of change at the federal level. In 2014, the U.S. Departments of Education and Justice recognized the persistent and systemic problem of discriminatory school discipline in the nation's public schools and issued a guidance package steering schools away from exclusionary school discipline (Benton, 2014). The "School Discipline Guidance Package" states that

1. Racial disparities in American school discipline are significant and persistent.
2. Those racial disparities cannot be explained by differential misbehavior by students of color.
3. Students lose important instructional time to exclusionary discipline.
4. Exclusionary discipline can significantly harm students' educational outcomes . . . and . . . contribute to the "school-to-prison pipeline."

The federal guidelines focus on how school discipline affects the entire school community, how school police and security forces exacerbate racial disparities, and how racial biases are expressed implicitly in discipline. The Department of Education recommends

5. Using positive interventions rather than exclusionary discipline.

6. Limiting exclusionary discipline to the most severe behavior that threatens school safety.

7. Referring students with social, emotional or behavioral needs for psychological testing and services.

8. Establishing clear and appropriate expectations for student behavior; and engaging school communities and families around student discipline.

Federal efforts, such as this, to move school districts away from exclusionary policies might begin to initiate a new set of practices that actively disengage the politics and economics of school suspension and expulsion.

Were we collectively to refuse exclusionary practices in schools and elsewhere, what would happen to the dependency economy? Might resources feeding the penal state shift back in the direction of the social welfare state, and could schools gain a larger share of resources to use in their quest to educate all children? I imagine that it's possible. As long as we participate in offering resources to the economy of dependency, it will be very difficult to obtain the resources to benefit academics in schools.

I have to acknowledge that the dynamics I have outlined in this book are disheartening—to say the least. As I have argued, intervention strategies must be broadly conceived and not limited to narrow conceptions of school discipline as a matter of sheer policy. A look into the economy of school discipline and youth corrections yields a miasma of intersecting and abusive relations that builds on the historical conditions of black oppression and reproduces them on the backs of children. The arguments that I make in this book point to violence that is entrenched in the traditions of American institutions, the fundamental principles of capitalism, and racism. Social, economic, and political oppression shapes human life far beyond these national borders, however, and keeps a choke hold on millions globally. When these forms of violence are perpetuated in any space, people, like Spider and others, will continue to die. As such, it may seem difficult to find a way out.

Other scholars in the sociology of education, like Bowles and Gintis, have argued that schools are so implicated in the stratifying forces of capitalism that they are stymied in the pursuit of egalitarianism and democracy. They might only be changed, then, by disempowering the capitalist system itself (Bowles & Gintis, 1976). But what if we were to act as agents on the fundamental principles of capitalism, such as supply and demand, and refuse to buy into the commodification of certain conditions, such as dependency? It means something different to "buy" into a pure social welfare state in which services are not privatized; we might thereby engage different sorts of capital—social, political, human—to sponsor a true commitment to education and opportunity and all that they can generate. By refusing to suspend, expel, or push students out of schools because of disciplinary infractions, and insisting instead on inclusion and equality, we defund the dependency model while shoring up resources for public education. This approach is centered on a politics of care and an insistence that humans are at every moment humanized.

I engaged in this book project as someone who believes in public education and its potential and is unwilling to let these institutions off the hook. I am not willing to give up on public schools or on any of the students in them. As such, this book has always been a project of faith and optimism for me. Having taught in many different kinds of schools, I do know that nothing is easy about what I am suggesting. But as educators and as a society, we really have no other ethical choice.

APPENDIX

In the fieldwork for this book, which I conducted between 2002 and 2010, I took on the role of participant observer (Adler & Adler, 1987). I spent over a thousand hours in the field doing formal research and lived in New Orleans for several years during this time period. In the field, I observed social and institutional dynamics as they unfolded and, when it was appropriate, jotted down observations in a small notebook that I carried with me. Soon afterward, I developed these jottings into ethnographic field notes with thick descriptions of events (Geertz, 1973). While conducting an ethnography of the present, I was attentive to historical dimensions. Using the methodologies of historical ethnography, I asked questions about how the past is known and represented.

I conducted informal, unrecorded interviews with approximately thirty people, most of whom, like Chui Clark, I interviewed on many occasions. I favored open-ended engagements that allowed my participants to take the interview in the direction that felt most comfortable to them. I conducted twenty-one semistructured and audio-recorded interviews—five on the telephone, and fifteen in people's homes or cars or at a local public library. I supplemented these data with a diverse set of secondary material, including school records, public school budgets, school-board meeting minutes, archived statistical data on local and state public schools, government and prison reports, media reports, and radio broadcasts, as well as unpublished local fliers distributed by school protestors (DeVault & Gross, 2007). To answer, in a broader sense, the question of how a public school came to be inside a prison, I conducted further research on the national phenomenon of school punishment in the context of the War on Crime and charted the social, economic, and political forces that were most at stake.

I transcribed all audio recordings myself in the interest of accuracy. Many of my research participants spoke in a thick New Orleans accent, and like many locals, they dropped hard final consonants like "er," making words like "water" sound more like "whattah." This made transcriptions challenging, even for me, and I had a distinct advantage. I was born in North Carolina and grew up speaking in a southern accent. I still do speak in a southern accent to some extent, especially when I am in the South or with family. The English spoken in New Orleans, though, is very different from that of North Carolina, which lies about eight hundred miles to the north, and I had to listen very carefully when gathering and analyzing data. I replayed sections of individual recordings as many as thirty or forty times to ensure full comprehension. Once I had a complete data set, I hand coded the data into emerging analytical categories using a grounded theory approach (Glaser and Strauss, 1967). The theories I develop in this book are generated from this data and analysis.

NOTES

INTRODUCTION

1. The Orleans Parish Prison, despite its name, is not actually a prison; it is a jail that serves Orleans Parish.

2. The principal was also in charge of education for juvenile inmates in the larger correctional institution.

3. In the 2002–03 school year, 13,831 students, representing nearly 19 percent of the K–12 student population, were suspended from school at least once in the Orleans Parish schools (Louisiana Department of Education, 2002–2003). A closer look at the data reveals that for African American males, the district rate of suspension in 2002–03 was 25 percent. In seven out of twenty-five middle schools in the district, the suspension rate was over 40 percent (Tuzzolo & Hewitt, 2006).

4. I later learned from Chui Clark that I was the only person at the conference who spent time talking with him or any of the protestors.

5. I use pseudonyms for these minors as a matter of human-subjects protocol.

6. Among the most promising research tools from this early era at the University of Chicago was a research focus on the city and a consequent research methodology that was leveled at the city street (Bogdan & Biklen, 1998; Matthews, 1977). The corpus of literature on racial and ethnic relations yielded by the Chicago School—including W. I. Thomas and Florian Znaniecki's *The Polish Peasant* (1918–1920), Charles Johnson's *The Negro in Chicago* (1922), Nels Anderson's *The Hobo* (1923), Frederic Thrasher's *The Gang* (1927), and Louis Wirth's *The Ghetto* (1928)—retains a clear critical purchase for contemporary studies on the social and economic margins of society (Bulmer, 1984; Matthews, 1977).

7. In the aftermath of the 2015 prayer-service massacre at Emanuel AME Church in Charleston, South Carolina, by a young white gunman who aimed to start a race war, pressure mounted to remove Civil War monuments wherever they stood and end the

symbolic reign of white supremacy. The Confederate flag flying over the grounds of South Carolina's capital and the Robert E. Lee statue in New Orleans were on the chopping block. With support from New Orleans Mayor Mitch Landrieu, the New Orleans City Council, and local jazz legend Wynton Marsalis, the statues of Robert E. Lee, Jefferson Davis, and two others were slated for removal (Marsalis, 2015; Rainey, 2015). In January 2016, the contractor hired to do the job reneged on his contract, citing death threats that had been made against him, his family, and his employees. In the same month, the contractor was a victim of arson: a car belonging to him, a Lamborghini valued at $200,000, was torched and destroyed while parked in his company parking lot (Lohr, 2016).

CHAPTER 1. PUBLIC SCHOOLS IN A PUNITIVE ERA

1. School crime is a long-standing public concern that Jonathan Simon, in his book *Governing through Crime*, traces back to the matter of school desegregation and the political will emerging from one side of that conflict to chart school-related crime in newly integrated school systems and name it as a problem to be addressed through new governmental solutions (i.e., crime control; Simon, 2007).

2. Serious violent victimization includes robbery, aggravated assault, sexual assault, and rape.

3. About three-quarters of SROs are trained by police departments, and the remainder are trained by sheriffs (James & McCallion, 2013).

4. The officer who beat up Marshawn Pitts was placed in a school security post at the Academy of Learning High School in Dolton, Illinois, shortly after having been placed on leave from the police department in the neighboring town of Robbins, Illinois, for his questionable involvement in the shooting death of his former wife's husband. The officer's ex-wife alleged that he had shot her current husband twenty-four times and killed him in front of the couple's home and in front of children. The officer received an acquittal at trial, based on a determination of self-defense, but he was suspended from his regular police duty in Robbins. Marshawn Pitts was admitted to the Academy of Learning High School in May 2009 after moving to Illinois from Iowa. He was attacked by the security officer shortly thereafter. Pitts was designated a special-needs student in childhood when he sustained injuries to his brain after being hit by a car. A year after he attacked Pitts, the officer served time in jail while awaiting trial on a rape charge (*Huffington Post*, 2010; Janssen & Gorner, 2009; CNN, 2009).

5. Figlio finds that this discrepancy exists only in grades that are scheduled to take high-stakes tests.

6. The term "zero tolerance" was coined in 1986 to name a strict U.S. policy to impound sea vessels that carried illicit drugs of any quantity. In 1988, it became the drug policy for vehicles at the U.S. border. By the late 1980s and early 1990s, zero tolerance was no longer simply a border-control policy. As Zweifler and De Beers (2002) explain, "zero tolerance captured the nation's imagination and was applied to an expansive range of topics."

7. There is some evidence that English-language learners may not be experiencing a disproportionate share of exclusionary school punishments (U.S. Department of Education, 2014).

8. This figure is a total of all populations in the custody of the criminal justice system and includes inmates in prisons and jails as well as individuals on probation.

CHAPTER 2. THE "AT-RISK YOUTH INDUSTRY"

1. The data on youth homicide capture incidents of violent deaths to youths ages five to eighteen (National Center for Education Statistics, 2011).

2. These market research data are based on qualitative interviews with industry representatives and school administrators, as well as corporate portfolio statistics, government reports, and trade publications (Packaged Facts, 2000).

3. This ranking is based on the number of facilities operated by CCA.

4. Ronnie Casella reports that this $35 million figure from CPS also represents money spent on tech support, character education, and other violence-prevention programs (Casella, 2003a). As Casella explains, the figure may not be an entirely accurate account of school security costs, because program expenditures are not adequately disaggregated. However, the published budget for the Chicago Public Schools in 2015–16 is significantly disaggregated, which suggests both that the $1 million school-security budget is accurate and that the reported tripling of school-security expenditures is an underestimation.

5. California, New York, Massachusetts, Mississippi, and Virginia authorize school districts to use state funds to finance school security. Connecticut has grants on the books for these expenditures, but they have not always been funded (Lohman & Shepard, 2006).

6. Free lunch is provided to students whose family income is below 130 percent of the poverty line. The figure cited is based on poverty guidelines published by the U.S. Department of Health and Human Services and not the poverty threshold, which is calculated differently.

7. The story of a lost inmate is a primary narrative thread in the television series *Treme,* David Simon's fictionalized account of post-Katrina New Orleans.

CHAPTER 3. UNDEREDUCATED AND OVERCRIMINALIZED IN NEW ORLEANS

1. Wallace was released from Angola in 2013, two days before he died of cancer. Woodfox was released on February 19, 2016, after serving forty-three years in solitary confinement—America's longest-held inmate in solitary confinement to date.

2. Foti served as attorney general of Louisiana from 2004 to 2008.

3. The sheriff's assistant claimed that two white boys were later added to the roster.

CHAPTER 4. THE PRISON SCHOOL

1. The Orleans Parish Prison, despite its name, is primarily a country jail. The federal government contracts with the OPP to house some federal inmates.

2. One male of Caucasian descent was later added to the roll. According to Chui, he came for two days and then ran from the program.

3. In 2013, a motion for a second consent-decree judgment was granted on the basis of "pervasive and longstanding problems" (*Jones v. Gusman*, 2013; Schwartz & Miller, 2008).

4. Moon Landrieu was elected mayor in 1970 on a pro–civil rights platform, winning almost 100 percent of the black vote (Donze, 2012). Explaining his success, Landrieu said that his campaign was "the first time a candidate solicited, met with, discussed black votes" (Bass & DeVries, 1974). During Landrieu's term in office, his relationship with the black community grew complicated. While he is lauded for overseeing the desegregation of city agencies, he also presided over a deceitful early-morning raid on the Black Panther Party (Moore, 2010). Police officers used dubious trespassing and attempted-murder charges as cause for disguising themselves as priests and firing at the Panthers, with the goal of evacuating the group's headquarters in the Desire neighborhood. Many in the African American community, who saw the Black Panthers as heroes because of their many social-welfare initiatives, were enraged by the violence and took their protest all the way to Moon Landrieu's front door (Moore, 2010). The Landrieu quotation I have used as an epigraph for the section "Jim Crow Lives Here" is from Harden (2013).

5. Moore explains that African Americans in New Orleans who had achieved middle-class status were often reluctant to get involved in matters of police brutality (Moore, 2010). While the black middle class was affected by police misconduct, they did not bear the brunt of the brutality, and their civil rights efforts were focused on less contentious subjects, which, at the time, included public education. The black middle class tended to hold a negative perception of black grassroots organizations that centered on police brutality and referred to these groups as "street niggas" (Moore, 2010). Drawing a distinction between illegitimate and legitimate blacks helped middle-class African Americans protect the socioeconomic privileges they had gained. Moore explains, for example, that "during the turbulent decades of the 1970s and 1980s, two of the city's most prominent black political organizations were largely silent concerning the issue of police brutality for fear of losing access to city hall patronage" (Moore, 2010). In order to maintain their own set of limited privileges, the efforts by middle-class blacks to delegitimize black grassroots organizations at times mimicked the rhetoric of white supremacists.

6. The St. Charles streetcar began service in 1835 and is the oldest streetcar in continuous operation. Hurricane Katrina disrupted the streetcar service, but it has since been restored.

7. Local legend holds that Armstrong fired a gun into the air on New Year's Eve in 1913 and was subsequently placed in the Colored Waifs' Home, where he first learned to play the horn.

8. The Milne Boys Home was originally intended to be an orphanage, as outlined in the 1838 bequest of Alexander Milne, a New Orleans philanthropist. Milne provided for children in New Orleans who had lost their parents to epidemics of diseases like yellow fever and malaria, which were common in that day (Richard, 2012). In spite of Milne's bequest, the facility, which was not built until 1933—almost a century later—served as a home for juvenile delinquents, with entirely segregated facilities (Richard, 2012).

9. The Virginia court's ruling in *Ruffin v. Commonwealth* was revisited in a number of subsequent cases, whereby prisoners' rights were augmented such that, as Angela Davis claims, prisoners "are no longer the living dead" but continue to reside "beyond the boundaries of liberal democracy" (Davis, 2012). In a law review article, legal scholar Grace Chin describes punishment in the era of mass incarceration as "the new civil death" because contemporary forms of punishment revive a set of civil deprivations that reflect the traditional status of civil death (Chin, 2012).

10. Inmates only keep half of what they earn in the fields at Angola (Schenwar, 2008). The remainder is held in an account to benefit inmates upon release. Because 90 percent of inmates die at Angola, in part because Louisiana has led the country in life sentences, these wages are rarely recouped (Cohen, 2013).

11. Various entities controlled the physical facility where the Prison School was sited. The building was owned by the New Orleans Public Schools and had once been a segregated school. Sheriff Foti held a lease to the property and had used it for many years as a correctional building. In opening a public school in the space, a school board member explained that "it has been Foti's facility, but we are taking it back and using it as our facility. . . . It is our facility coming back to us to be used by our men with our instruction." When the program advertised for teachers, however, applicants were instructed to apply to the Orleans Parish Criminal Sheriff's Office (*Times-Picayune*, 2002).

12. Another newspaper published a story after a few weeks. By contrast, the African American weekly paper published a story immediately and continued its solid coverage.

13. Losen clarifies that disciplinary alternative schools are not charter schools by definition, though some may be operated by charters.

14. Not all schools show evidence of having been incentivized by No Child Left Behind to mete out harsher discipline at test time. Aaron Kupchik found no evidence of this in the schools he studied while conducting research for his book *Homeroom Security* (Kupchik, 2010).

REFERENCES

ACLU. (2006, January 11). *Orleans Parish Prison: A big jail with big problems.* Washington, DC: Author. www.aclu.org/prisoners-rights/orleans-parish-prison-big-jail-big-problems.

———. (2008, December). *Louisiana has highest incarceration rate in the world; ACLU seeks changes.* Washington, DC: Author. www.aclu.org/news/louisiana-has-highest-incarceration-rate-world-aclu-seeks-changes.

ACLU National Prison Project. (2006, August). *Abandoned & abused: Orleans Parish prisoners in the wake of Hurricane Katrina.* Washington, DC: Author. www.aclu.org/prisoners-rights/abandoned-and-abused.

ACLU of Northern California. (2014, September). *California enacts first-in-the-nation law to eliminate student suspensions for minor misbehavior.* San Francisco, CA: Author. www.aclunc.org/news/california-enacts-first-nation-law-eliminate-student-suspensions-minor-misbehavior.

Acorn, A. E. (2004). *Compulsory compassion: A critique of restorative justice.* Vancouver, Canada: University of British Columbia Press.

Adler, P. A. & Adler, P. (1987). *Membership roles in field research.* Newbury Park, CA: Sage.

Advancement Project. (2010, March). *Test, punish, and push out: How "zero tolerance" and high-stakes testing funnel youth into the school-to-prison pipeline* (revised). Washington, DC: Author. http://b.3cdn.net/advancement/d05cb2181a4545db07_r2im6caqe.pdf.

Advancement Project and Civil Rights Project. (2000). *Opportunities suspended: The devastating consequences of zero tolerance and school discipline* (Report from a National Summit on Zero Tolerance, June 15–16, 2000, Washington, DC). Washington, DC: Authors.

Alexander, M. (2010). *The new Jim Crow: Mass incarceration in the age of colorblindness.* New York, NY: New Press.

Altheide, D. L. (2009). The Columbine shootings and the discourse of fear. *American Behavioral Scientist, 52*, 1354–1370.

Anderson, N. (2010, January 30). Education Secretary Duncan calls Hurricane Katrina good for New Orleans schools. *The Washington Post.* www.washingtonpost.com /wp-dyn/content/article/2010/01/29/AR2010012903259.html.

Anyon, J. (1997). *Ghetto schooling: The political economy of urban educational reform.* New York, NY: Teachers College Press.

Apple, M. (1990/2004). *Ideology and curriculum* (2nd ed.). New York, NY: Routledge.

Arum, R. & Beattie, I. (1999). High school experience and the risk of adult incarceration. *Criminology, 37*, 515–540.

Arum, R. & LaFree, G. (2008). Teacher–student ratios and the risk of adult incarceration. *Sociology of Education, 81*, 397–421.

Ashley, J. & Burke, K. (2009). *Implementing restorative justice: A guide for schools.* Chicago, IL: Illinois Criminal Justice Information Authority.

Aud, S., Fox, M. A. & KewalRamani, A. (2010, July). *Status and trends in the education of racial and ethnic groups* (NCES 2010–015). Washington, DC: U.S. Department of Education, National Center for Education Statistics. http://nces.ed.gov /pubs2010/2010015.pdf.

Austria, Rubén, Rev. (2015, October 29). 'Disturbing schools' *[sic]* law and school resource officers criminalize teens. *Juvenile Justice Information Exchange.* http://jjie.org /disturbing-schools-law-and-school-resource-officers-criminalize-teens/148344/.

Ayers, W., Dohrn, B. & Ayers, R. (Eds.). (2001). *Zero tolerance: Resisting the drive for punishment in our schools.* New York, NY: New Press.

Bahena, S., Cooc, N., Currie-Rubin, R., Kuttner, P. & Ng, M. (Eds.). (2012). *Disrupting the school-to-prison pipeline.* Cambridge, MA: Harvard Educational Review.

Balfanz, R. & Legters, N. (2004). *Locating the dropout crisis: Which high schools produce the nation's dropouts? Where are they located? Who attends them?* Baltimore, MD: Center for Research on the Education of Students Placed at Risk, Johns Hopkins University.

Bankston, C., III & Caldas, S. (2002). *A troubled dream: The promise and failure of school desegregation in Louisiana.* Nashville, TN: Vanderbilt University Press.

Bass, J. & DeVries, W. (1974). Interview with Moon Landrieu (Interview A-0089, January 10–11, 1974). Documenting the American South: Southern Oral History Program Collection no. 4007. Chapel Hill, NC: University Library, University of North Carolina. http://docsouth.unc.edu/sohp/A-0089/A-0089.html.

Beaumont, G. A. de & Tocqueville, A. de (1833/1979). *On the penitentiary system in the United States and its application in France.* Carbondale, IL: Southern Illinois University Press.

Beckett, K. (1997). *Making crime pay: Law and order in contemporary American politics.* New York, NY: Oxford University Press.

Beckett, K. & Herbert, S. (2010). *Banished: The new social control in urban America.* New York, NY: Oxford University Press.

Bell, R. (2001, December 11). New school to serve troubled students. *The Times-Pica-yune*, p. 1B.

Benton, H. (2014). *Federal guidance seeks to end discriminatory school discipline.* Oakland, CA: National Center for Youth Law. http://youthlaw.org/publication/federal-guidance-seeks-to-end-discriminatory-school-discipline/.

Bernstein, N. (2005). *All alone in the world: Children of the incarcerated.* New York, NY: New Press.

Berube, A. & Holmes, N. (2015, August 27). *Concentrated poverty in New Orleans 10 years after Katrina* (Metropolitan Opportunity Series no. 66). Washington, DC: Brookings Institution. www.brookings.edu/blogs/the-avenue/posts/2015/08/27-concentrated-poverty-new-orleans-katrina-berube-holmes.

Berube, A. & Katz, B. (2005, October). *Katrina's window: Confronting concentrated poverty across America.* Washington, DC: Brookings Institution. www.brookings.edu/research/reports/2005/10/poverty-berube.

Bervera, X. (2004, June 24). The death of Tallulah prison: An extraordinary campaign against racism and corruption takes down Louisiana's notorious Tallulah youth prison. *Alternet.* www.alternet.org/story/19040/the_death_of_tallulah_prison.

Blackmon, D. (2008). *Slavery by another name.* New York, NY: Anchor Books.

Bloomberg. (2014, April 15). *Most income inequality: U.S. cities* (Bloomberg Visual Data). www.bloomberg.com/graphics/best-and-worst/#most-income-inequality-us-cities.

Blow, C. (2012, May 25). Plantations, prisons and profits. *The New York Times.* www.nytimes.com/2012/05/26/opinion/blow-plantations-prisons-and-profits.html.

Board of Education of the City of Chicago. (2015–2016). Chicago Public Schools: Approved budget. http://cps.edu/fy16budget/documents/fy16budget.pdf.

Bobo, L. (2011). The importance of research on race, crime and punishment. Keynote address, National Institute of Justice Conference, June 20–22, 2011, Arlington, VA. www.youtube.com/watch?v = 6h2jTFxwF-M).

Body Positive. (1999, September). HIV-positive prisoners forced to wear stun belts. *The Body: The Complete HIV/AIDS Resource.* www.thebody.com/bp/sept99/news.html#prisoners.

Bogdan, R. & Biklen, S. (1998). *Qualitative research in education.* Boston, MA: Allyn and Bacon.

Bonczar, T.P. (2003). *Prevalence of imprisonment in the U.S. prison population, 1874–2001* (Special Report 197976). Washington, DC: U.S. Department of Justice, Office of Justice Programs, Bureau of Justice Statistics.

Bonilla-Silva, E. (2006). *Racism without racists: Color-blind racism and the persistence of racial inequality in the United States.* Lanham, MD: Rowman & Littlefield.

Bourdieu, P. & Passeron, J.C. (1977). *Reproduction in education, society and culture.* Beverly Hills, CA: Sage.

Bourgois, P. (1996). *In search of respect.* Cambridge, UK: Cambridge University Press.

Bowles, S. & Gintis, H. (1976). *Schooling in capitalist America.* New York, NY: Basic Books.

Braden, J. & Schroeder, J. (2004). High-stakes testing and No Child Left Behind: Information and strategies for educators. In *Helping children at home and school II: Handouts for families and educators*. Bethesda, MD: National Association of School Psychologists. www.nasponline.org/communications/spawareness/highstakes.pdf.

Braithwaite, J. (2002). *Restorative justice and response regulation*. New York, NY: Oxford University Press.

Breton, A. (1928/1960). *Nadja*. New York, NY: Grove Press.

Bridgeland, J. M., DiIulio, J. J., Jr. & Morrison, K. B. (2006, March). *The silent epidemic: Perspectives of high school dropouts*. Washington, DC: Civic Enterprises. www.civicenterprises.net/MediaLibrary/Docs/the_silent_epidemic.pdf.

Brown, E. (2003). Freedom for some, discipline for 'others': The structure of inequality in education. In K. Saltman & D. Gabbard (Eds.), *Education as enforcement: The militarization and corporatization of schools*. New York, NY: Routledge.

Bulmer, M. (1984). *The Chicago school of sociology*. Chicago, IL: University of Chicago Press.

Burawoy, M., Burton, A., Ferguson, A., Fox, K., Gamson, J., Gartrell, N., Hurst, L., Kurzman, C., Salzinger, L., Schiffman, J. & Ui, S. (1991). *Ethnography unbound: Power and resistance in the modern metropolis*. Berkeley, CA: University of California Press.

Bureau of Governmental Research. (1998, December). *BGR Outlook on Orleans: Orleans Parish School Board*. New Orleans, LA: Author. www.bgr.org/files/reports/OutlookOrleansSchoolBoard98.pdf.

Bush, M., Ryan, M. & Rose, S. (2011, August). Number of instructional days/hours in the school year. *School calendar: Length of school year*. Denver, CO: Education Commission of the States. www.ecs.org/clearinghouse/95/05/9505.pdf.

Butterfield, F. (1998a, July 15). Hard time: A special report; profits at a juvenile prison come with a chilling cost. *The New York Times*. www.nytimes.com/1998/07/15/us/hard-time-special-report-profits-juvenile-prison-come-with-chilling-cost.html.

———. (1998b, July 24). Louisiana seizes management of privately run youth prison. *The New York Times*. www.nytimes.com/1998/07/24/us/louisiana-seizes-management-of-privately-run-youth-prison.html.

Byrd, W. M. & Clayton, L. A. (2002). *Race, medicine, and health care in the United States 1900–2000*. New York, NY: Routledge.

———. (2003). Racial and ethnic disparities in health care: A background and history. In B. D. Smedley, A. Y. Stith & A. R. Nelson (Eds.), *Unequal treatment: Confronting racial and ethnic disparities in health care*. Washington, DC: National Academy of Sciences.

Campbell-Rock, C. C. (2002). Letter to the editor. *The Louisiana Weekly* (May 13–19).

Carnoy, M. & Levin, H. (1985). *Schooling and work in the democratic state*. Stanford, CA: Stanford University Press.

Carr, S. (2012, May 14). Recovery School District grapples with discipline policies. *The Times-Picayune*. www.nola.com/education/index.ssf/2012/05/recovery_school_district_getti.html.

Carroll, M. (2008). Educating expelled students after No Child Left Behind: Mending an incentive structure that discourages alternative education and reinstatement. *UCLA Law Review, 55*, 1909–1969.

Casella, R. (2001). *At zero tolerance: Punishment, prevention, and school violence.* New York, NY: Peter Lang.

———. (2003a). The false allure of security technologies. *Social Justice, 30*(3).

———. (2003b). Punishing dangerousness through preventive detention: Illustrating the institutional link between school and prison. *New Directions for Youth Development, 2003,* 55–70.

———. (2003c). Zero tolerance policy in schools: Rationale, consequences, and alternatives. *Teachers College Record, 105,* 872–892.

———. (2006). *Selling us the fortress: The promotion of techno-security equipment for schools.* New York, NY: Routledge.

———. (2010). Safety or social control: The security fortification of schools in a capitalist society. In T. Monahan & R. Torres (Eds.), *Schools under surveillance: Cultures of control in public education* (pp. 73–86). New Brunswick, NJ: Rutgers University Press.

Cash, J. (1972). Orleans Parish Prison [song recording]. *Murder* [CD]. New York, NY: Columbia Records, 2010.

Casserly, M. (2006). Double jeopardy: Public education in New Orleans before and after the storm. In C. Hartman and G. Squires (Eds.), *There is no such thing as a natural disaster: Race, class, and Hurricane Katrina.* New York, NY: Routledge.

Center for Education Reform. (2012). K–12 facts. www.edreform.com/2012/04/k-12-facts/.

Centers for Disease Control and Prevention. (2014, January). *School-associated violent death study.* Atlanta, GA: CDC. www.cdc.gov/violenceprevention/youthviolence/schoolviolence/savd.html.

Chaddock, G. (1999, August 24). Safe schools, at a price. *The Christian Science Monitor,* p. 15.

Chambliss, D.F. & Schutt, R.K. (2014). *Making sense of the social world: Methods of investigation.* Thousand Oaks, CA: Sage.

Chang, C. (2012a, May 13). Louisiana incarcerated. *The Times-Picayune.* http://media.nola.com/prisons/other/tp-2012-prisons-part-1e.pdf.

———. (2012b, May 14). North Louisiana family is a major force in the state's vast prison industry. *The Times-Picayune.* www.nola.com/crime/index.ssf/2012/05/jonesboro_family_is_a_major_fo.html.

Chang, C. (2013, January 11). Prisons for profit. *Public Broadcasting Service.* www.pbs.org/wnet/religionandethics/2013/01/11/january-11-2013-prisons-for-profit/14485/.

Chin, G. (2012). The new civil death: Rethinking punishment in the era of mass conviction. *University of Pennsylvania Law Review, 160,* 1789–1833.

Civil Rights Project & Advancement Project. (2000, June 15–16). *Opportunities suspended: The devastating consequences of zero tolerance and school discipline.* Washington, DC: Authors. https://civilrightsproject.ucla.edu/research/k-12-education

/school-discipline/opportunities-suspended-the-devastating-consequences-of-zero-tolerance-and-school-discipline-policies/crp-opportunities-suspended-zero-tolerance-2000.pdf.

Clausing, J. (2011, December 2). Suit filed after NM teen cuffed for burp in class. *The Seattle Times*. www.seattletimes.com/nation-world/suit-filed-after-nm-teen-cuffed-for-burp-in-class/.

Clear, T. (2007). *Imprisoning communities: How mass incarceration makes disadvantaged neighborhoods worse*. New York, NY: Oxford University Press.

CNN. (2009, October 8). Officer resigns after alleged beating of student caught on tape. www.cnn.com/2009/US/10/08/special.needs.student.beating/index.html?eref = rss_topstorie.

Coates, T.-N. (2015). *Between the world and me*. New York, NY: Random House.

Cohen, A. (2013, October). At Louisiana's most notorious prison, a clash of testament [*sic*]. *The Atlantic Monthly*. www.theatlantic.com/national/archive/2013/10/at-louisianas-most-notorious-prison-a-clash-of-testament/280414/.

Contractor, D. & Staats, C. (2014, May). *Interventions to address racialized discipline disparities and school "push out"* (Kirwan Institute Policy Brief). Columbus, OH: Kirwan Institute for the Study of Race and Ethnicity, The Ohio State University.

Cooper, A. & Smith, E. (2011, November). *Homicide trends in the United States, 1980–2008* (NCJ 236018). Washington, DC: U.S. Department of Justice, Office of Justice Programs, Bureau of Justice Statistics. www.bjs.gov/content/pub/pdf/htus8008.pdf.

Cooper, E. F. (2005, February). *The Safe and Drug-Free Schools and Communities Act: Reauthorization and appropriations* (CRS Report for Congress, order code RS20532). Washington, DC: Library of Congress, Congressional Research Service. www.law.umaryland.edu/marshall/crsreports/crsdocuments/RS2053202152005.pdf.

Cornell University Law School. (2002). 20 U.S. Code 7137: School Security Technology and Resource Center. www.law.cornell.edu/uscode/text/20/7137?qt-us_code_tabs = 1#qt-us_code_tabs.

Cowen Institute. (2010). *The state of public education in New Orleans: Five years after Hurricane Katrina*. New Orleans, LA: Cowen Institute for Public Education Initiatives, Tulane University. www.coweninstitute.com/wp-content/uploads/2010/07/katrina-book.final_.CIpageSmaller.pdf.

———. (2011). *Transforming public education in New Orleans: The Recovery School District 2003–2011*. New Orleans, LA: Cowen Institute for Public Education Initiatives, Tulane University. www.coweninstitute.com/wp-content/uploads/2011/12/History-of-the-RSD-Report-2011.pdf.

Darling-Hammond, L. (2001). Apartheid in American education: How opportunity is rationed to children of color in the United States. In T. Johnson, J. Boyden & W. Pittz (Eds.), *Racial profiling and punishment in U.S. public schools* (pp. 39–44). Oakland, CA: Applied Research Center.

Davis, A. Y. (1998). The prison of slavery and the slavery of prison. In Joy James (Ed.), *The Angela Davis reader*. Malden, MA: Blackwell.

———. (2003). *Are prisons obsolete?* New York, NY: Seven Stories Press.

————. (2005). *Abolition democracy: Beyond empire, prisons, and torture*. New York, NY: Seven Stories Press.

————. (2012). *The meaning of freedom and other difficult dialogues*. San Francisco, CA: City Lights Books.

DeSilver, D. (2014, July 14). Despite recent shootings, Chicago nowhere near U.S. 'murder capital.' *Pew Research Center*. www.pewresearch.org/fact-tank/2014/07/14 /despite-recent-shootings-chicago-nowhere-near-u-s-murder-capital/.

DeVault, M. & Gross, G. (2007). Feminist interviewing: Experience, talk, and knowledge. In S. N. Hesse-Biber (Ed.), *Handbook of feminist research: Theory and praxis*. Thousand Oaks, CA: Sage.

Devine, J. (1996). *Maximum security: The culture of violence in inner-city schools*. Chicago, IL: University of Chicago Press.

Dewey, J. (1944/1916). *Democracy and education*. New York, NY: Free Press.

Dohrn, B. (2001). "Look out kid/It's something you did": Zero tolerance for children. In W. Ayers, B. Dohrn & R. Ayers (Eds.), *Zero tolerance: Resisting the drive for punishment in our schools*. New York, NY: New Press.

Donze, F. (2012, January 29). Moon Landrieu: The *Times-Picayune* covers 175 years of New Orleans history. *The Times-Picayune*. www.nola.com/175years/index .ssf/2012/01/moon_landrieu_the_times-picayu.html.

Douglass, F. (1846, May 12). An appeal to the British people [reception speech at Finsbury Chapel, Moorfields, England]. In P. Foner (Ed.), *The life and writings of Frederick Douglass*, vol. 1. New York, NY: International Publishers, 1950.

Downtown Neighborhood Improvement Association and Fyre Youth Squad Position Papers (2007). New Orleans, LA.

Drye, W. (2005, August 31). New Orleans flooded in wake of Hurricane Katrina. *National Geographic News*. http://news.nationalgeographic.com/news/2005/08 /0831_050831_katrina_flooding.html.

Du Bois, W. E. B. (1899/1996). *The Philadelphia negro: A social study*. Philadelphia, PA: University of Pennsylvania Press.

————. (1903/2007). *The souls of black folk* (B. H. Edwards, Ed.). Oxford, UK: Oxford University Press.

Editorial Board. (2010, October 16). Trapped in jail purgatory after Hurricane Katrina: An editorial. *The Times-Picayune*. www.nola.com/opinions/index.ssf/2010/10 /trapped_in_jail_purgatory_afte.html.

Ellison, R. (1952). *Invisible man*. New York, NY: Vintage Books.

Equitable Trust. (2014). Home page: www.equitableco.com/investment-advisory /equity-investing/assets.

European Commission. (2016, June). *Forced displacement—refugees and internally displaced persons (IDPs)* (Echo Fact Sheet). Brussels, Belgium: Author. http:// ec.europa.eu/echo/files/aid/countries/factsheets/thematic/refugees_en.pdf.

Fabelo, T., Thompson, M. D., Plotkin, M., Carmichael, D., Marchbanks, M. P., III & Booth, E. A. (2011, July). *Breaking schools' rules: A statewide study of how discipline relates to students' success and juvenile justice involvement*. New York, NY: Council of State Governments Justice Center. http://knowledgecenter.csg.org/kc/content /breaking-schools-rules-statewide-study.

Fausset, R. & Southall, A. (2015, October 26). Video shows officer flipping student in South Carolina, prompting inquiry. *The New York Times*. www.nytimes.com /2015/10/27/us/officers-classroom-fight-with-student-is-caught-on-video.html?_ r = 0.

Fellner, J. (2008). *Prisoner abuse: How different are U.S. prisons?* New York, NY: Human Rights Watch. www.hrw.org/english/docs/2004/05/14/usdom8583.htm.

Fenske, M. (2007). Micro, macro, agency: Historical ethnography as cultural anthropology practice [translated by J. Bendix]. *Journal of Folklore Research, 44*, 67–99.

Ferguson, A. (2000). *Bad boys*. Ann Arbor, MI: University of Michigan Press.

Ferguson, B. (2013, January). *RSD skews its performance score by omitting nearly 20% of schools*. Louisiana: Research on Reforms. www.researchonreforms.org/html /documents/RSDSkewsResults.pdf.

Ferriss, S. (2012, September 28). Florida to close controversial juvenile detention center. *Youth Services International—News and Investigations*. www.publicintegrity.org /news/Youth-Services-International.

Fields, G. (2005, May 18). As inmates age, a prison carpenter builds more coffins. *The Wall Street Journal*. www.wsj.com/articles/SB111637661650736440.

Figlio, D. (2006). Testing, crime and punishment. *Journal of Public Economics, 90*, 837–851.

Finch, S. (2002, May 5). "School safety net also seen as a trap." *The Times Picayune*, pp. B1, B4.

Fisher, I. (1993, November 24). Kelly bans choke holds by officers. *The New York Times*. www.nytimes.com/1993/11/24/nyregion/kelly-bans-choke-holds-by-officers.html.

Forte, L. (1996). Numbers missing for twenty-one schools. *Catalyst Chicago* (June).

Foti, C. (2001). Let's save the children [Letter to the Editor]. *The Louisiana Weekly* (December 17–23).

———. (2002). Honoring 10 New Directions graduates. *The Louisiana Weekly*.

Foucault, M. (1979/1995). *Discipline and punish: The birth of the prison*. New York, NY: Vintage Books.

Freeman, R. (1992). Crime and the employment of disadvantaged youth. In W. Vroman & G. Peterson (Eds.), *Urban labor markets and job opportunities*. Washington, DC: Urban Institute.

Freudenberg, N. & Ruglis, J. (2007). Reframing school dropout as a public health issue. *Preventing Chronic Disease: Public Health Research, Practice, and Policy, 4*(4).

Frey, S. (2013, December 31). Largest school districts vary widely in use of 'willful defiance' to suspend students. *EdSource*. https://edsource.org/today/2013/largest-school-districts-vary-widely-in-use-of-willful-defiance-to-suspend-students/54381# .UwaBrP1FM8M.

———. (2014, February 26). San Francisco Unified eliminates 'willful defiance' as a reason to expel or suspend students. *EdSource*. https://edsource.org/2014/san-francisco-unified-eliminates-willful-defiance-as-a-reason-to-expel-or-suspend-students/58105# .U2PrF_3iw8M.

Fuentes, A. (2005, September 19). Failing students, rising profits. *The Nation.* www .thenation.com/article/failing-students-rising-profits/.

Furness, A. (Host). (2002a). *Exodus Live* [radio series]. New Orleans, LA: WBYU.

——. (2002b). New Directions program comes under fire. *The Louisiana Weekly* (April 15–22), pp. A1, A8.

Fussell, E. (2007, December). Constructing New Orleans: A population history of New Orleans. *Journal of American History, 94,* 846–855.

Gabor, A. (2015, August 22). The myth of the New Orleans school makeover. *The New York Times.* www.nytimes.com/2015/08/23/opinion/sunday/the-myth-of-the-new-orleans-school-makeover.html.

Garland, D. (2001a). *The culture of control: Crime and social order in contemporary society.* Chicago, IL: University of Chicago Press.

——. (2001b). Introduction: The meaning of mass imprisonment. In D. Garland (Ed.), *Mass imprisonment: Social causes and consequences.* London, UK: Sage.

Gates, H. L., Jr. (2014, January 6). How many slaves landed in the US? *The Root.* www .theroot.com/articles/history/2014/01/how_many_slaves_came_to_america_fact_ vs_fiction/.

Geertz, C. (1973). *The interpretation of cultures: Selected essays.* New York, NY: Basic Books.

Georgia Public Radio. (2013, January 11). Prisons for profit. *Religion & Ethics News-Weekly.* Public Broadcasting System. www.gpb.org/television/shows/religion-ethics-newsweekly/episode/2609e0bc-6ff8–44f9–8d5a-9f6728037bd6.

Gerharz, B. & Hong, S. (2006). Down by law: Orleans Parish Prison before and after Katrina. *Dollars & Sense* (Boston, MA). www.dollarsandsense.org/archives /2006/0306gerharzhong.html.

Germany, K. (2007). *New Orleans after the promises: Poverty, citizenship and the search for the Great Society.* Athens, GA: University of Georgia Press.

Giroux, H. (2003). Foreword: Governing through crime and the pedagogy of punishment. In K. Saltman & D. Gabbard (Eds.), *Education as enforcement: The militarization and corporatization of schools.* New York, NY: Routledge.

——. (2011a). Shattered bonds: Youth in a suspect society and the politics of disposability. *PowerPlay, 3*(1).

——. (2011b). *Zombie politics and culture in the age of casino capitalism.* New York, NY: Peter Lang.

Glaser, B. (2001). *The grounded theory perspective: Conceptualization contrasted with description.* Mill Valley, CA: Sociology Press.

——. (2002). Constructivist grounded theory? *Forum: Qualitative Social Research, 3*(3), article 12.

Glaser, B. & Strauss, A. (1967). *The discovery of grounded theory: Strategies for qualitative research.* Chicago, IL: Aldine.

Glaze, L. & Parks, E. (2012, November 29). *Correctional populations in the United States, 2011* (NCJ 239972). Washington, DC: U.S. Department of Justice, Office of Justice Programs, Bureau of Justice Statistics.

Goffman, A. (2014). *On the run: Fugitive life in an American city.* Chicago, IL: University of Chicago Press.

Goldberg, E. & Evans, L. (1997). *The prison industrial complex and the global economy.* Berkeley, CA: Prison Activist Resource Center.

Goodman, A. (2005, September 27). After the hurricane: Where have all the prisoners gone? More than 500 from New Orleans jail still unaccounted for [radio transcript]. *Democracy Now.* www.democracynow.org/2005/9/27/after_the_hurricane_where_have_all.

Goodman, A. & Gonzalez, J. (2013, October 23). Prisoners for profit: Despite widespread abuse, private juvenile jail firm expands empire. *Democracy Now.* www.democracynow.org/2013/10/23/prisoners_of_profit_despite_widespread_abuse.

Goodman, A. & Gonzalez, J. (2014, February 4). Kids for cash: Inside one of the nation's most shocking juvenile justice scandals. *Democracy Now.* https://kpfa.org/program/democracy-now-9am/page/68/.

Gordon, R., Piana, L. D. & Keleher, T. (2001). *Facing the consequences: An examination of racial discrimination in U.S. public schools.* Oakland, CA: Applied Research Center.

Green, E. (2013a, November 11). Pre-K suspensions common in Maryland schools. *The Baltimore Sun.* www.baltimoresun.com/news/maryland/education/blog/bal-prek-suspensions-common-in-maryland-schools-20140123-story.html.

———. (2013b, November 15). City principal say pre-K suspensions are a matter of safety. *The Baltimore Sun.* www.baltimoresun.com/news/maryland/education/blog/bal-principal-pre-k-suspensions-20131115-story.html.

Green, J. L. (2014). Can bioinformed design promote healthy indoor ecosystems? *Indoor Air, 24,* 113–115.

Greenfield, S. (2016). Simple Justice: A criminal defense blog. http://blog.simplejustice.us/2013/05/09/schools-have-rules-tuck-your-shirt-in-or-else-edition/.

Gregory, J. (2012). Internal migration: Twentieth century and beyond. In L. Dumenil (Ed.), *Oxford encyclopedia of American social history.* New York, NY: Oxford University Press.

Hamilton v. Morial, 644 F.2d 351 (5th Cir. 1981).

Harden, K. D. (2013, March 4). Panel reflects on integration era. *The Advocate.* http://theadvocate.com/news/5313406–123/jesuit-marks-50th-anniversary-of.

Harlow, C. W. (2003, January). *Education and correctional populations* (Special Report NCJ 195670). Washington, DC: U.S. Department of Justice, Office of Justice Programs, Bureau of Justice Statistics. www.bjs.gov/content/pub/pdf/ecp.pdf.

Haygood, W. & Tyson, A. S. (2005, September 15). "It was as if all of us were already pronounced dead." *The Washington Post.* www.washingtonpost.com/wp-dyn/content/article/2005/09/14/AR2005091402655.html.

Heilig, J. V. (2015, August). *Should Louisiana and the Recovery School District receive accolades for being last and nearly last?* (Policy Brief). Tucson, AZ: Network for Public Education. www.networkforpubliceducation.org/2015/08/policy_brief_louisiana/#_edn15.

Heyer, R. & Wagner, P. (2004). *Too big to ignore: How counting people in prisons distorted Census 2000.* Northampton, MA: Prison Policy Initiative. www.prisonersofthecensus .org/toobig/datasearch.php.

Hirsch, A. (Ed.). (1992). *Creole New Orleans: Race and Americanization.* Baton Rouge, LA: Louisiana State University Press.

Hirsch, A., Dietrich, S., Landau, R., Schneider, P., Ackelsberg, I., Bernstein-Baker, J. & Hohenstein, J. (2002). *Every door closed: Barriers facing parents with criminal records.* Washington, DC: Center for Law and Social Policy and Community Legal Services.

Hirschfield, P. (2008). Preparing for prison? The criminalization of school discipline in the USA. *Theoretical Criminology, 12,* 79–101.

Hirschfield, P. & Celinska, K. (2011). Beyond fear: Sociological perspectives on the criminalization of school discipline. *Sociology Compass, 5,* 1–12.

Holzer, H., Raphael, S. & Stoll, M. (2003, May). *Employment barriers facing ex-offenders.* Paper presented at Urban Institute Reentry Roundtable, New York University Law School, New York, NY. www.urban.org/uploadedpdf/410855_ holzer.pdf.

Huffington Post. (2010, March 18). Christopher Lloyd, cop in taped beating of special ed student, jailed on rape charge. www.huffingtonpost.com/2009/10/09/christopher-lloyd-cop-who_n_315445.html.

Human Rights Watch. (2005, October 12). *Louisiana: Justice obstructed, not restored.* New York, NY: Author. www.hrw.org/news/2005/10/12/louisiana-justice-obstructed-not-restored.

Hunter, G. & Wagner, P. (2007). Prisons, politics, and the census. In T. Herivel and P. Wright (Eds.), *Prison profiteers: Who makes money from mass incarceration.* New York, NY: New Press.

Hyde, L. (1998). *Trickster makes this world: Mischief, myth and art.* New York, NY: North Point Press.

IHS Research. (2013, July 17). *High-profile shootings spur rapid growth of market for US school security system integration* (Press Release). https://technology.ihs.com/488177 /high-profile-shootings-spur-rapid-growth-of-market-for-us-school-security-system-integration.

International Committee of the Red Cross. (2000, June). *Internally displaced persons: The mandate and role of the International Committee of the Red Cross* (International Review of the Red Cross No. 838). www.icrc.org/eng/resources/documents /misc/57jqhr.htm.

Jackson, P. (1968/1990). *Life in classrooms.* New York, NY: Teachers College Press.

James, N. & McCallion, G. (2013, June 26). *School resource officers: Law enforcement officers in schools.* Washington, DC: Library of Congress, Congressional Research Service. www.fas.org/sgp/crs/misc/R43126.pdf.

Janssen, K. & Gorner, J. (2009, October 9). Dolton cop caught on camera in student's beating is in jail on rape charge. *Chicago Tribune.* http://articles.chicagotribune .com/2009-10-09/news/0910080737_1_charles-lloyd-jail-camera.

Johnson, T., Boyden, J. & Pittz, W. (2001). *Racial profiling and punishment in U.S. public schools: How zero tolerance and high stakes testing subvert academic excellence and racial equity.* Oakland, CA: Applied Research Center.

Jones v. Gusman, No. 2:12-cv-00859-LMA-ALC, 2013 WL 2458817 (E.D. La. Jun. 6, 2013).

Judah, E. H. (2004). *Criminal justice: Retribution vs. restoration.* Binghamton, NY: Haworth Press.

Juvenile Justice Project of Louisiana. (2004–2008). Louisiana Center for Children's Rights, New Orleans. www.laccr.org/press-room/.

———. (2011, November 29). New Orleans school suspends students for singing (Community Briefs: South). *Equal Voice: America's Family Story.* www.equalvoiceforfamilies .org/new-orleans-school-suspends-ten-students-for-singing-in-cafeteria/.

Karp, S. (2010). Suspensions down in CPS, but stats for black boys still highest. *Catalyst Chicago* (June).

Katz, A. & Columbus, D. (2012, December 14). Allan Katz and Danae Columbus: Consent decree will eventually improve jail. *Uptown Messenger.* http://uptownmessenger .com/2012/12/allan-katz-and-danae-columbus-consent-decree-will-eventually- improve-jail/.

Katznelson, I. (1976). The crisis of the capitalist city: Urban politics and social control. In W. Hawley & M. Lipsky (Eds.), *Theoretical perspectives on urban politics.* Englewood Cliffs, NJ: Prentice Hall.

Kearney, M., Harris, B., Jácome, E. & Parker, L. (2014). *Ten economic facts about crime and incarceration in the United States* (Policy Memo). Washington, DC: Hamilton Project, Brookings Institution.

Kebhaj, S., Shahidinia, N., Testa, A. & Williams, J. (2013). Collateral damage & the War on Drugs: Estimating the effect of zero tolerance policies on drug arrest rates, 1975–2002. *The Public Purpose, 9,* 1–25. www.american.edu/spa/publicpurpose /upload/2013_Collateral-Damage.pdf.

Keen, C. (2006, June 12). Schools suspend poor students to raise test scores, study shows. *University of Florida News.* http://news.ufl.edu/archive/2006/06/schools- suspend-poor-students-to-raise-test-scores-study-shows.html.

Khadaroo, S. T. (2014, March 1). New Orleans goes all in on charter schools. Is it showing the way? *The Christian Science Monitor.* www.csmonitor.com/USA/2014/0301 /New-Orleans-goes-all-in-on-charter-schools.-Is-it-showing-the-way.

Kim, C., Losen, D. & Hewitt, D. (2010). *The school-to-prison-pipeline: Structuring legal reform.* New York, NY: New York University Press.

Kimball, M. (2012, April 20). Louis Armstrong, the Colored Waifs' Home & Milne Boys Home [blog post]. New Orleans, LA: Preservation Resource Center. http:// blog.prcno.org/2012/04/20/louis-armstrong-the-colored-waifs-home-milne-boys- home/.

Kimmett, C. (2015, August 28). 10 years after Katrina, New Orleans' all-charter school system has proven a failure. *In These Times.* http://inthesetimes.com/article/18352/10- years-after-katrina-new-orleans-all-charter-district-has-proven-a-failur.

King, R. H. (2012). *From the bottom of the heap: The autobiography of Black Panther Robert Hillary King.* Oakland, CA: PM Press.

Kirp, D. (1982). *Just schools: The idea of racial equality in American education.* Berkeley, CA: University of California Press.

Kozol, J. (1991/2012). *Savage inequalities: Children in America's schools.* New York, NY: Crown.

Krupa, M. & Donze, F. (2010, February 6). Mitch Landrieu claims New Orleans mayor's office in a landslide. *The Times-Picayune.* www.nola.com/politics/index .ssf/2010/02/mitch_landrieu_claims_new_orle.html.

Kupchik, A. (2010). *Homeroom security: School discipline in an age of fear.* New York, NY: New York University Press.

Kupchik, A. & Bracy, N. L. (2010). To protect, serve and mentor: Police officers in public schools. In T. Monahan & R. Torres (Eds.), *Schools under surveillance: Cultures of control in public education.* New Brunswick, NJ: Rutgers University Press.

Kupchik, A. & Monahan, T. (2006). The new American school: Preparation for postindustrial discipline. *British Journal of Sociology of Education, 27,* 617–632.

Kurgan, L. (2009). *Justice Re-investment New Orleans.* Spatial Information Design Lab, Columbia University. http://spatialinformationdesignlab.org/sites/default /files/publication_pdfs/JR_NewOrleans.pdf.

Kurgan, L. (2013). *Close up at a distance: Mapping, technology and politics.* New York, NY: Zone Books.

Lacour, G. (2015, October 28). 'Disturbing' arrest of black S. Carolina student sparks federal, local probes. *Reuters.* www.reuters.com/article/us-south-carolina-police-idUSKCN0SL02320151028.

Ladson-Billings, G. (2001). America still eats her young. In W. Ayers, B. Dohrn & R. Ayers (Eds.), *Zero tolerance: Resisting the drive for punishment in our schools.* New York, NY: New Press.

Lee, E. (1966). A theory of migration. *Demography, 3,* 47–57.

Lee, S. (2012, June 20). By the numbers: The U.S.'s growing for-profit detention industry. *ProPublica.* www.propublica.org/article/by-the-numbers-the-u.s.s-growing-for-profit-detention-industry.

Lehr, C. A., Johnson, D. R., Bremer, C. D., Cosio, A. & Thompson, M. (2004, May). *Essential tools: Increasing rates of school completion: Moving from policy and research to practice.* Minneapolis, MN: National Center on Secondary Education and Transition, Institute on Community Integration, University of Minnesota.

Leonard, J. (2010, February 10). 'Pizza thief' walks the line. *Los Angeles Times.* http:// articles.latimes.com/2010/feb/10/local/la-me-pizzathief10–2010feb10.

Lewis, E. (2002). Letter to the editor. *The Louisiana Weekly* (June).

Lewis, P. (2003, June). *New Orleans: The making of an urban landscape.* Santa Fe, NM: Center for American Places.

Liu, A. & Holmes, N. (2010, August 28). The state of New Orleans. *The New York Times.* www.nytimes.com/2010/08/29/opinion/29liu.html?_r=0.

Lohman, J. & Shepard, A. (2006, November). *School security technologies* (OLR Research Report 2006-R-0668). Hartford, CT: Connecticut General Assembly. www.cga.ct.gov/2006/rpt/2006-R-0668.htm.

Lohr, D. (2016, January 20). Man hired to remove Confederate monuments in New Orleans has $200,000 Lamborghini torched. *The Huffington Post*. www.huffingtonpost.com/entry/confederate-monuments-new-orleans_us_569f9ec2e4b0fca5ba760b0f.

Losen, D. (2011, October). *Discipline policies, successful schools, and racial justice.* Boulder, CO: National Educational Policy Center, School of Education, University of Colorado. http://nepc.colorado.edu/files/NEPC-SchoolDiscipline.pdf.

Losen, D. & Edley, C. (2001). The role of law in policing abusive disciplinary practices: Why school discipline is a civil rights issue. In W. Ayers, B. Dohrn & R. Ayers (Eds.), *Zero tolerance: Resisting the drive for punishment in our schools.* New York, NY: New Press.

Losen, D. & Gillespie, J. (2012, August). *Opportunities suspended: The disparate impact of disciplinary exclusion from school.* Los Angeles, CA: Center for Civil Rights Remedies, Civil Rights Project, University of California.

Losen, D., Hodson, C., Keith, M., II, Morrison, K. & Belway, S. (2015, February). *Are we closing the school discipline gap?* Los Angeles, CA: Center for Civil Rights Remedies, Civil Rights Project, University of California.

Losen, D. & Martinez, T. (2013, April). *Out of school & off track: The overuse of suspensions in American middle and high schools.* Los Angeles, CA: Center for Civil Rights Remedies, Civil Rights Project, University of California.

Losen, D. & Skiba, R. (2010, September). *Suspended education: Urban middle schools in crisis.* Los Angeles, CA: Center for Civil Rights Remedies, Civil Rights Project, University of California.

Louisiana Department of Education. (2001–2002). School performance label, growth label, corrective action status, and rewards eligibility by district. Retrieved October 9, 2003, from www.leadr.info/runreport.php?did = 149372.

———. (2002). District performance score (DPS) sorted by 2002 K–12. *District Accountability Report.* Retrieved October 9, 2003, from www.doe.state.la.us/lde/pair/1355.html.

———. (2002–2003). School report cards: Principal report card. www.louisianabelieves.com/data/reportcards/2003/.

———. (2003, January). 2001–2002 district composite report: Orleans Parish. www.louisianabelieves.com/data/files/CompReports/DCR0304/DCR036.pdf.

———. (2004, April). 2002–2003 district composite report: Orleans Parish. http://files.eric.ed.gov/fulltext/ED483660.pdf.

———. (2005, April). 2004–2005 district composite report: Orleans Parish. www.louisianabelieves.com/data/files/CompReports/DCR0304/DCR036.pdf.

———. (2013, October). Multiple statistics by site for elementary/secondary school students.

Louisiana Public Health Institute. (2007, January 11). 2006 Louisiana Health and Population Survey: Survey report. Orleans Parish. *Louisiana Health and Population*

Survey. www.popest.org/popestla2006/files/PopEst_Orleans_SurveyReport_01_11_07.pdf.

Louisiana School Report Card. (2002–2003). Louisiana Educational Assessment Program, LEAP. www.louisianabelieves.com/data/reportcards/.

Louisiana Schools. (2002, October). SIS report. Retrieved September 15, 2003, from www.louisianaschools.net.

Louisiana Weekly. (2002, July 14–20). [photograph]. New Orleans, LA.

Loury, G. (2008). *Race, incarceration, and American values*. Cambridge, MA: MIT Press.

Lyon, D. (1994). *The electronic eye: The rise of the surveillance society*. Minneapolis, MN: University of Minnesota Press.

Lyons, W. & Drew, J. (2006). *Punishing schools: Fear and citizenship in American public education*. Ann Arbor, MI: University of Michigan Press.

MacLeod, J. (1987). *Ain't no makin' it: Leveled aspirations in a low–income neighborhood*. Boulder, CO: Westview Press.

Mallik-Kane, K., Parthasarathy, B. & Adams, W. (2012, September). *Examining growth in the federal prison population 1998 to 2010*. Washington, DC: Urban Institute.

Manza, J. & Uggen, C. (2008). *Locked out: Felon disenfranchisement and American democracy*. New York, NY: Oxford University Press.

Marsalis, W. (2015, December 15). Why New Orleans should take down Robert E. Lee's statue. *The Times-Picayune*. www.nola.com/politics/index.ssf/2015/12/confederate_monuments_new_orle_6.html.

Massey, D. & Denton, N. (1993). *American apartheid: Segregation and the making of the underclass*. Cambridge, MA: Harvard University Press.

Matthews, F. (1977). *The quest for an American sociology*. Montreal, Canada: McGill–Queen's University Press.

Mauer, M. (1999). *Race to incarcerate*. New York, NY: New Press.

Mauer, M. & Chesney-Lind, M. (Eds.). (2002). *Invisible punishment: The collateral consequences of mass imprisonment*. New York, NY: New Press

McCloskey, F. (2011, April 28). America's jobless men: Decline of the working man. *The Economist*. www.economist.com/node/18618613/print.

McCulley, R. (2006, June 18). The crime that stunned New Orleans. *Time Magazine*. http://content.time.com/time/nation/article/0,8599,1205340,00.html.

Meiners, E. R. (2007). *Right to be hostile: Schools, prisons, and the making of public enemies*. New York, NY: Routledge.

Molnar, M. (2013, September 24). Districts invest in new measures to boost security. *Education Week*. www.edweek.org/ew/articles/2013/09/25/05security_ep.h33.html.

Monahan, R. (2010, July 6). Schoolkids' suspensions through the roof: Expert says 40% rise in 'major crisis' in discipline. *Daily News* (New York). www.nydailynews.com/new-york/education/schoolkids-suspensions-roof-expert-40-rise-major-crisis-discipline-article-1.464043.

Monahan, T. (2006a). The new American school: Preparation for post-industrial discipline. *British Journal of Sociology of Education, 27*, 617–631.

————. (2006b). The surveillance curriculum. In T. Monahan (Ed.), *Surveillance and security: Technological politics and power in everyday life*. New York, NY: Routledge.

Monahan, T. & Torres, R. (Eds.). (2010). *Schools under surveillance: Cultures of control in public education*. New Brunswick, NJ: Rutgers University Press.

Moore, L. (2010). *Black rage in New Orleans: Police brutality and African American activism from World War II to Hurricane Katrina*. Baton Rouge, LA: Louisiana State University Press.

Mora, R. & Christianakis, M. (2013). Feeding the school-to-prison pipeline: The convergence of neoliberalism, conservatism and penal populism. *Journal of Educational Controversy, 7*(5).

Morgan Quitno Press. (2003, September 25). *Results of the 2003 Smartest State Award* (Press Release). Lawrence, KS: Author. www.morganquitno.com/edpress03 .htm.

Morse, E. & Glazer, D. (2002, May 17). Alternative school's supporters dispute criticism. *The Louisiana Weekly*.

Mukherjee, R. J. (2007). *Criminalizing the classroom: The over-policing of New York City schools*. New York, NY: New York Civil Liberties Union.

Mullins, D. (2014, April 4). New Orleans to be home to nation's first all-charter school district. *Al Jazeera America*. http://america.aljazeera.com/articles/2014/4/4/new-orleans-charterschoolseducationreformracesegregation.html.

Murphy, E. & Dingwall, R. (2001). The ethics of ethnography. In P. Atkinson, A. Coffey, S. Delamont, J. Lofland & L. Lofland (Eds.), *Handbook of ethnography* (pp. 339–351). Los Angeles, CA: Sage.

National Association for the Advancement of Colored People [NAACP]. (2011, April). *New NAACP report ties state spending on prisons to low education achievement* (Press Release). Baltimore, MD: Author. www.naacp.org/press/entry/naacp-report-ties-state-spending-on-prisons-to-low-education-achievement.

————. (2012). Criminal justice fact sheet. www.naacp.org/pages/criminal-justice-fact-sheet.

————. (2009–2016). Criminal justice fact sheet. www.naacp.org/pages/criminal-justice-fact-sheet.

National Center for Education Statistics. (2004). Serious disciplinary actions taken by public schools. Indicators of school crime and safety. Violence and crime at school. Public school reports. Washington, DC: U.S. Department of Education. Retrieved August 2, 2004, from http://nces.ed.gov/pubs2004/crime03/8.asp? nav = 2.

————. (2011). Indicators of school crime and safety. Violent deaths at school and away from school. Washington, DC: U.S. Department of Education. Retrieved February 3, 2015, from http://nces.ed.gov/programs/crimeindicators/crimeindicators2011 /ind_01.asp.

————. (2013). Fast facts. Washington, DC: U.S. Department of Education. http:// nces.ed.gov/fastfacts/display.asp?id = 372.

———. (2014a). Rates of school crime. Washington, DC: U.S. Department of Education. http://nces.ed.gov/programs/coe/pdf/Indicator_CLD/coe_cld_2014_04 .pdf.

———. (2014b). Table 203.10: Enrollment in public elementary and secondary schools, by level and grade: Selected years, fall 1980 through fall 2024. *Digest of Education Statistics.* Washington, DC: U.S. Department of Education. http://nces.ed.gov /programs/digest/d14/tables/dt14_203.10.asp.

National Public Radio. (2012, June 5). How Louisiana became the world's 'prison capital.' *Fresh Air.* www.npr.org/2012/06/05/154352977/how-louisiana-became-the-worlds-prison-capital.

National Research Council. (2014). Crime and imprisonment rates 1960–2008. In *The growth of incarceration in the United States: Exploring causes and consequences.* Washington, DC: National Academies Press.

National School Boards Association. (1994). *Violence in schools: How America's school boards are safeguarding our children.* Alexandria, VA: Author.

National Substance Abuse and Mental Health Services Administration. (2008). *Results from the 2007 National Survey on Drug Use and Health: National findings* (Office of Applied Studies, DHHS Publication no. SMA 08–4343). Rockville, MD: SAMHSA.

Natural Resources Defense Council. (2011, December 29). *Katrina's toxic legacy.* www .nrdc.org/living/healthreports/katrinas-toxic-legacy.asp.

New Orleans Public Schools. (2001, October 1). Interagency Agreement.

Noguera, P. (1995). Preventing and producing violence. *Harvard Educational Review,* 65, 189–212.

———. (2001). Finding safety where we least expect it. In W. Ayers, B. Dohrn & R. Ayers (Eds.), *Zero tolerance: Resisting the drive for punishment in our schools.* New York, NY: New Press.

———. (2003). Schools, prisons, and social implications of punishment: Rethinking disciplinary practice. *Theory Into Practice,* 42(4).

———. (2008a). *The trouble with black boys: And other reflections on race, equity and the future of public education.* San Francisco, CA: Jossey-Bass.

———. (2008b). What discipline is for: Connecting students to the benefits of learning. In M. Pollack (Ed.), *Everyday antiracism: Getting real about race in school.* New York, NY: New Press.

Nolan, K. (2011). *Police in the hallways: Discipline in an urban high school.* Minneapolis, MN: University of Minnesota Press.

Oakes, J. (1985). *Keeping track: How schools structure inequality.* New Haven, CT: Yale University Press.

Olsen, L. (2010, August 30). 5 years after Katrina, storm's death toll remains a mystery. *Houston Chronicle.* www.chron.com/news/nation-world/article/5-years-after-Katrina-storm-s-death-toll-remains-1589464.php.

Orfield, G. & Eaton, S. (1996). *Dismantling desegregation: The quiet reversal of Brown v. Board of Education.* New York, NY: New Press.

Orleans Parish School Board. (2002, June 24). [Minutes.] Orleans Parish School Board meeting, New Orleans, LA.

Packaged Facts. (2000). *The U.S. school security market*. Rockville, MD: Market-Research.com. http://academic.marketresearch.com/.

Palmie, S. & Stewart, C. (2013, November 20). *Beyond the historic turn: Toward an anthropology of history*. Panel session at American Anthropological Association Annual Meeting, Chicago, IL.

Parke, R. & Clarke-Stewart, A. (2003). Effects of parental incarceration on children: Perspectives, promises, and policies. In J. Travis & M. Waul (Eds.), *Prisoners once removed: The impact of incarceration and reentry on children, families, and communities* (pp. 189–232). Washington, DC: Urban Institute Press.

Peters, E. (1995). Prison before the prison: The ancient and medieval worlds. In N. Morris & D. Rothman (Eds.), *The Oxford history of the prison: The practice of punishment in Western society*. New York, NY: Oxford University Press.

Peterson, R., Krino, L. & Hagan, J. (2006). *The many colors of crime: Inequalities of race, ethnicity, and crime in America*. New York, NY: New York University Press.

Pettit, B. (2012). *Invisible men: Mass incarceration and the myth of black progress*. New York, NY: Russell Sage Foundation.

Pettit, B. & Western, B. (2004). Mass imprisonment and the life course: Race and class inequality in U.S. incarceration. *American Sociological Review, 69*, 151–169.

Pew Center on the States. (2008). *One in 100: Behind bars in America 2008*. Washington, DC: Pew Charitable Trusts.

———. (2009). *One in 31: The long reach of American corrections*. Washington, DC: Pew Charitable Trusts.

Pew Charitable Trusts. (2015, August). *Federal drug sentencing laws bring high cost, low return*. Washington, DC: Author. www.pewtrusts.org/en/research-and-analysis/issue-briefs/2015/08/federal-drug-sentencing-laws-bring-high-cost-low-return.

Pitts, T. (1999). *Cops and classrooms: How school security spending affects school quality*. Oakland, CA: Applied Research Center.

Planty, M., Hussar, W., Snyder, T., Kena, G., KewalRamani, A., Kemp, J., Bianco, K. & Dinkes, R. (2009). *The condition of education 2009* (NCES 2009–081). Washington, DC: U.S. Department of Education, National Center for Education Statistics, Institute of Education Sciences.

Platt, A. (1969). *The child savers*. Chicago, IL: University of Chicago Press.

Polakow-Suransky, S. (2000). America's least wanted: Zero-tolerance policies and the fate of expelled students. In V. Polakow (Ed.), *The public assault on America's children: Poverty, violence, and juvenile justice*. New York, NY: Teachers College Press.

Press, E. & Washburn, J. (2002, December). The at-risk-youth industry. *The Atlantic Monthly*. www.theatlantic.com/magazine/archive/2002/12/the-at-risk-youth-industry/302645/.

Provine, D. M. (2011). Race and inequality in the War on Drugs. *Annual Review of Law and Social Science, 7*, 41–60.

Rainey, R. (2015, December 17). Lee Circle no more: New Orleans to remove 4 Confederate statues. *The Times-Picayune.* www.nola.com/politics/index.ssf/2015/12/confederate_monuments_lee_circ.html.

Rand, M. R. (2009, September). *National Crime Victimization Survey: Criminal victimization, 2008* (NCJ 227777). Washington, DC: U.S. Department of Justice, Office of Justice Programs, Bureau of Justice Statistics. www.bjs.gov/content/pub/pdf/cv08.pdf.

Recovery School District. (2006). Legislatively required plan. Retrieved September 13, 2007, from www.nolapublicschools.net/rsdupdate.aspx?RSDU = 837—46k.

Regional Transit Authority. (2013). About the RTA. www.norta.com/About-the-RTA.aspx.

Richard, N. (2012). *Milne Boys Home: Historical land use analysis and future land use recommendations.* New Orleans, LA: University of New Orleans.

Ridgeway, J. & Casella, J. (2012, April 6). "Complete lawlessness" at Orleans Parish Prison. *Mother Jones.* www.motherjones.com/politics/2012/04/new-orleans-parish-prison-conditions-lawsuit-splc.

Rimer, S. (2004, January 4). Unruly students facing arrest, not detention. *The New York Times,* p. A1.

Rios, V. (2011). *Punished: Policing the lives of black and Latino boys.* New York, NY: New York University Press.

Robertson, C. (2016, February 20). For 45 years in prison, Louisiana man kept calm and held fast to hope. *The New York Times.* www.nytimes.com/2016/02/21/us/for-45-years-in-prison-louisiana-man-kept-calm-and-held-fast-to-hope.html.

Rodriguez, D. (2010). The disorientation of the teaching act: Abolition as pedagogical position. *Radical Teacher, 88*(Summer), 7–10.

Rogers Park Young Women's Action Team & NIA. (2013). Brain dead. *Suspension Stories.* www.suspensionstories.com/brain-dead/.

Ross, S. & Jackson, J. (1991). Teachers expectations for black males' and black females' academic achievement. *Personality and Social Psychology Bulletin, 17,* 78–82.

Rott, N. (2013, March 15). LA schools throw out suspensions for 'willful defiance.' *All Things Considered* (National Public Radio). www.npr.org/2013/05/15/184195877/l-a-schools-throw-out-suspensions-for-willful-defiance.

Ruffin v. Commonwealth, 62 Va. 790, 796 (Va. 1871).

S. Res. 638, 106th Cong., First Session. March 17. School Technology Center (1999) [enacted].

Saltman, K. (2003). Introduction. In K. Saltman & D. Gabbard (Eds.), *Education as enforcement: The militarization and corporatization of schools.* New York, NY: Routledge.

Saltman, K. & Gabbard, D. (Eds.). (2003). *Education as enforcement: The militarization and corporatization of schools.* New York, NY: Routledge.

Sandia National Laboratories. (1999). About Sandia. www.sandia.gov/about/index.html.

Schenwar, M. (2008, August 28). Slavery haunts America's plantation prisons. *Truthout*. http://truth-out.org/archive/component/k2/item/79840:slavery-haunts-americas-plantation-prisons.

Schept, J. (2015). *Progressive punishment: Job loss, jail growth, and the neoliberal logic of carceral expansion*. New York, NY: New York University Press.

Schiraldi, V. & Ziedenberg, J. (2001, September 1). *Schools and suspensions: Self-reported crime and the growing use of suspensions*. Washington, DC: Justice Policy Institute. www.justicepolicy.org/uploads/justicepolicy/documents/school_suspensions.pdf.

Schiraldi, V. & Ziedenberg, J. (2002). *Cellblocks or classrooms? The funding of higher education and corrections and its impact on African American men*. Washington, DC: Justice Policy Institute.

Schlossman, E. (1995). Delinquent children. In N. Morris & D. Rothman (Eds.), *The Oxford history of the prison: The practice of punishment in Western society*. New York, NY: Oxford University Press.

Schmitt, J. & Warner, K. (2010, November). *Ex-offenders and the labor market*. Washington, DC: Center for Economic and Policy Research. http://cepr.net/documents/publications/ex-offenders-2010–11.pdf.

Schwartz, J. & Miller, R. (2008, October 10). *An operational review of the Orleans Parish jails* (TA no. 08J1109). Washington, DC: U.S. Department of Justice, National Institute of Corrections Technical Assistance.

Scruggs, L. (2015). *Separation of church and school: Guidance for public charter schools using religious facilities*. Washington, DC: National Alliance for Public Charter Schools.

Segura, L. (2011). Dispatch from Angola: Faith-based slavery in a Louisiana prison. *Colorlines*. Retrieved from http://colorlines.com/archives/2011/08/dispatch_from_angola_faith-based_slavery_in_a_louisiana_prison.html.

Sentencing Project. (2016). The lifetime likelihood of imprisonment. Racial Disparity. www.sentencingproject.org/.

Shaw, S. R. & Braden, J. P. (1990). Race and gender bias in the administration of corporal punishment. *School Psychology Review, 19*, 378–383.

Simerman, J. (2013, April 23). Sheriff Marlin Gusman: Don't hate the jailer; hate the jail. *The Times-Picayune*.

Simmons, L. (2007). Research off-limits and underground: Street corner methods for finding invisible students. *Urban Review, 39*, 319–347.

———. (2009a). The docile body in school space. In T. Monohan & R. Torres (Eds.), *Schools under surveillance: Cultures of control in public education*. New Brunswick, NJ: Rutgers University Press.

———. (2009b). End of the line: Tracing racial inequality from school to prison. *Race/Ethnicity: Multidisciplinary Global Contexts, 2*, 215–241.

———. (2012). Profiting from punishment: Public education and the school security market. *Social Justice Journal, 41*(4), 81–95.

Simon, J. (2007). *Governing through crime: How the War on Crime transformed American democracy and created a culture of fear*. New York, NY: Oxford University Press.

Sims, P. & Vaughn, D. (2014). *The state of public education in New Orleans.* New Orleans, LA: Cowen Institute for Public Education Initiatives, Tulane University.

Skiba, R. (2000). *Zero tolerance, zero evidence: An analysis of school disciplinary practice.* Bloomington, IL: University Education Policy Center.

———. (2001). When is disproportionality discrimination? In W. Ayers, B. Dohrn & R. Ayers (Eds.), *Zero tolerance: Resisting the drive for punishment in our schools.* New York, NY: New Press.

Skiba, R., Chung, C., Trachok, M., Baker, T., Sheya, A. & Hughes, R. (2012). Parsing disciplinary disproportionality: Contributions of interaction, student, and school characteristics to out-of-school suspension and expulsion. *American Educations Research Journal, 51,* 640–670.

Skiba, R. & Leone, P. (2001). Zero tolerance and school security measures: A failed experiment. In *Racial profiling and punishment in the U.S. public schools: How zero tolerance and high stakes testing subvert academic excellence and racial equity.* Oakland, CA: Applied Research Center.

Skiba, R., Michael, R., Nardo, C. & Peterson, R. (2002). The color of discipline: Sources of racial and gender disproportionality in school punishment. *Urban Review, 34,* 317–342.

Skiba, R. & Peterson, C. (1999, January). The dark side of zero tolerance: Can punishment lead to safe schools? *Phi Delta Kappan.* http://curry.virginia.edu/uploads /resourceLibrary/dark_zero_tolerance.pdf.

Skolnick, J. & Fyfe, J. (1993). *Above the law: Police and the excessive use of force.* New York, NY: Free Press.

Sojoyner, D. M. (2013). Black radicals make for bad citizens: Undoing the myth of the school-to-prison pipeline. *Berkeley Review of Education, 4,* 241–263.

———. (2014). Changing the lens: Moving away from the school-to-prison pipeline. In A. J. Nocella, P. Parmar & D. Stovall (Eds.), *From education to incarceration: Dismantling the school-to-prison pipeline.* New York, NY: Peter Lang.

Southern Education Foundation. (2015). *Low income students now a majority in the nation's public schools* (New Majority Research Bulletin). Atlanta, GA: Author. www.southerneducation.org/Our-Strategies/Research-and-Publications/New-Majority-Diverse-Majority-Report-Series/A-New-Majority-2015-Update-Low-Income-Students-Now.

Spring, J. (2000). *American education* (9th ed.). Boston, MA: McGraw-Hill.

State of California, Legislative Counsel. (2012). Education Code Section 48900–48927. Official California Legislative Information: California Education Codes. http:// leginfo.legislature.ca.gov/.

State of Louisiana, Office of Juvenile Justice. (2013). *History of juvenile justice in LA.* http://ojj.la.gov/.

Stearns, E., Moller, S., Blau, J. & Potochnick, S. (2007). Staying back and dropping out: The relationship between grade retention and school dropout. *Sociology of Education, 80,* 210–240.

Street, P. (2005). *Segregated schools: Educational apartheid in post civil-rights America.* New York, NY: Routledge.

Stuart, S. (2010). In loco parentis in the public schools: Abused, confused and in need of change. *University of Cincinnati Law Review, 78,* 969–1005.

Sturgis, S. (2014, March 13). *Institute Index: A brief history of the hell that is Louisiana's Angola prison.* Durham, NC: Institute for Southern Studies. www.southernstudies .org/2014/03/institute-index-a-brief-history-of-the-hell-that-i.html.

Sugrue, T. (1996). *The origins of the urban crisis: Race and inequality in postwar Detroit.* Princeton, NJ: Princeton University Press.

Sullivan, E. & Morgan, D. (2010, spring). *Pushed out: Harsh discipline in Louisiana schools denies the right to education.* New York, NY: National Economic and Social Rights Initiative & New Orleans, LA: Families and Friends of Louisiana's Incarcerated Children. www.njjn.org/uploads/digital-library/resource_1587.pdf.

Sum, A., Khatiwada, I., McLaughlin, J. & Palma, S. (2009). *The consequences of dropping out of school: Joblessness and jailing for high school dropouts and the high cost for taxpayers.* Boston, MA: Center for Labor Market Studies.

Sumter, M. (2008, August). The correctional work force faces challenges in the 21st century. *Research Notes.* American Correctional Association. www.aca.org/ACA_PROD_ IMIS/Docs/Corrections%20Today/ResearchNotes/ResearchNotes_Aug08.pdf.

Sundius, J. & Farneth, M. (2008). *Putting kids out of school: What's causing high suspension rates and why they are detrimental to students, schools, and communities.* Baltimore, MD: Open Society Institute.

SunTrust Equitable Securities. (1997). At-risk youth … A growth industry. *Youth Services/Juvenile Corrections Industry.* [Report to investors.]

Swanson, C. B. (2004). *Who graduates? Who doesn't? A statistical portrait of public high school graduation, class of 2001.* Washington, DC: Urban Institute.

Sweeten, G., Bushway, S. & Paternoster, R. (2009). Does dropping out of school mean dropping into delinquency? *Criminology, 47,* 47–91.

Telfair, J. & Shelton, T. (2012). Educational attainment as a social determinant of health. *North Carolina Medical Journal, 73,* 358–365.

Terriquez, V., Chlala, R. & Sacha, J. (2013). *The impact of punitive high school discipline policies on the postsecondary trajectories of young men* (California Young Adult Study Research Brief). Pathways to postsecondary success. Los Angeles, CA: UC/ ACCORD. http://pathways.gseis.ucla.edu/publications/Discipline_Report .pdf.

Thevenot, B. (2002, June 25). Alternative school to be closed. *The Times-Picayune.*

Think Progress. (2006, August 28). *Katrina timeline* (Special Report). Washington, DC: Center for American Progress. www.thinkprogress.org/katrina-timeline.

Times-Picayune. (2002, April 24). Certified teachers wanted [advertisement].

Tonry, M. (2004). *Thinking about crime: Sense and sensibility in American penal culture.* New York, NY: Oxford University Press.

———. (2013). Sentencing. Presentation at "Sentencing Reform in America: 1975–2025," the first Robina Institute Annual Conference, November 15–16, 2013, University of Minnesota Law School. www.robinainstitute.org/.

Travis, J., Solomon, A. L. & Waul, M. (2001). *From prison to home: The dimensions and consequences of prisoner reentry.* Washington, DC: Urban Institute Press.

Tuzzolo, E. (2007, fall). Homegrown heroes fight for support not security. *Education Organizing,* no. 28. Washington, DC: Center for Community Change. www.communitychange.org/.

Tuzzolo, E. & Hewitt, D. (2006). Rebuilding inequality: The re-emergence of the school-to-prison pipeline in New Orleans. *High School Journal, 90,* 59–68.

UCLA-IDEA. (2006). *Suspension and expulsion at a glance.* Los Angeles, CA: Institute for Democracy, Education, and Access.

United Nations Human Rights. (2016). Questions and answers about IDPs. UN Office of the High Commissioner. www.ohchr.org/EN/Issues/IDPersons/Pages/Issues.aspx.

U.S. Census Bureau. (2000a). Census Online Access. Retrieved September 15, 2003, from factfinder.census.gov/servlet/DTTable?_ts = 82166404913.

———. (2000b). Census Online Access [census tract 0071]. Retrieved September 15, 2003, from Tier2.census.gov/cgi-win/ctsl/tracbrws.exe.

———. (2005). General characteristics for Orleans Parish, Louisiana. *American Community Survey.* www.census.gov/programs-surveys/acs/.

———. (2013). QuickFacts. http://quickfacts.census.gov/qfd/states/00000.html.

U.S. Congress. (1999). H.R. 2034. Safe School Security Act of 1999. 106th Congress. (1999–2000). Introduced June 8, 1999. http://beta.congress.gov/.

U.S. Congressional Record. (2001, May 22–June 11). *Congressional Record.* House of Representatives. Government Printing Office. V. 147, part 7. 107 Congress.

U.S. Department of Education. (1996, September). Searches for drugs and weapons. In *Creating safe & drug-free schools: An action guide.* Washington, DC: Author. www.ed.gov/offices/OESE/SDFS.

———. (2001, October 10). *More than $38 million in grants going to communities to prevent violence among youth* (Press Release). Washington, DC: Author. www.ed.gov/PressReleases/.

———. (2002, September 26). *More than $80 million in grants goes to communities to prevent violence among youth* (Press Release). Washington, DC: Author. www.ed.gov/PressRelease/09-2002/09262002.html.

———. (2007). *The condition of education 2007* (NCES 2007–064). Washington, DC: U.S. Government Printing Office.

———. (2011). Office of Safe and Drug-Free Schools: Archived information. www2.ed.gov/about/offices/list/osdfs/index.html.

U.S. Department of Education, Office for Civil Rights. (1998, fall). *Elementary and secondary school rights compliance report: National and state projections, June 2000.* Washington, DC: Author.

————. (2014, March). *Civil Rights Data Collection: Data snapshot (school discipline)* (Issue Brief No. 1). Washington, DC: Author.

U.S. Department of Health and Human Services. (2005). *The 2005 HHS Poverty Guidelines: One version of the [U.S.] federal poverty measure.* Washington, DC: Author. http://aspe.hhs.gov/poverty/05poverty.shtml.

U.S. Department of Homeland Security. (2013). School safety. www.dhs.gov/school-safety.

U.S. Department of Justice. (2007, September 7). Office of Community Oriented Policing Services (COPS): Secure Our Schools grant announcement. http://cops .usdoj.gov/pdf/GrantAnnounce/2007SOSGranteeList.pdf.

————. (2008). *COPS FY2008 application guide: Secure Our Schools (SOS).* Washington, DC: Author. www.cops.usdoj.gov/html/funding/applying/SOSGuide_ e030827129.pdf.

————. (2011a). Statistical briefing book: Juveniles in corrections. Office of Justice Programs, Office of Juvenile Justice and Delinquency Prevention. www.ojjdp.gov /ojstatbb/corrections/qa08201.asp?qaDate = 2011.

————. (2011b). Statistical briefing book: Offending by juveniles. Office of Justice Programs, Office of Juvenile Justice and Delinquency Prevention. http://ojjdp.gov /ojstatbb/offenders/qa03105.asp?qaDate = 2011.

————. (2011c, September 8). *U.S. Department of Justice office announces over $13 million in school safety grants* (Press Release). Washington, DC: Author. www.cops.usdoj .gov/Default.asp?Item=2599.

————. (2013a). Office of Community Oriented Policing Services (COPS), Secure Our Schools (SOS) Grant Program. CFDA no. 16.710. www.k12grants.info /GrantDetails.aspx?gid = 14769.

————. (2013b). Prisoners and prisoner re-entry. www.justice.gov/archive/fbci /progmenu_reentry.html.

————. (2015, March 4). Justice Department announces findings of two civil rights investigations in Ferguson, Missouri. *Justice News.* www.justice.gov/opa/pr/justice-department-announces-findings-two-civil-rights-investigations-ferguson-missouri.

Valrey, J.R. (Host). (2006, August 3). *Flashpoints* [radio series]. Berkeley, CA: KPFA.

Vanacore, A. (2013, October 23). Blame for jail's problems to dominate sheriff's race. *The New Orleans Advocate.* www.theneworleansadvocate.com/.

Van Dijk, T.A., Goldberg, D.T. & Essed, P. (Eds). (2002). *Race critical theories: Text and context.* Malden, MA: Blackwell.

Vargas, R.A. (2012, December 11). After unveiling of proposed consent decree, Orleans sheriff disputes inmates' abuse claims. *The Times-Picayune.* www.nola.com/crime /index.ssf/2012/12/after_unveiling_of_proposed_co.html.

Vaughan, D., Mogg, L., Zimmerman, J. & O'Neill, T. (2011). *Transforming public education in New Orleans: The Recovery School District.* New Orleans, LA: Cowen Institute for Public Initiatives, Tulane University.

Vera Institute of Justice. (2014). Status Offense Reform Center and Center on Youth Justice, New York, NY. Home page: www.vera.org/. Contact: Vidhya Ananthakrishnan.

Vorrasi, J. & Garbarino, J. (2000). Poverty and youth violence: Not all risk factors are created equal. In V. Polakow (Ed.), *The public assault on America's children: Poverty, violence, and juvenile justice*. New York, NY: Teachers College Press.

Wacquant, L. (2001). Deadly symbiosis: When ghetto and prison meet and mesh. *Punishment and Society, 3*, 95–133.

———. (2008). *Urban outcasts: A comparative sociology of advanced marginality*. Malden, MA: Polity Press.

———. (2009). *Punishing the poor: The neoliberal government of social insecurity*. Durham, NC: Duke University Press.

———. (2010). Prisoner reentry as myth and ceremony. *Dialectical Anthropology, 34*, 605–620.

Wakefield, S. & Wildeman, C. (2014). *Children of the prison boom: Mass incarceration and the future of American inequality*. New York, NY: Oxford University Press.

Wald, J. & Kurlaender, M. (2003). Connected in Seattle? An exploratory study of student perceptions of discipline and attachments to teachers. In J. Wald & D. Losen (Eds.), *Deconstructing the school-to-prison pipeline* (New Directions for Youth Development, No. 99) (pp. 55–70). Hoboken, NJ: Jossey-Bass.

Wald, J. & Losen, D. (Eds.). (2003a). *Deconstructing the school-to-prison pipeline* (New Directions for Youth Development, No. 99). Hoboken, NJ: Jossey-Bass.

Wald, J., & Losen, D. (2003b, May). *Defining and redirecting a school-to-prison pipeline*. Paper presented at "Reconstructing the School-to-Prison Pipeline: Charting Intervention Strategies of Prevention and Support for Minority Children," a conference conducted by the Civil Rights Project, Harvard University, and the Institute on Race and Justice, Northwestern University, Cambridge, MA.

———. (2004). *Defining and redirecting a school-to-prison pipeline*. Paper presented at the "2004 Midwest Conference on the Dropout Crisis: Assessing the Problem and Confronting the Challenge," Civil Rights Project at Harvard University, Cambridge, MA.

Ware, W. (2011, July). *Locked up and out: Lesbian, gay, bisexual and transgender youth in Louisiana's juvenile justice system*. New Orleans, LA: Juvenile Justice Project of Louisiana. http://jjpl.org/.

Webster, R. (2012, April 2). Orleans sheriff faces class action suit for alleged prison abuse. *New Orleans City Business*. http://neworleanscitybusiness.com/blog/2012/04/02/orleans-sheriff-faces-class-action-suit-for-alleged-prison-abuse/.

Weis, L. & Fine, M. (Eds.). (1993). *Beyond silenced voices: Class, race, and gender in United States schools*. Albany, NY: State University of New York Press.

West, C. (2005, September 10). Exiles from a city and from a nation. *The Guardian*. www.theguardian.com/world/2005/sep/11/hurricanekatrina.comment.

West, H. (2010, June 23). *Prisoners at yearend 2009—advance counts* (NCJ 230189). Washington, DC: U.S. Department of Justice, Office of Justice Programs, Bureau of Justice Statistics.

Western, B. (2006). *Punishment and inequality in America.* New York, NY: Russell Sage Foundation.

Western, B., Pettit, B. & Guetzkow, J. (2002). Black economic progress in the era of mass imprisonment. In M. Mauer and M. Chesney-Lind (Eds.), *Invisible punishment: The collateral consequences of mass imprisonment.* New York, NY: New Press.

White House, Office of the Press Secretary. (1998, October 15). *Conference on school safety* (Press Release). Washington, DC: Author. http://inet.ed.gov/PressReleases /10–199/.

Wildeman, C. (2014). Mass incarceration. *Oxford Bibliographies.* www.oxfordbiblio graphies.com/.

Wilf, R. (2012, March). *Disparities in school discipline move students of color toward prison.* Washington, DC: Center for American Progress. www.americanprogress.org/issues /race/news/2012/03/13/11350/disparities-in-school-discipline-move-students-of-color-toward-prison/.

Williams, J. (2012, September 12). Despite state mandate to keep students in class, some schools continue to have high suspension rates. *The Lens.* http://thelensnola .org/2011/09/12/suspension-rates/.

Williams, R. (1977). *Marxism and literature.* New York, NY: Oxford University Press.

Willis, C. (2012, March 26). *School officials 'reassess' students' punishment for nasal spray.* Atlanta, GA: WSB-TV 2. www.wsbtv.com/news/news/local-education/5th-grade-students-suspended-over-nasal-spray/nLckS/.

Willis, P. (1977). *Learning to labor: How working class kids get working class jobs.* New York, NY: Columbia University Press.

Wilson, W. J. (1987). *The truly disadvantaged: The inner city, the underclass and public policy.* Chicago, IL: University of Chicago Press.

Winant, H. (2004). *The new politics of race: Globalism, difference, and justice.* Minneapolis, MN: University of Minnesota Press.

WWLTV. (2011, October 12). La. leads nation in high school dropouts [television news report]. www.wwltv.com/news/.

Yancey, G. & Butler, J. (2015, January 12). What's wrong with 'all lives matter'? *The New York Times.* http://opinionator.blogs.nytimes.com/2015/01/12/whats-wrong-with-all-lives-matter/.

Youth Services International. (2016). Home page: www.youthservices.com.

Yudof, M., Kirp, D., Levin, B. & Moran, R. (2002). *Educational policy and the law* (4th ed.). Belmont, CA: West-Thomson Learning.

Zimring, F. (2007). *The great American crime decline.* New York, NY: Oxford University Press.

Zweifler, R. & De Beers, J. (2002). The children left behind: How zero tolerance impacts our most vulnerable youth. *Michigan Journal of Race and Law, 8,* 191–220.

INDEX

absenteeism: ban on suspensions resulting in improved attendance records, 150; as basis for Prison School assignment, 86; of peers, 91–92; as status offense, 12, 86. *See also* exclusionary school discipline; status offenses and offenders

accountability/access problems: Hurricane Katrina and abused/lost/escaped/dead prisoners from OPP, 69, 107–108; and local prisons authorized to house Louisiana state inmates, 69, 159n7; lost school records, 17–19, 88; Prison School and, 8–10, 11, 117, 118–120, 121, 127; securitization of schools and, 118–119. *See also* police harassment and brutality; systemic concealment strategies

achievement ideology, 92

Adams, W., 32

adequate yearly progress (AYP), 37–38

Adler, P., 155

Adler, P.A., 155

African Americans: activism against police brutality in New Orleans, 109–110, 160n5; the color line and, 73, 74, 77, 92; and double consciousness, 74, 92; percentage of population, 32. *See also* black male bodies; black prison diaspora; incarceration rates for African American males; invisibility, racialized; police harassment and brutality; public schools; racism/racist ideologies

Alexander, Michelle, *The New Jim Crow*, 4, 5, 26, 63, 115

"all is data," 17, 18

alternative disciplinary schools: assignments to, as racially disproportionate, 123; charter schools differentiated from, 161n13; as conduit for school-to-jail pipeline, 119; disabled students overrepresented in, 123–124; disparities in, as civil rights issue, 124; isolation of students in, 119, 124; lack of access/accountability in, 8–10, 11, 117, 118–120, 121, 127; private, contracted by New Orleans School Board, 10, 134–135, 138; standardized testing and timing of assignments to, 124; suspension and expulsion of students and assignment to, 66, 123. *See also* Prison School

American Civil Liberties Union (ACLU), 21, 70, 103, 106–107, 150–151; and Hurricane Katrina aftermath in OPP, 107–108

Anderson, N., 146

Anderson, Nels, *The Hobo*, 157n6

Angola 3, 17, 80–82, 102, 109, 113, 159n1

Angola State Prison (Louisiana), 59, 70, 71, 79; Angola 3, 17, 80–82, 102, 109, 113, 159n1; death and burial of 90% of inmates, 113; slavery as extension of, 113, 115, 161n10

Anton, Anatole, 121

Anyon, Jean, *Ghetto Schooling*, 28–29, 45

Apple, M., 45, 50

Arena, Jay, 110

Arendt, Orissa, 7–8, 17, 76

Armstrong, Louis, 111, 160n7